Doing Research about Education

Social Research and Educational Studies Series

Series Editor: Robert G. Burgess, Professor of Sociology,
University of Warwick

Doing Research about Education

Edited by

Geoffrey Walford

FALMER PRESS

Taylor & Francis Group

UK Falmer Press, 1 Gunpowder Square, London, EC4A 3DE
USA Falmer Press, Taylor & Francis Inc., 1900 Frost Road, Suite 101, Bristol, PA 19007

First published in 1998

A catalogue record for this book is available from the British Library

ISBN 0 7507 0783 6 cased
ISBN 0 7507 0782 8 paper

Library of Congress Cataloging-in-Publication Data are available on request

Jacket design by Caroline Archer

Typeset in 10/12pt Garamond by
Graphicraft Typesetters Ltd., Hong Kong

Printed in Great Britain by Biddles Ltd., Guildford and King's Lynn on paper which has a specified pH value on final paper manufacture of not less than 7.5 and is therefore 'acid free'.

Contents

Contents

Series Editor's Preface

The purpose of the *Social Research and Educational Studies* series is to provide authoritative guides to key issues in educational research. The series includes overviews of fields, guidance on good practice and discussions of the practical implications of social and educational research. In particular, the series deals with a variety of approaches to conducting social and educational research. Contributors to this series review recent work, raise critical concerns that are particular to the field of education and reflect on the implications of research for educational policy and practice.

Each volume in the series draws on material that will be relevant for an international audience. The contributors to this series all have wide experience of teaching, conducting and using educational research. The volumes are written so that they will appeal to a wide audience of students, teachers and researchers. Altogether the volumes in the *Social Research and Educational Studies* series provide a comprehensive guide for anyone concerned with contemporary educational research.

The series includes individually authored books and edited volumes on a range of themes in education including qualitative research, survey research, the interpretation of data, self-evaluation, research and social policy, analysing data, action research and the politics and ethics of research.

Among the volumes that have contributed to our understanding of social research methodology in the last 20 years have been those devoted to research autobiographies where researchers are encouraged by editors to 'tell it as it is'. Such accounts have helped to extend our understanding of the research process and the ways in which research problems have been handled. They have also highlighted the ways in which the context of research has changed over time. It is for this reason that autobiographical essays need to be regularly commissioned if we are to understand the preoccupations of contemporary researchers. Geoffrey Walford's collection of essays examines the ways in which researchers working on education in the 1990s face a diverse range of social, political and methodological issues in the delivery of high quality work.

Robert G. Burgess
University of Warwick

1 Introduction: Research Accounts Count

Geoffrey Walford

There are very many books about how to do educational research. But many undergraduate and postgraduate research methodology courses are based on just one or two of the well-known textbooks that have been often reprinted and have served successive cohorts of students (examples are Moser and Kalton, 1992; Cohen and Manion, 1994). While these 'cook-book' textbooks have much to offer, they present research largely as an unproblematic process. When considering more quantitative and statistical research, their concern is with sampling, questionnaire design, interview procedures, response rates, observation schedules, and so on. Even when focusing on qualitative research, there is often an emphasis on such tactical aspects as gaining entry to sites, generating rapport with interviewees, and strategies for the analysis of data. In short, many well-known textbooks present an idealized conception of how educational research is designed and executed, where research is carefully planned in advance, predetermined methods and procedures followed, and the 'results' are the unavoidable conclusion. The effect of the researcher is excluded from the process.

The limitations of traditional research methods textbooks have been gradually recognized over the last decade or more, and there is now a growing range of 'alternative' books for students and practitioners that present more personal accounts of the particular research practices that led to specific research reports. In these books the authors of well-known research reports have written semi-autobiographical reflexive accounts of the process of doing research, in the hope that others will benefit from this sharing of practical experience. Such accounts have become common within the wider discipline of anthropology (e.g. Lareau and Shultz, 1996) and it is the more qualitative researchers who have been in the forefront of such 'alternative' writing within educational research. Within Britain one of the first collections or articles that present the practical, political and personal side of educational research was edited by Martin Shipman (1976) who persuaded six authors of highly respected research reports to write about the origins, organization and implementation of their projects.

During the mid-1980s Robert Burgess gathered together about 40 accounts of the research process that were published in four separate volumes (Burgess, 1984, 1985 a–c). The first of these was used widely on educational research methods courses but, while offering a valuable corrective to existing textbooks, it had the disadvantage of concentrating only on qualitative research. A critical reader might have gained the impression that the 'flexibility' of method and the effect of the personal on the way in which research is conducted is a feature of only qualitative research, and that quantitative methods escape from these problems. That this is not correct is shown by some of the chapters in my own edited collections. Both *Doing Sociology of Education* (Walford, 1987) and *Doing Educational Research* (Walford, 1991) included some chapters about quantitative work as well as qualitative. This present volume should be seen as a sequel to these two earlier volumes and to the work of Shipman and Burgess.

Much has changed within education and educational research since the publication of *Doing Educational Research*. This volume deals with the issues of the 1990s, and includes accounts that cover the various stages of the research process, a sampling of research topics, the diversity of methodologies used in educational research, and a range of theoretical perspectives. There is coverage of qualitative and quantitative methodologies and of large and smaller scale research. It also includes discussions of ESRC programme research, contract research and theoretical research.

Critique

During the late 1980s and early 1990s the rise in semi-autobiographical accounts of the research process led to the publication of more specialist volumes. Some concentrated on education evaluation (e.g. Adelman, 1984) or research ethics (Burgess, 1989) while others focused on researching education policy (Halpin and Troyna, 1994) or researching the powerful in education (Walford, 1994). While these and similar books have been widely used by students and other researchers, they have not been without criticism.

One of the most important criticisms has developed from a growing interest in language use and representations within educational writing (Van Maanen, 1995). For example, in a recent book, Atkinson (1996) discusses the genre of the autobiographical or 'confessional' account in which ethnographers, in particular, 'tell it like it was' and reveal the personal and practical issues they experience in the course of their own fieldwork. Such stories often recount hardships, deprivations, danger and fortitude but, Atkinson argues, such accounts are no less contrived or more authentic than any other genre of sociological reportage. He explains,

> It must be remembered that however 'intimate' and revealing confessionals may be, they are themselves artful products of writing. The genre is used by authors to invite particular kinds of readings and responses: the moral character and analytic acumen of the narrator are assembled out of the textual elements offered by the confessional. It would be quite wrong to assume that

the 'confessional' embodies a 'true' and transparently unvarnished account, in contrast to the more worked-up 'realist' ethnographic text. There is nothing uniquely privileged or authentic about the autobiographical story. The confessional is as conventional as any other style or genre. (Atkinson, 1996, p. 55)

Atkinson goes on to show that the accounts are shaped by narrative and other conventions. Their form is as culturally shaped as is other writing. One aspect of this is that such accounts often present the author as a strange mixture of 'hero' and 'anti-hero':

There is the wry tradition whereby we rehearse the second-worst thing that ever happened to us in the field, the first being too painful or embarrassing. We paint ourselves in unflattering colours: we are by turns naïve, vulnerable and incompetent. Of course, we mean to present ourselves as 'socially acceptable incompetents' for the purpose of data collection. (Atkinson, 1996, p. 91)

In his edited collection of reflexive accounts, Barry Troyna (1994) has also raised several questions about such alternative accounts of research. He has three major reservations. His first echoes that of Atkinson, for he claims that the accounts tend to suffer from delusions of grandeur, and that they parade a pretence that it is possible to 'tell it like it is' in a way that is not done in conventional research methodology textbooks. Where accounts are presented in this way it helps to legitimize a realist view that there is 'something out there' that can be written about and transmitted to others. Troyna argues that, while these additional narratives about the research process may be of social, historical and intellectual interest, and may also demystify a researcher's particular experiences in the framing, execution or dissemination of a study, the methodological significance of such accounts cannot be taken for granted.

Troyna's second concern is about the effect that such reflexive accounts may have on the credibility of certain types of educational research. The particular problem here is the imbalance in expectations and practice that exists between qualitative and quantitative researchers. While there are now many reflexive accounts of qualitative research, and some researchers such as Ball (1990) argue that methodological rigour demands that every ethnography should be accompanied by such an account, there are still relatively few comparable reports about the process of conducting quantitative research. Troyna argues that this imbalance may have serious negative implications for qualitative research. The result of the availability of alternative accounts of qualitative research processes could mean that non-qualitative researchers, policy-makers, researcher-funders and lay people may be less likely to take qualitative research seriously. The reflexive accounts available might be interpreted to show that qualitative research is subjective and value-laden, and thus unscientific and invalid. As there are few corresponding accounts of quantitative research, it is more able to retain its illusion of being objective, value-free, scientific and valid.

Troyna's third concern is with the impact of such 'confessional tales' within the power relations of the research community. He argues that the activity of writing such accounts is akin to self-appraisal. However, while self-appraisal is conducted in a highly structured and local environment, such reflexive accounts lead the researcher to open himself or herself to wider scrutiny by the research community. Troyna claims that while this is potentially threatening to anyone, it holds less danger for those already with established posts and reputations than it does to those on the fringes of the research community such as postgraduate students and contract researchers.

This last concern has also been voiced by Paechter (1996) whose insightful article compares reflexive accounts of the research process with Bentham's Panopticon and the Christian ritual of confession. Using a Foucaultian analysis of the relationship between knowledge and power, she argues that the increasing imperative on researchers to produce reflexive accounts acts to control those with little power within the research community. For the powerless, the act of confession is an enactment of a power relation. She argues that Ball's exhortation for all researchers to produce a research biography alongside their ethnographic account should be ignored. For doctoral students, in particular, the inequalities of power between examiners and students are great, such that the practice becomes strongly coercive.

All three of Troyna's concerns are worthy of further examination, but it is first necessary to recognize that not all reflexive accounts serve a similar purpose or attempt to cover the same type of issue. Even within this volume, where all the accounts are by established authors, there is considerable variation in the nature of the accounts. However, the primary aim in practically all cases is to show other less well-established authors that the research process is rarely straightforward, and that personal, political and practical matters play significant parts in shaping what was done in particular research projects. Here, these established researchers are able to give accounts that show some of the 'warts-and-all' nature of their practice. These reflexive accounts are separated in time and place from the original research reports, and the security of their academic positions gives the authors some autonomy to admit the 'second worst thing that happened'. In answer to Troyna's third point, it is undoubtedly correct that the publication of such reflexive research accounts could potentially have a rather different impact on a doctoral student from that on established researchers. But this does not mean that doctoral students should not write a reflexive account of their research — it just needs to be a different type of account.

The doctorate is, in part, a learning process, but I believe the doctoral thesis should be a record of successful learning and research rather than a blow-by-blow account of the whole learning process. In essence, the doctorate must be a 'contribution to knowledge' that can be used by others and not just a contribution to the student's self-knowledge. Thus, I do not believe that it is particularly useful for doctoral theses to record all of the false starts, errors, disappointments, feelings of despair and so on that everyone who has actually done research already knows about. These aspects will have been important to the student, but an examiner or any other reader wishes to know about the research that has been successfully conducted as a result of the learning process. I find navel-gazing accounts from doctoral students that record every detail of their own learning process very boring to read, and I see them as the worst examples of 'vanity ethnography' (Maynard, 1993). For doctoral students, the reflexive account should certainly include consideration of the importance of the researcher within the research and a discussion of personal influences on the research process, but the essence of the account is to show that a success-ful piece of research has been conducted, and to explain where justifiable decisions were made. No novice researcher (or any other researcher for that matter) should feel obliged to emulate the type of reflexive account that details all the problems, mistakes and meanderings of their research process. How-ever, in contrast to student accounts, accounts from experienced researchers are valuable simply because they are concerned with academic research that has been already accepted by the wider research community. They show that recognized researchers experience many difficulties, which may make the novice researcher's problems seem more manageable.

I am in broad agreement with Troyna's first and second concerns about reflexive accounts, but I believe that these potentially negative effects can be reduced. His first point was that they can tend to legitimize a realist view of research. However, I would argue that, while some of the early reflexive accounts may have been cast within the framework of 'telling it as it is', this is now a rarity. Most such accounts are now written by researchers who accept that their descriptions are selective and constructed according to narrative and other conventions. They recognize that they do not present a complete 'true' account of what 'really' went on, but offer another perspective. In themselves, reflexive accounts do not necessarily support a realist perspective of educational research. Indeed, they may act to challenge such a view.

Troyna's second concern about the potential effects of reflexive accounts on the credibility of qualitative research is one that also concerns me. The particular effect of a bias towards more reflexive accounts of qualitative rather than quantitative research can be potentially corrected by editors encouraging more quantitative researchers to contribute to volumes such as this. This is far from easy to achieve. This volume is still heavily biased towards more qualit-ative research in spite of my desire to have a more even balance. However, if it were possible to get such a balance, this might have the effect of reducing the credibility of *all* educational research rather than just qualitative educational research, which is not necessarily desirable. A more reasonable answer to the concern is that it probably overestimates the impact of such accounts. They are unlikely to be read by anyone other than those involved in research them-selves — who will either already know about the uncertainties and vagaries of research or will very soon find out for themselves. If policy-makers, research funders and other powerful individuals do read them, it is likely that they will already have a wide-ranging knowledge of the practicalities of research. My feeling here is that the potential benefits to those conducting research out-weigh the risks of reducing the wider credibility of research. The intention of the chapters collected together here is certainly not to devalue educational research. In practice, all of the contributors have a very strong commitment to improving the quality of educational research, and believe that the publication of accounts such as those included here will assist in that task.

The Chapters

My aim in this collection of reflexive accounts is to provide discussions that deal with some of the research issues of the 1990s. The book includes accounts that cover the various overlapping stages of the research process, a range of research topics, some of the range of methodologies used in educational research, and a diversity of theoretical perspectives. There is coverage of qualitative and quantitative methodologies and of large and smaller scale research. It also includes discussions of ESRC programme research, contract research and the development of theory.

The first two chapters that follow this introduction are based on ethnographic work conducted by single researchers. Sally Power's study of the significance of pastoral care and its relationship to the academic dimension was originally undertaken as a doctoral research project. She explains her choice of ethnography in terms of her desire to illuminate and evaluate Bernstein's theoretical framework through a specific example. In the chapter she describes the selection of two secondary schools, and discusses in detail the variety of sources of data used in ethnography. The second part of the chapter is concerned with issues of reliability and replicability. Power pays particular attention to the potential effects of the attributes and values of the researcher. She also examines the advantages and disadvantages of conducting ethnography using a pre-existing theoretical framework.

Debbie Epstein's ethnography investigated the gendered cultures of a Year 5 primary school class, and had a focus on issues of sexuality and gender identity. In Chapter 3 she explains why this research was conducted and some of the problems that she encountered during the research. A particular feature of her approach was that Epstein spent virtually all of her time in school with the children, but tried to adopt a 'least adult' role rather than be seen by them as acting as any sort of teacher. This was far from easy to achieve. Epstein also describes some of the ways that the children attempted to 're-search' the researcher and examines issues of informed consent with young children.

The next three chapters begin to move from a focus on the individual researcher to the researcher as part of a small team. Peter Woods has now been conducting ethnographic work in secondary and primary schools for many years. His initial research in what has come to be a series of studies of 'creative teaching' was conducted alone, but more recent additions have been the result of a teamwork approach. In this chapter Woods examines some of the critical moments in the research process, where particular people and events can change the course of the research and the attitudes of the researcher.

He describes two such events which were part of his primary school research and one that relates to a case study of a secondary school's award-winning dramatic production of Godspell, and explains how new studies can develop from chance encounters.

The way that relatively small-scale studies can grow into projects that take over a decade to complete is well illustrated in Chapter 5 by Ann Filer with Andrew Pollard. What started as a single ethnographic study developed into a dual site, longitudinal study of the educational careers of a group of children from their Reception year to Year 11. Filer describes the way this research was organized and conducted, and examines some of the difficulties encountered in such long-term collaborative and comparative research. The current secondary stage involves a small team of academics and presents its own new challenges.

Some of the problems and advantages of collaborative team research are discussed by Gwen Wallace and her colleagues in the next chapter. They undertook a longitudinal ethnographic study that tracked a group of young people through their last four years of secondary schooling. They give an account of the influences that changes in membership of the team, political climate, and educational and academic debate had on the progress of the research. They show the complexities of organizing and conducting research on multiple sites, and some of the personal and ethical realities of in-depth research with young people.

The longitudinal research described in Chapter 6 was just one of 10 projects funded by the ESRC within their 'Innovation and Change in Education' Research Programme which is the subject of the next chapter. Martin Hughes was the programme coordinator, appointed just after the 10 projects had been selected. These 10 projects ranged in methodology, scale, focus, and disciplinary base. Hughes gives an account of the complex role of the coordinator and the way that he worked with the various project teams. He shows that the task was far from straightforward, especially as a major shift in ESRC priorities occurred during the life of the programme. He examines the task of creating coherence within the programme, and discusses issues of dissemination of results and, in particular, some of the problems encountered with the media.

David Reynolds and his colleagues report some of the problems and challenges of large-scale quantitative international comparative research. The full list of authors of this chapter runs to 23 names, and is a reflection of the vast scale of this project. The authors explain how research involving 3 countries gradually expanded to 9 countries, each with 6 or 12 schools, with 1 to 12 classes per school, and between 20 to 40 pupils per class. They examine some of the cultural and practical difficulties encountered during the study and then show the major potential benefits of such collaborative projects. Eventually, we learn that the project reported here and widely discussed in the media is just a pilot study for a far larger study that is due to begin in 1999!

The next two chapters return to smaller scale research projects and have a focus on the role of the theoretician in educational research. In Chapter 9 Chris Haywood and Máirtín Mac an Ghaill reflect on their work that has tried to make sense of how schools generate student masculinities and heterosexualities. Their chapter raises questions of methodology and epistemology about an ethnographic study conducted by Mac an Ghaill. They describe the theoretical background from which the work emerged, and discuss the importance of its theory-led grounded methodology, and its use of a multi-layered approach where theoretical frameworks and empirical material from the field interrogated each other. The final part of the chapter raises ethical questions about this type of ethnographic work.

In Chapter 10, Martyn Hammersley examines his own career as a 'methodological purist'. He describes the origins of his interest in methodological work and in investigating the standards by which he believes social and educational research ought to be assessed. He then discusses some of the reactions to his work by fellow researchers, in particular the claims that have been made that his 'methodological purism' demands unobtainably high standards. As this debate has become particularly acrimonious, Hammersley's discussion examines the issues involved within the wider context of the importance of methodology and theory.

One of the greatest changes in educational research since the 1980s has been the growth of contract research. Many of those currently involved in educational research do not have the tenured academic's luxury of being able to choose their own research topics, but must obtain externally funded research contracts, with their associated insecurity of short-term funding and temporary employment contracts. Chapters 11 and 12 are both concerned with these developments. In the first, Robert Burgess describes the development of the Centre for Educational Development, Appraisal and Research (CEDAR) at Warwick which he directs. He describes the genesis of that research centre and how it gradually grew into one of the largest university-based educational research centres in the country. He discusses the importance of sponsorship, of developing substantive themes of research, and of building and maintaining teams. Finally, he raises a number of problems associated with such contract research centres.

Valerie Wilson gives a vivid account in Chapter 12 of her experiences of managing contract research in the Scottish Council for Research in Education (SCRE). She recounts the story of a research project, and details the challenges, compromises and short-cuts which she *knowingly* undertook as part of a pragmatic and performative role as a manager of research contracts. But the account also provides insights into the interrelationship between contract research and the construction of meanings at a time when notions of linear progress and modernity are much debased. Finally, the chapter begins to challenge some of the conventions of reporting educational research and questions the nature of 'readerly' texts.

This focus on publication and text is continued in the final chapter where I give a personal account of some aspects of my own relationship to the process of writing and publication. My objective in this chapter is to demystify some aspects of the academic publication process, such that new writers in particular will have a more realistic view of how publication occurs. In the chapter I describe the nature of academic publishing for books and for articles in refereed journals. I then use a series of examples of my own publications that were linked to a research project that examined a political campaign to enable faith-based private schools to become grant-maintained schools. Through these examples, I show how publication was achieved, and I reflect on the nature of my 'compulsive writing behaviour'.

The chapters are thus diverse. The book as a whole does not present a single, simple understanding of the process of doing research about education. Indeed, it almost revels in the complexities and uncertainties of that process. It is hoped that readers will find the collection useful, and will be encouraged to read research reports with a new scepticism. Yet, I also hope that the collection will encourage readers to undertake their own research and to develop a questioning of their own research processes which can only lead to an enhancement of the quality of research about education.

References

ADELMAN, C. (1984) (ed.) *The Politics and Ethics of Fieldwork*, Beckenham: Croom Helm.

ATKINSON, P. (1996) *Sociological Readings and Re-readings*, Aldershot: Avebury.

BALL, S.J. (1990) 'Self-doubt and soft data: Social and technical trajectories in ethnographic fieldwork', *International Journal of Qualitative Studies in Education*, **3**, 2, pp. 157–71.

BURGESS, R.G. (1984) (ed.) *The Research Process in Educational Settings: Ten Case Studies*, London: Falmer Press.

BURGESS, R.G. (1985a) (ed.) *Field Methods in the Study of Education*, London: Falmer Press.

BURGESS, R.G. (1985b) (ed.) *Strategies of Educational Research: Qualitative Methods*, London: Falmer Press.

BURGESS, R.G. (1985c) (ed.) *Issues in Educational Research: Qualitative Methods*, London: Falmer Press.

BURGESS, R.G. (1989) (ed.) *The Ethics of Educational Research*, London: Falmer Press.

COHEN, L. and MANION, L. (1994) *Research Methods in Education (4th edition)*, London: Routledge.

HALPIN, D. and TROYNA, B. (1994) (eds) *Researching Education Policy: Ethical and Methodological Issues*, London: Falmer Press.

LAREAU, A. and SHULTZ, J. (1996) (eds) *Journeys through Ethnography: Realistic Accounts of Fieldwork*, Oxford: Westview Press.

MAYNARD, M. (1993) 'Feminism and the possibilities of a postmodern research practice', *British Journal of Sociology of Education*, **14**, 3, pp. 327–31.

MOSER, C.A. and KALTON, G. (1992) *Survey Methods and Social Investigation (2nd edition)*, Aldershot: Dartmouth.

PAECHTER, C. (1996) 'Power, knowledge and the confessional in qualitative research', *Discourse*, **17**, 1, pp. 75–84.

SHIPMAN, M. (1976) *The Organization and Impact of Social Research*, London: Routledge and Kegan Paul.

TROYNA, B. (1994) 'Reforms, research and being reflexive about being reflective', in HALPIN, D. and TROYNA, B. (eds) *Researching Education Policy: Ethical and Methodological Issues*, London: Falmer Press.

VAN MAANEN, J. (1995) *Representation in Ethnography*, London: Sage.

WALFORD, G. (1987) (ed.) *Doing Sociology of Education*, London: Falmer Press.

WALFORD, G. (1991) (ed.) *Doing Educational Research*, London: Routledge.

WALFORD, G. (1994) (ed.) *Researching the Powerful in Education*, London: UCL Press.

2 Researching the 'Pastoral' and the 'Academic': An Ethnographic Exploration of Bernstein's Sociology of the Curriculum

Sally Power

Introduction

It would be something of an exaggeration to say that reading Basil Bernstein changed my life. But it is true to say that his paper 'On the classification and framing of educational knowledge' (Bernstein, 1971) altered the way I looked at education. Even though it had been published for over 10 years and was widely recognized as a seminal text by the time I came across it, it seemed to offer a perspective that was not only entirely novel but eminently convincing. Overriding the long-established assumption that the division and ranking of school knowledge into different categories reflects the various properties of its subject matter, Bernstein claimed '. . . there is nothing intrinsic to the relative status of various contents, there is nothing intrinsic to the relationships between contents' (1971, p. 49). Rather than focus our attention on the content of school knowledge we might, therefore, more fruitfully analyse the curriculum 'in terms of the principle by which units of time and their contents are brought into a special relationship with each other' (p. 48). Bernstein argued that this relationship could be analysed through two structural dimensions. 'Classification' indicates the degree of closure or openness between constituent elements. 'Framing' indicates the degree of rigidity or leeway within the mode of pedagogy. Seduced by both the scope and precision of the arguments, my understanding of education became itself increasingly structured through sets of oppositions: Where were the boundaries between subjects 'strong' or 'weak'? How open or closed were the principles of transmission? Whose knowledge categories were 'pure' or 'mixed'? Which knowledge was 'sacred' and which 'profane'?

In the English secondary school, many of these oppositions seemed to be embodied within the division that had emerged between the teaching of school subjects and the organizational structures designed to foster students' personal and social development. Although the term 'pastoral care' has been around for some time, its widespread institutionalization within secondary schools as a distinctive and systematized form of provision dates back no further than 30 years. Yet despite its relatively rapid and extensive emergence, the significance of pastoral care and its relationship to the academic dimension had received hardly any critical analysis. Investigation of this relationship — its background, manifestation and consequences became the focus of my PhD research undertaken in the late 1980s. This chapter looks at the process of that research — an aspect that I have been criticized by Bates (1996) for neglecting within the subsequent account of the findings (Power, 1996).

The Research

Investigation of the relationship between the pastoral and the academic involved exploring accounts of the curriculum both past and present and analysing the principles of pastoral texts. But the bulk of the research, and that which provides the focus of this chapter, involved ethnographic fieldwork in two secondary schools.

The preference for ethnography stemmed not so much from a distaste for 'quantitative' approaches, but rather because none of the methods of data collection usually characterized in this way appeared sufficiently sensitive to do the work required of them in illuminating and evaluating the theoretical framework. Although there is an increasing amount of research that draws on Bernstein's formulations on the curriculum and pedagogy (Domingos, 1989; Daniels, 1988 and 1989; Singh, 1993), many empirical explorations, such as those by King (1976 and 1981), have met with criticism that his theories have been misinterpreted or misapplied (e.g. Davies, 1995). However, as Edwards (1995) points out, Bernstein's own frustration and subsequent defence of his work (e.g. Bernstein, 1990)

> illustrates the perennial difficulty of drawing testable propositions from a theory of structuration which is located so deeply within pedagogic practice and which insists on being tested in its own terms. (Edwards, 1995, p. 106)

Indeed, Tyler has argued that:

> . . . Bernstein's structural interpretation of school organisation is so differently conceived from other theories of the school, it does not lend itself easily to conventional empirical testing. Not only does it reconstitute the elements of a theory of school organisation, it also generates its own methodological principles which make any 'objective' empirical test to some degree self-validating. Since the instrumentation of empirical research is an aspect of coding practices, an inappropriate choice of a method could produce a very distorting result. The main danger with such structuralist theories is that they are not testable by the usual empiricist methods which deal by definition with 'surface' appearance or phenomena. (1988, pp. 159–60)

In relation to my research, it is clear that undertaking a survey of the relationship between the pastoral and the academic may well only confirm the existence of classifications rather than provide data that would enable one to unpick organizing principles and interrelationships. It is hard to envisage how such data could be obtained other than by 'entering' the organization and monitoring the ways in which the underlying classificatory principles of each domain structured practices and positioned staff and students.

Those who take a 'naturalistic' approach to qualitative research might argue that this kind of research is not ethnographic at all. It takes from ethnography the possibility of understanding 'the meanings that give form and content to social processes' (Hammersley and Atkinson, 1995, p. 2). It does not hold, however, that these meanings are then taken as valid interpretations of social processes; rather, they become manifestations of the classificatory principles through which the speakers are discursively structured.

This is some distance from the 'grounded theory' approach that is often seen as the distinctive feature of ethnography. As Tyler argues, Bernstein's methods of analysis, like those of Foucault:

> . . . deny that the intentions and meanings of the individual subject can be the beginnings of explanation, since the conditions of experience depend on the possibilities which the individual does not himself control. (1988, p. 164)

With reference to Hammersley's (1992) typology of the possible relationships between theory and ethnography, this research was closest to the 'study of critical cases' using a hypothetico-deductive method. I did not start the fieldwork with tightly framed hypotheses, but I did have theories I wished to address. Although these could not be 'experimentally' controlled, I still structured the research around principles of comparison and contrast.

The Fieldwork

Selecting the Schools

As Hammersley (1992) points out, there are considerable difficulties with applying the hypothetico-deductive approach to ethnographic research. As ethnography can only draw on a small number of cases, it is hard to find ones 'that vary the independent variable and control relevant extraneous variables' (p. 21). Given the focus on the relationship between the pastoral and the academic, two schools were needed that were structured along contrasting principles. One school was to be organized on a 'specialist' basis (Marland, 1980) in which the pastoral and the academic were explicitly demarcated. Here I could examine the principles and practices of each domain, the relationship between the two areas and the extent to which demarcation structured professional and pupil identities. The second school was to exhibit a 'whole school' approach (Marland, 1980) where explicit attempts were being made to erode the pastoral/academic boundary. It was my intention to use this second site further to expose the structural dimensions of curricular classifications. In particular, it would enable me to examine the depth or superficiality of integration across areas of the curriculum. If the boundary proved resistant to integrative initiatives, it would tell me about the endurance of curricular classifications and the processes through which they are constructed and maintained under pressure.

Several schools were considered in consultation with the relevant LEA advisers, and as is often the case, the final selection of two schools, Elmfield and Kings Marsh (pseudonyms), was made on the basis of proximity and access as well as research-driven criteria. I was fortunate that both schools agreed to cooperate. The most intensive research took place in the 'specialized' school, Elmfield, over a period of 15 months. An initial 'immersion' of two months was followed up by regular visits of at least two days each week. Kings Marsh, the school which was integrating the pastoral and the academic, was visited on average three days each week over a period of four months.

Sources of Data

One of the wonderful things about ethnography is the lack of restrictions on what can be taken as data. Conventional techniques of classroom observation and prearranged interviewing can be supplemented by an endless variety of data sources. Indeed, it is difficult to think of anything that might not count as valid data. In order to examine the relative strength and organizational principles of the academic and pastoral dimensions, all manner of evidence was collected.

The ways in which space and time were distributed were taken as indicators of 'dimensions of non-verbal, non-gestural symbolic reality' (Bennett and Bennett, 1971). Analysis of the spatial and temporal features showed that, at Elmfield, the academic curriculum was organized along the principles of Bernstein's specialized collection code (1971). The timetable was used as graphic illustration of the clear-cut demarcations and lack of ambiguity over where, when and what each pupil or teacher was doing at any given time. Syllabuses revealed how subjects were organized into series of discrete units; each clearly bounded and sequential in character. The academic career of the secondary school pupil was divided into prearranged stages; from the single unit of 35 minutes that comprises the 'lesson', to the term and then the school year.

Within the academic domain, it was also possible to identify strong segregation of space. Subjects had 'homes', whether on the scale of the science block or the single geography room. The subject identity of these rooms was clearly visible through the display material and/or specialist equipment. Through observation of staff movements, it was also possible to see that these areas took on the significance of 'territory'. Workrooms were the exclusive meeting place of subject members, where entry of non-members was perceived as intrusion. These areas not only strengthened subject allegiance they also diminished interaction with other staff, thus perpetuating subject insulation.

For the main part, the academic dimension was transmitted through a 'visible' pedagogy (Bernstein, 1977 and 1990). The rules of hierarchy tended to be explicit and unambiguous. Through observing interactions and analysing conversations it was clear that relations between teachers and pupils, but also between teachers and other teachers, pupils and other pupils, were based on the possession of various kinds and degrees of subject specialism. The subjects tended to have explicit sequencing rules and criteria for evaluation, visible to both staff and pupils. The terminology of academic development was shot through with sequential reference; pupils were 'advanced', 'forward', or 'lagging behind' and in need of help to 'catch up'. Through the complex but visible grading and setting processes, pupils knew how they were positioned relative to their peers.

Just as the academic dimension at Elmfield can be represented in terms of the specialized collection code, it was also possible to find strong parallels between Bernstein's model of the integrated code and Elmfield's provision of pastoral care. While the collection code can be characterized in terms of strong boundary maintenance, hierarchical ordering of subjects and progressive screening of students, the integrated code signifies weak insulation between areas, lack of hierarchy and no formal student screening. Indeed, the very invisibility of its organization and lack of formal structure rendered observation more difficult.

Although there was a formally demarcated slot of 'pastoral time' at Elmfield, for the main part, pastoral care was administered on an ad hoc basis throughout the day. The lack of insulation meant there were no formal divisions into periods, nor even any formal separation of 'contact' time from 'non-contact' time for those with primarily pastoral responsibilities. Neither was the spatial demarcation of pastoral provision at Elmfield as clear cut as that of the academic. Although tutor periods were located in tutor-rooms, these rooms did not have the status of 'territory'. Pastoral staff areas were likewise not as exclusive as subject work-rooms. Staff and pupils could, and often did, enter unaccompanied and uninvited. It is hard to see how these subtle but significant details could be garnered through anything other than ethnographic means.

Observation of sessions and the ways in which 'work' was recorded provided data that revealed that pastoral transmissions were structured along the lines of 'invisible pedagogy' (Bernstein, 1977 and 1990). There were attempts to diminish hierarchies between staff and students. In one case, for instance, the tutor used his, and my (as observer), first names with the class. Efforts were also made to dissolve hierarchy between pupils. Tutor groups, unlike 'classes', were deliberately constructed to be heterogeneous social units. Like other invisible pedagogies, tutor periods emphasized features of flexibility, spontaneity and the cyclical rather than linear nature of learning. This was clear from the way staff and students used resources. For tutor work, learning materials were at most worksheets, lacking the permanency of the textbook. Tutees' work was not recorded in a linear fashion. In the lower years, they used exercise books that were significantly referred to as 'notebooks', reflecting their casual, disposable nature. These were apparently designed for the tutees' own use inasmuch as staff rarely looked at them. In the upper years, tutees used files, associated with models of further/higher education and indicative of looser structure and greater tutee control over learning. In the exercise book that records academic progress, the order of work is unalterable. Missing or spoilt work remains visible. But with files, pages can be added or removed. Criterial rules were also less visible. There was no visible, gradable standard against which pupils could measure themselves. Pastoral carers often emphasized that it was the *process* rather than the *product* of learning which counted. As Bernstein claims of invisible pedagogies, difference reveals uniqueness. It is certainly the central tenet of pastoral care that every child is unique. Pastoral staff were often heard to assert 'we are all individuals'. However, this does not mean that there were no criteria for evaluation. As with all invisible pedagogies, the tutor learns to 'read' the child; to look for key indicators of difference; and to assess what stage they are at, but the processes of pastoral assessment remain hidden. What was perceived by the tutee to be 'chatting' could hold great weight for the tutor. The following comments come from a Year 10 tutor:

> They'll hopefully chat for ten minutes and get through last night before the lessons start . . . It's what I like to do, it's how I get to know them a lot better.

Her strategies however were not visible to her tutees, e.g.:

> *P*:   And then she comes round to all the tables and she talks to all the groups about them and everything.
> *SP*:   Is that to get to know you or something?
> *P*:   No, she never does that. This is my second year in her class and she's never done that to me before.

Again these subtle shifts of emphasis and visibility are unlikely to be elicited through formal survey methods or structured interviewing. Being 'on site' enables one to gather contrasting meanings and perceptions. The situated nature of ethnography also enables one to delve beneath the official versions of organizations that tend to be elicited from questionnaire data or formal interviewing. For instance, despite claims that the pastoral and the academic have parity, or even claims by the academic specialists that pastoral care was taking control, it became clear that academic concerns dominated. Again a variety of indicators can be used, based on both analysis of the distribution of time and space and observation of how such time and space was allocated. For instance, at Elmfield, tutor work was carried out in the teaching classrooms, but any notion of 'sharing' was only nominal. While noticeboards displayed administrative notices of the tutor groups, these were marginal when compared to the dominant subject identity of the room. Furniture and equipment was arranged for academic lessons, and hardly ever altered for tutorial work. Tutor work was rarely displayed on the walls. Blackboards were often covered with academic classwork with instructions for this to be left alone. When a particular room was required for other purposes, usually academic, the tutor group moved. It appeared, therefore, that although these rooms could be designated as both pastoral and academic, the pastoral was very much the 'guest', and at times of conflicts of interest, it was academic needs that prevailed.

It had been suggested by senior pastoral staff that teachers should be moved from their subject bases for tutor periods to stop them using this time for lesson preparation. Gareth Evans, Head of Physics, warning his science department of this over their regular Friday pub lunch, commented:

> Have you heard of their latest ploy? They're trying to make us move out of our rooms for tutor periods.

The adversarial nature of the language ('them' and 'us'), the inference of subversive tactics ('ploy'), and the territorial claims ('our rooms') within this small but revealing snatch of conversation belied official claims that the relationship between pastoral staff and subject specialists was one of cooperation and complementarity.

The opportunistic nature of ethnography, the endless variety of data sources and the ability to scratch beneath the surface mean that insights can be derived from unexpected incidents. One such incident was a cross-curricular survey on social education that was being carried out by pastoral staff while I was at Elmfield. What was more important for my research than the survey findings was the way in which teachers responded to the exercise. The survey elicited a variety of reactions from teachers, including a significant amount of hostility, particularly from those with primary allegiance to the academic. These staff distanced themselves through a number of tactics from 'spoiling' their questionnaire to trivializing it. The following comments were among many negative reactions elicited at meetings set aside to complete the survey: 'I think I've finished mine — have I passed?' and 'Sir, will you check that for me?'

While the examples above illustrate the potential of ethnography to draw on a wide variety of sources and to take advantage of unanticipated events, there are also limitations. As mentioned earlier, the dependency on, in this instance, just two research sites limits the number of 'cases' that can be considered. But there are also restrictions within even these case studies. As Schatzman and Strauss (1973) argue, it is not just a question of 'getting in', but also of 'staying in'. Managing field relations involves being sensitive to what areas and issues are 'out of bounds'. Although some of these boundaries were overcome with time, others were not. On a number of occasions, I failed to get access to data of any quality.

However, even *not* getting data can be informative. The ease with which I gained access can be seen to reflect the degree of openness/closure of the settings. The strong departmental structure of the 'academic' at Elmfield meant that large numbers of the staff were almost 'invisible'. Indeed, even after several weeks within the school I had never seen a large proportion of the science department. Subject identity was so powerful that these staff remained in their workrooms at both break and lunchtime and presented themselves as a tightly knit group with their own well-defined territory. Access to this territory was never informal or casual, and I always felt I was intruding.

The strong insulation of the school subjects meant that throughout the fieldwork there were difficulties about observing lessons. Where I had imagined access would be a problem, for instance at meetings where pupils' problems were discussed, I was welcomed. I also experienced no problems in studying their confidential records. It is significant that while I was granted easy access to pupils' private lives, I was often excluded from the 'sanctity' of the classroom.

Difficulties in gaining access to pastoral encounters stemmed not from the strength of boundaries but from their very absence. Again, as already mentioned, pastoral care operates largely on an informal and ad hoc basis. Observation depended on being in the right place at the right time. For this reason, accounts of many incidents were obtained 'second hand' through the staff or pupils. Of course, it would have been ideal to witness more 'first-hand' encounters of pastoral significance, but it also became increasingly clear that, in most cases, 'second-hand' accounts provided the main source of data for staff as well. This underscored the realization that the various ways in which events were represented and interpreted was at least as significant as what may have 'really' occurred. Indeed, understanding the weak evidential basis and differential interpretations behind pastoral diagnoses became an important dimension of the analysis. As the following comments reveal, hearsay and gossip, particularly concerning 'promiscuous' mothers, was given great explanatory power by pastoral carers:

> It sounds as if he might have been sexually abused . . . father's in and out of prison, mother sleeps with loads of different men.

> She's off the ropes again, drinking a lot, sleeping with any man she can.

> Apparently mum said 'I've never liked Matthew'. That might be the source of the problem.

Even where there was direct evidence of incidents, there appeared to be vast discrepancies between what was considered 'serious' and what could be discounted. One boy, for instance, set fire to a pile of aerosol sprays in a hotel while on a skiing trip. However, according to his tutor:

> He's a silly lad, a nice lad who got involved. It's his first and last time. It's unlikely to happen again.

On the other hand, apparently trivial behaviours were attributed with great significance and even used to justify outside intervention:

> What about Gary Page . . . There's something wrong there . . . His handwriting's gone weird.

I think we should look at Martin; he's always forgetting his dinner money.

Just as the underlying principles of the academic and pastoral domains structured access to settings and the nature of data made available, so too did the tense and oppositional relationship between them. In Elmfield, staff could not easily hold dual identities, and neither could my research.

Several staff expressed hostility to educational research itself and elevated the 'experienced' over the 'well-qualified' teacher or the 'theoretician'. But given the fact that non-graduates are disproportionately represented in the 'pastoral' side (Lyons, 1981), it is not surprising that it was from here that most hostility to the 'degree' aspect of my research was encountered. But overall both my research and therefore myself became identified as being on the pastoral side. Although in the introductory letter and conversations with staff I had emphasized that the research would focus on the relationship *between* the 'pastoral' and the 'academic', it appeared to be almost universally assumed that I was really only interested in pastoral care. At Elmfield, I was formally introduced solely to pastoral staff and initially told only about aspects of pastoral organization. Even after I managed to extend my contacts, I was always seen as the responsibility of the pastoral 'team'. As Hammersley and Atkinson (1995) point out, relationships can be both obstructive and facilitative.

The strength of the pastoral/academic boundary was clearly evident in the patchy success I had entering into close relationships with subject specialists. Helpful as the pastoral staff were towards me, the tension between them and their academic colleagues hindered my entry into 'subject' circles. Staff who were hostile towards the idea of pastoral care were also hostile towards me. While those with key pastoral responsibilities were always happy to chat, other members of staff seemed more wary, as if I were 'checking' up on them. As Simons (1981) points out, teachers 'may use the interview to enhance their position either indirectly by eliciting your advocacy for their innovatory activities . . . or more directly by confirming their "good work"'. Where staff feel their activities are unlikely to elicit the researcher's approval it is probable that they will resist involvement. Some teachers were always 'too busy' to speak to me, some kept cancelling appointments, and in other instances they agreed to be interviewed but were preoccupied with tasks in conditions where I could not sit down or had to keep moving out of the way — making it impossible even to take notes.

The identification of my research with the pastoral side of the curriculum also affected access to pupils. I had originally intended to interview a cross-section of pupils. In the event pupils were selected for me, though not in the way I had anticipated. Simons, for instance, reports that 'gaining access to sixth formers or "prize" pupils is less of a problem than getting the opportunity to talk to the "trouble makers" or low achievers' (Simons, 1981, p. 31). Within my research, the reverse was true. In both schools there was reluctance from staff to extract pupils from classes, with the significant exception of tutor time. Where pupils were offered to me for interview, they were nearly always identified as 'trouble-makers' from bottom sets, or pupils who couldn't do PE because they had forgotten their kit. Some pastoral staff hoped these interviews might act as some sort of therapy. One teacher asked me to talk to three particularly 'trouble-some' boys as he 'would like to know what made them tick'. It was often difficult to reconcile confidentiality with pupil respondents and closeness with staff.

The partial nature of ethnography, in particular its dependency on case studies and critical incidents, and, particularly with this research, the difficulty of achieving equal access to both academic and pastoral settings and staff, raise serious questions about the reliability of the research.

Reliability and Replicability

In order to address whether similar conclusions would be reached by other researchers and in other schools, we need to consider how far the research findings were dependent on the idiosyncrasies of these two schools, the personal attributes and values of the researcher, or the product of the theoretical framework being used.

The Idiosyncrasies of Case Studies

Within case-study research, it is possible to argue that the strength and applicability of the findings lie in the high logical validity of the data (Mitchell, 1983) rather than their generalizability. However, although we often surround this kind of research with disclaimers about extending beyond the case, we always want our investigations to have wider relevance. As I mentioned earlier, I selected two particular schools that I hoped would enable me to make comparisons that would reveal general principles about the strength and significance of boundary maintenance in secondary schools. But to what extent were the features that I identified as significant actually related to the particular attributes of pastoral care and the academic curriculum rather than other extraneous variables?

Certainly, on initial entry I was dismayed at the extent of peculiarities and was concerned that these would 'interfere' with the search for generalities. For instance, Elmfield had undergone a relatively recent amalgamation and inherited an awkwardly split site. However, rather than seeing such a legacy as 'interference', the ways in which the various tensions were resolved — or not — provided further useful insights. The amalgamation and consequent redistribution of teachers resulted in retrenched allegiances which reinforced curricular divisions — and particularly that of the pastoral and the academic. One of the schools had had a much weaker academic tradition and the staff, who consequently lacked strong subject identities, were more likely to be displaced into pastoral positions than those from the school where traditional academic priorities were well established. Similarly, the resulting split site created questions concerning which teachers should travel most, when and for what. Again, this issue was resolved to the advantage of the high status subject specialists to the extent that it was impossible for pastoral staff to achieve any progression with tutor groups as they moved up the school or even to see them on a regular daily basis.

The Attributes and Values of the Researcher

Given the close proximity between the researcher and respondents within ethnographic research, it is clear that the personal attributes of the researcher and how they are perceived are going to have some bearing on the data collection process. As I have already argued, I was strongly identified by staff as being with the pastoral side. Given the strong gendered dimension of pastoral care, I have often speculated whether this identification would have been less pronounced had I been male. While access to all kinds of confidential pastoral data may have been less easy, I may have been able to develop closer relations with some of the subject specialists — particularly those from traditionally masculine subjects.

Another gender-related issue was motherhood. In Elmfield, great emphasis was placed by pastoral carers upon the marital status of parents, in particular mothers. As comments cited earlier suggest, many problems were laid at the door of single and unmarried mothers. Pastoral staff were quite open in their attributions of blame, until they learnt that I too was a parent. My failure to anticipate the importance of the distinction between being a 'mother' and being a 'single mother' created the dilemma of whether to regain their confidence through presenting myself as 'appropriately' married or whether to refuse to endorse their prejudice but risk losing data.

Thus, while it is undoubtedly the case that aspects of our own identity will influence our position in the field, reflection upon the processes of inclusion and exclusion can further inform the analysis. Perhaps a greater risk to the status of the data are those personal values and commitments that lie beyond critical reflection. I am struck, for example, by the differences between my account of the relationship between the pastoral and the academic, and that conducted by Redican.

Redican (1985), in 'Subject Teachers under Stress', found that pastoral staff were gaining such control that they were damaging the subject-centred curriculum. Using interviews and observation, Redican constructed a variety of indicators to determine the relative status of subject teachers and pastoral staff: access to confidential information, office space and negotiation procedures. He claims that pastoral care represented an intrusion into the 'real job of teaching' and the 'sanctity of the lesson' and that the supervisory and guidance aspects of welfare had been extended by pastoral staff to exert control over subject teachers. Moreover pastoral staff were 'selectively promoted' despite 'inferior qualifications'. Through the delegation of authority outside their areas of competence, they employed strategies to erode the base of the subject teacher.

Perhaps, the contrast between Redican's findings and my own is a further illustration of the strength of the pastoral/academic boundary and the way in which it demands allegiance to either side. He can only refer to those on the 'pastoral side' with thinly disguised hostility. Those on the pastoral side are, in his own words, 'petty administrators', 'managers' and 'supervisory' staff. Subject teachers, on the other hand, are the 'doers', the 'real' teachers of 'proper' subjects displaying the qualities of 'academic leadership' over 'administrative management'. In contrast, it is perhaps more likely that Redican took on board one side's definition of the situation too uncritically and mistook phenomenal forms for more fundamental transformations.

That surface appearances can be deceptive is illustrated by the second of my case studies, Kings Marsh. In this school, the headteacher and his senior management team had embarked upon a radical programme of integration that might at first sight lead one to conclude that the pastoral dimension had indeed risen to a position of dominance. Attempts had been made to diminish the pastoral/academic boundary by resisting demarcation within senior management levels and generally elevating pastoral priorities throughout the school. At the same time, there were deliberate strategies to weaken the power of departments through diminishing the role of subject department heads and reorganizing subjects into clusters.

But while there was some erosion of the pastoral/academic boundary at Kings Marsh, ethnographic investigation revealed that this was often partial and superficial. It tended to be 'at the fringes' of the academic curriculum with the academic 'core' retaining strong boundaries. Paradoxically, the case of Kings Marsh might lead one to suggest that superficial integration may *strengthen* insulation at deeper levels with the 'loss' of 'marginal' academic subjects resulting in greater definition for those that remained intact. There is certainly no evidence to suggest that students were less differentiated within Kings Marsh. Indeed, such partial integration seemed to result in *sharper* stratification than at Elmfield.

Imposing the Theoretical Framework

Entering the field with a theoretical framework in mind may help prevent the researcher from being drawn too far into the perspectives of the researched, but it may also lead to a different kind of blindness. As I noted earlier, there have been concerns that Bernstein's theories in particular are to some extent self-confirming (e.g. Tyler, 1988).

Much of the research rested on highlighting the opposition between the pastoral and the academic dimensions. Where the academic was visible, the pastoral was invisible. Where the academic had strong insulation, the pastoral had weak insulation. It is perhaps worth questioning whether these were substantive differences or merely analytical caricatures. Were they real contrasts, or are they simply contrived, as Pring argues 'on the interesting logical device of dividing things into two types which . . . depends upon making one category simply the negative of the other' (1975, p. 71).

At first sight it does appear as if pastoral care is always defined in the negative — less boundaries, less identity, less screening. Is this because, as Pring suggests, the nature of the categories is essentially flawed? Is the use of Bernstein's framework helpful in understanding the relationship between the two areas, or is it simply making a point of difference through unhelpful contrast?

It is certainly the case that the division of the school curriculum into mutually exclusive areas is an analytical convenience which glosses over a degree of messiness within and between each dimension. There are some areas of the curriculum which it is hard to identify unambiguously as either academic or pastoral. However, the ambivalence of these elements, rather than disproving the fundamental nature of the opposition, can again be used to illustrate further the tension that resides between the pastoral and the academic dimensions.

Some subjects, for instance, that appeared on the timetable at Elmfield were not considered to be 'proper' subjects at all in the eyes of academic specialists. Although they may have had all the trappings of a subject — a demarcated slot on the timetable, syllabuses, textbooks and even some kind of formal assessment — they had never successfully established themselves within the academic framework (Goodson, 1987). The ambiguous status of these areas, such as Education in Personal Relationships, Community Studies and Citizenship, highlights the tension between the pastoral and the academic. Whether the pastoral or the academic dimension of these areas is emphasized, the force of the tension is such that dual identity was uncomfortable and undesirable.

But even if we establish that there are underlying oppositions between different practices that are manifest within the curriculum, to what extent can we attribute to them any explanatory power? Hammersley (1992) argues that much ethnography is essentially about description rather than theorized explanation. It is certainly the case that much of the fieldwork and subsequent account depended upon reconstituting data in line with elements of Bernstein's models. But in doing this I hoped to do more than simply replace common-sensical or naturalistic understandings of the relationship between the pastoral and the academic with a new set of descriptors. It seemed to me that through focusing on, dissecting and abstracting the underlying structure of the relationship it might be possible to identify the principles that accounted for the differentiation not just of teachers' professional identities but of students' careers.

However, exploring the significance of the boundary in these terms meant getting to grips with the messages embodied not just within one element of the curriculum, but those produced by the relationship *between* the pastoral and the academic. It could be argued that it is in looking at complex interrelationships such as these that ethnography is perhaps at its weakest. As Bernstein himself argues:

> Power is never more eloquent and penetrating than in the insulation it pro-
> duces between categories. From this point of view, research which focuses on
> communication within a classroom (that is, upon framing) misses entirely the
> complex messages transmitted *indirectly* by the principle of classification.
> (1977, pp. 198–9, his emphasis)

But, given the indirect nature of these transmissions, and the circumstantial
nature of any attributed consequences, it is difficult to ascertain what mode of
research could provide appropriately robust evidence. My research may not
have enabled me to present hard and fast 'findings' about the messages transmitted through classificatory principles and their consequences, but it did, I
believe, make it possible for me to construct empirically grounded and theoretically informed connections.

For instance, most simply, and yet crucially, it was possible to argue that
the pastoral/academic boundary perpetuates the 'objectivity' of the academic
dimension just by being there. Some of the consequences of perpetuating this
fiction were evident in differentiated staff identities. For example, the oppositional
nature of the relationship meant teachers were attributed with being 'clever' or
'caring', but not both. And there are, of course, significant gender dimensions
to this opposition. In addition, through examining the ways in which effort
and ability were differently and, and most importantly, *alternatively* rewarded,
it was possible to propose that the division between the pastoral and the
academic creates a mismatch between 'trying' and 'succeeding' that endorses
the naturalness of academic ability. One of the consequences of divorcing
effort from achievement is likely to be the promotion of the 'ideology of
aptitudes' (Bisseret, 1979) that obscures the extent to which children are differentially privileged.

Whether propositions such as these are seen to have any value beyond
'mere' speculation is likely to depend upon personal preference for structural
explanations of social phenomena. Some people, maybe with justification,
think that if connections cannot be empirically demonstrated they add little to
our understanding. But for some of us this may well mean losing sight of those
deeply embedded connections that contribute most to our understanding.

In addressing the way in which our understandings are themselves structured it is perhaps appropriate to come back to where the research started. I
shall therefore conclude with Bernstein's own account of how he came to
develop the ideas behind 'On the classification and framing of educational
knowledge':

> We cannot reflect the world, how it is, and any sociology which attempts this,
> which attempts to understand the practices whereby individuals construct
> order by disconnecting these practices from the structural relationships of
> which they are the outcome, is inevitably a sociology without history; either
> of members or of the sociologist. (1977, p. 13)

Acknowledgments

The research discussed in the chapter was funded by a grant from the Economic and Social Research Council. I'd also like to take this opportunity to thank again the staff and students at the two case-study schools and my supervisors Geoff Whitty and Len Barton. In addition, Geoff Whitty also provided helpful comments on an earlier draft of this chapter.

References

BATES, I. (1996) 'Review symposium on The Pastoral and the Academic: Conflict and Contradiction in the Curriculum (Sally Power)', *British Journal of Sociology of Education*, **17**, 3, pp. 351–65.

BENNETT, D.J. and BENNETT, J.D. (1971) 'Making the scene', in COSIN, B.R., DALE, I.R., ESLAND, G.M. and SWIFT, D.F. (eds) *School and Society: A Sociological Reader*, London: Routledge and Kegan Paul.

BERNSTEIN, B. (1971) 'On the classification and framing of educational knowledge', in YOUNG, M.F.D. (ed.) *Knowledge and Control*, London: Collier Macmillan.

BERNSTEIN, B. (1977) *Class, Codes and Control, Volume 3 (Second Edition)*, London: Routledge and Kegan Paul.

BERNSTEIN, B. (1990) *The Structuring of Pedagogic Discourse: Class Codes and Control, Volume 4*, London: Routledge.

BISSERET, N. (1979) *Education, Class, Language and Ideology*, London: Routledge and Kegan Paul.

DANIELS, H.J.J. (1988) 'An enquiry into different forms of special school organization, pedagogic practice and pupil discrimination', *CORE*, **12**, 2.

DANIELS, H.J.J. (1989) 'Visual displays as tacit relays of the structure of pedagogic practice', *British Journal of Sociology of Education*, **10**, 2, pp. 123–40.

DAVIES, B. (1995) 'Bernstein on classrooms', in ATKINSON, P., DAVIES, B. and DELAMONT, S. (eds) (1995) *Discourse and Reproduction: Essays in Honor of Basil Bernstein*, New Jersey: Hampton Press.

DOMINGOS, A.M. (1989) 'Influence of the social context of the school on the teacher's pedagogic practice', *British Journal of Sociology of Education*, **11**, 2, pp. 155–69.

EDWARDS, A.D. (1995) 'Changing pedagogic discourse', in ATKINSON, P., DAVIES, B. and DELAMONT, S. (eds) *Discourse and Reproduction: Essays in Honor of Basil Bernstein*, New Jersey: Hampton Press.

GOODSON, I. (1987) *School Subjects and Curriculum Change (2nd Edition)*, London: Falmer Press.

HAMMERSLEY, M. and ATKINSON, P. (1995) *Ethnography: Principles and Practice (2nd Edition)*, London: Tavistock.

HAMMERSLEY, M. (1992) *What's Wrong with Ethnography?*, London: Routledge.

KING, R. (1976) 'Bernstein's sociology of the school: Some propositions tested', *British Journal of Sociology* **27**, pp. 430–43.

KING, R. (1981) 'Bernstein's sociology of the school — a further testing', *British Journal of Sociology*, **32**, pp. 259–65.

LYONS, G. (1981) *Teacher Careers and Career Perception*, Windsor: NFER.

MARLAND, M. (1980) 'The pastoral curriculum', in BEST, R., JARVIS, C. and RIBBINS, P. (eds) *Perspectives on Pastoral Care*, London: Heinemann Educational, pp. 151–70.

MITCHELL, J.C. (1983) 'Case and situation analysis', *Sociological Review*, **32**, 2, pp. 187–211.

POWER, S. (1996) *The Pastoral and the Academic: Conflict and Contradiction in the Curriculum*, London: Cassell.

PRING, R. (1975) 'Bernstein's classification and framing of knowledge', *Scottish Educational Studies*, November, pp. 67–74.

REDICAN, B. (1985) 'Subject teachers under stress', in WALFORD, G. (ed.) *Schooling in Turmoil*, London: Croom Helm.

SCHATZMAN, L. and STRAUSS, A.L. (1973) *Field Research: Strategies for a Natural Sociology*, Englewood Cliffs, New Jersey: Prentice Hall.

SIMONS, H. (1981) 'Conversation piece: The practice of interviewing in case study research', in ADELMAN, C. (ed.) *Uttering, Muttering: Collecting, Using and Reporting Talk for Social and Educational Research*, London: Grant McIntyre.

SINGH, P.L. (1993) 'Institutional discourse and practice: A case study of the social construction of technological competence in the primary classroom', *British Journal of Sociology of Education*, **14**, 1, pp. 39–58.

TYLER, W. (1988) *School Organization: A Sociological Perspective*, London: Croom Helm.

3 'Are you a girl or are you a teacher?' The 'Least Adult' Role in Research about Gender and Sexuality in a Primary School

Debbie Epstein[1]

During 1995–96, I did a small-scale piece of ethnography in a Year 5 class of a London primary school (Edenfield School)[2] to investigate the gendered cultures of the children and how questions around sexuality were involved in the ways gendered identities were put in place. The substantive findings of the project have been published elsewhere (Epstein, 1997; Epstein and Johnson, 1998, especially Chapters 5 and 6) so the purpose of this paper is to consider some of the methodological and ethical questions that arose during the course of the project ('warts and all' as Geoffrey Walford said when he invited me to write this chapter).

The project arose from several different strands of my work and networks. During the early 1990s I had worked on some connected projects around sexuality, gender and ethnicity on which I had collaborated with Richard Johnson (Epstein and Johnson, 1998), Peter Redman (1994) and others in the Politics of Sexuality Group (Steinberg, Epstein and Johnson, 1997). Our work in secondary schools, along with evidence from other researchers,[3] had convinced us that it was necessary to investigate what, at the time, we called 'sexual cultures' of primary schools and some of us (myself, Maírtín Mac an Ghaill and Peter Redman) had put in a bid to the Economic and Social Research Council (ESRC) for funding for a project which would have followed children from Year 6 into Year 7. This proposal, though alpha-rated did not receive funding,[4] so we were left with the problem of whether to try again and of what to do next.

Second, I had spent approximately 17 years in primary (mainly early years) schools/classrooms and two as a Teacher Adviser in a Local Education Authority (LEA) before giving up my job in 1989 to finish my PhD, so it was some time since I had had regular contact with schools. Since I had left my LEA job just as the National Curriculum was coming in, I felt that not only had I been too long outside the classroom but that the changes in UK schools which had taken place during the 1990s (following the Education Reform Act 1988 and the Education Act 1993) were so vast that my research would be seriously weakened if I did not soon spend some significant time in schools on some basis.

Third, I happened to know a teacher of a Year 5 class ('Mr Stuart') who was concerned about many of the issues we were interested in investigating. These issues revolved around questions about what young children understand when they talk, as so many of them do, about boyfriends/girlfriends, dating, 'dumping', 'two-timing', 'going out' and so on. How, we wanted to know, are these discursive practices (including talk) gendered and how far are they part of the construction of gender within and through schooling? Can they be seen as strategies for establishing gender boundaries (see Thorne, 1993)? To what extent can we see, played out in the primary school context, the imposition, policing and performance of 'compulsory heterosexuality' (Butler, 1990; Rich, 1980)? And in what ways, when children 'do (heterosexual) gender', is this performed through ethnicity, class and other social divisions? Conversations with Mr Stuart led to the idea that I could spend time in his class conducting a small-scale study as a pilot for developing our previously unsuccessful research proposal in order to have another go at obtaining funding. This more or less haphazard combination of theoretical/research interests, pragmatic approaches and personal networks is fairly typical, I believe, of most research projects, though often accounts are much more seamless than this one might appear.

In this chapter, I will try to trace the development of the research as well as considering some of the issues which are raised by doing research on such sensitive topics as gender and sexuality in primary schools. Here, I will be particularly concerned with three issues: first, the limitations of the adoption of the 'least adult role' by the researcher; second, and related, how children understand the presence of the researcher, and what this might mean in the production of meaning within the research process; and third, ethical questions, particularly around 'informed consent' which arise when doing research on children and which may be made even more acute when dealing with sensitive topics like gender, sexuality, 'race', and identity (all key areas of interest for me). Much of this is grist to the feminist mill and this chapter arises directly out of my engagement with feminist methodological debates. I do not, in this context, intend to lay out in detail either the case for feminist research or the ins and outs of previous writing, which readers can, in any case, follow up for themselves.[5] Rather, my focus will be on those issues which intrigued, worried or pleased me as a feminist researcher during the course of this particular small-scale project.

Calling on the 'Child Inside': Seeking the 'Least Adult' Role

Part of my preparation for going into school, was to discuss with Mr Stuart, the head teacher ('Mr Snowden'), and other teachers the role that I would take up in the classroom and playground during the course of my research. We agreed that I would not adopt anything like a 'teacherly' role but would, as far as possible, integrate with the pupils, learning from them and trying to see things from their point of view. This was a contrast to my previous research in primary schools which had been conducted from the position of teacher-as-researcher and of Teacher Adviser within the Local Education Authority (Epstein, 1993), when my aim was to learn about school processes and teaching strategies.

Barrie Thorne (1993) writes evocatively about her experience of trying to learn from (rather than about) children for *Gender Play: Boys and Girls in School*, a book which significantly influenced my thinking in this work:

> I slowly came to realize that within the ethnographer, many selves were at play. Responding to our shared positions as adult women and as teachers, I easily identified with Miss Bailey and the other school staff. Being around so many children also stirred my more maternal emotions and perspectives . . . Occasionally I felt much like the fourth- and fifth-grader I used to be, and the force of this took me by surprise. This jangling chorus of selves gave me insight into the complexity of being an adult trying to learn from kids. (pp. 11–12)

I found that resisting the role of teacher was significantly more difficult than I had anticipated. This difficulty is not surprising, given the fact that most of my adult life has been spent teaching young children and that I have invested a great deal of psychic, emotional and social energy in 'becoming' and 'being' a teacher. I often found it hard not to intervene, not to ask 'teacherly' rather than 'researcherly' questions about their work and play. Corsaro (1985) draws attention to the necessity of reminding oneself constantly not to act like other adults when doing field work with children, pointing out that, in his observation:

> . . . adults primarily initiated contacts with the children; that is, they were primarily *active* rather than *reactive*. The teachers directed and monitored the children's play, helped in times of trouble, or told the children what they could or could not do. The adults would frequently move from one group of children to another, and initiate conversations without any real intention of engaging in extended interaction. (p. 28, original emphasis)

I spent virtually all my time in school with the children. Arriving about half an hour before school began, I would hang around in the playground as the pupils arrived; when school started, I would go in with 'my' class; at playtime and dinner break I would go out into the playground with the class, going into the dining room to have lunch with them, sometimes eating a school dinner and sometimes taking sandwiches and eating with those children who brought packed lunches to school. Occasionally, after school, I would wait until the children had left and then, gasping, go into the staffroom to have a cup of coffee and a chat with Mr Stuart and other teachers. Like Corsaro, I tried to be reactive, waiting for children to approach me, rather than initiating conversations or play with them. I studiously avoided adopting a disciplinary stance towards the children (apart from one occasion when I did stop a child from rushing out of the playground) and tried to speak to the children on their own terms at all times. In short, I tried to adopt a 'least adult role' in relation to the children.

I wanted to adopt this 'least adult role' for two main reasons. First, it is well known that children have different kinds of conversation with different kinds of adults and with each other. Children's talk in the home, for example, is very different to children's talk in schools (see, for example, Sealey, 1993). I thought that it might produce a different kind of information to that collected by the 'adult-as-teacher'. Second, and particularly in the light of my reading of Barrie Thorne's *Gender Play: Boys and Girls in School* (1993), I was interested in exploring my own perception from a different kind of ethnographic researcher position, one in which I could identify more with the children than the teachers.

There were, I think, some advantages to the 'least adult role'. Children did open up to me in ways which do not usually happen with teachers, even at this age. They also seemed to appreciate the fact that I was intensely interested in their thoughts and feelings in a way which is unusual in schools, partly because of the practical constraints on teachers trying to deal with many children at the same time, and partly because of the discursive position of teachers as being 'in charge'. Nevertheless, the 'least adult' position was not without its problems. Others, (for example, Corsaro, 1985; Davies, 1989; Fine and Sandstrom, 1988; Mandell, 1988; Thorne, 1993) have traced some of the difficulties in playing out this role. Bronwyn Davies (1989), for example, points out 'how tricky it is as adult to participate in this subtle, shifting complex world of childhood relations' (p. 37). This is partly because of children's expectations of adult behaviour, particularly in schools. Children would turn to me in class, expecting me to help them with their work; they would rush up to me in the playground with reports of misdemeanours by other children or to show me their scraped knees; in the dining room they would point out who was not eating their dinner. My usual response was to say that I was not worried about any of the 'naughty' things that children did, or to suggest they ask the dinner supervisor or teacher to help them, but this response did not come easily and I often found myself struggling to find words which did not compromise my 'least adult' status.

I have mentioned above the constant temptation to fall into the familiar and comfortable role of teacher, but my difficulty in not responding to children in this way was not only about my own autobiography and teacher identity but also, in a large degree, to do with the structures of schooling. The discursive space of the school is one in which there are a small number of adults responsible for the care and control of a very much larger number of children. Those adults who are regularly present in schools often (usually? nearly always?) insert themselves, or are positioned, within the discourses through which this space is organized — as instructors, demonstrators, discipliners, carers, first aiders, comforters, substitute mothers. As a researcher one can resist these discourses but it is impossible to refuse them completely or to step right outside of them, partly because the expectations of both children and other adults are so strongly organized through the discourses of adult-as-teacher.

When the children turned to me as an adult, the situation in which I was most likely to fall into a more teacherly role was when they asked me for help with their work. However, I did try to avoid doing this when the requests for help were more complicated than, for example, helping a child with spelling (which I would simply give them). Geoffrey Walford, in his editorial response to the first draft of this chapter, commented that helping children with their work when asked 'is what any adult might do and, more importantly, it is what friends would do. It seems to me that if you know that someone can help and refuses to do so, doesn't exactly help that relationship!' His point is well made, and may help to explain some of the discomfort I felt in refraining from helping children with their work at the time. Indeed, what he points up is the very contradictory way in which power relations operate. In one sense, the adoption of the 'least adult role' is an attempt to reduce power differential with the children, but, at the same time, it reinforces that very differential by imposing on them a 'least adult' construction when they might prefer to position the researcher in a more familiar adult position. And, clearly, the power differential does not go away and the children will not be convinced — however much the researcher tries to perform the 'least adult' role — that she or he is not an adult!

On the other hand, as Barrie Thorne (1993) points out, her size, adult status and relationships with teachers and, particularly, the head, created barriers to learning from the kids.[6]

> I knew that if I were too associated with adult authority, I would have difficulty gaining access to kids' more private worlds. Nor did I want the tasks of a classroom or playground aide. The practical constraints of keeping order and imposing an agenda would, I quickly realized, run against the open-ended curiosity and witnessing that ethnography requires. (p. 16)

Like Thorne and Davies, I worked hard to adopt the 'least adult role' possible, but ended up feeling that, as an adult, a teacher, a researcher, observing and writing about children, I was constantly re-inscribed within the discourse of adult-in-school, which is, primarily, that of teacher.

Bronwyn Davies (1989, pp. 35–38, 95–110) writes about one occasion on which she was able to 'gain complete access' to the pre-school children's world, playing as a child, within a pre-school group which she describes as being 'in part defined through the adoption of hegemonic masculine practices' (p. 35). As the boys' aggression towards her increased, she tried various well-known child strategies to defend herself — for example, saying she was in her 'safe hideaway' (p. 37) — and ultimately adopted the strategy of climbing to the top of the climbing frame and announcing that she was 'Queen of the World and that there was nothing they could do to hurt [her]' (p. 38). Davies provides a very lengthy set of transcripts to take the reader through the game (pp. 96–106) which actually ends when she 'reverts' to adult status.

Her reading of the game as an occasion when she was admitted fully into the children's world seems to me to be questionable. Reading the transcripts, it appears to me that part of what the boys are mad about is, precisely, that they know that she can revert to adult status. When she claims power as 'Queen of the World' their assertion of male power becomes an assault on her femaleness in a way which is somewhat reminiscent of Valerie Walkerdine's (1981) famous 'Miss Baxter-Paxter' — although in Bronwyn Davies' case, she is not positioned, as Miss Baxter was, as a sex object by the boys, but rather as powerless-because-female. Their furious aggression could be read as resistance to her adult power even while, at another level, she is positioning herself and being positioned as a child. In fact, at the penultimate moment of the game, Davies adopts a decidedly teacherly (or parental disciplinary) voice when she says to one of the children 'Don't do that. That's not very nice Brian' (p. 106).

What Davies does not discuss, however, is the extreme difficulty which a girl child, of the same age as the boys, would have in similarly refusing a hegemonic masculine discourse which rendered them powerless in an equivalent situation. I would suggest that one of the reasons why Davies could assert, with a degree of success, that she was 'Queen of the World' with absolute power was precisely her adult status. It seems likely that the scene, replayed with a girl asserting her authority as Queen of the World, would be more likely to result in physical injury to the girl rather than in the boys withdrawing, and that the girl's inability to emulate Davies in becoming an adult would, almost inevitably, result in her running to one. Moreover, a small girl would, most likely, not have been successful in preventing the teacher from intervening in the game, as Davies did at one point. In sum, Davies' adult status mitigated against her positioning as female-therefore-powerless, while, at the same time, her femaleness may have moderated her adult status.

Feminists have often written about the complex problems of representing the Other (see, for example, Wilkinson and Kitzinger, 1996). In this regard Christine Griffin (1996) asserts that:

> When, as a feminist and researcher, I 'speak for' other women (and sometimes 'for' men), I cannot avoid telling *my* story about *their* lives. I can use the voices of Others from (my understanding of) their positions, but I can never speak/write *from* their positions. I cannot become them, I can only pass on selected aspects of (what they have shown me about) their lives. (p. 189, original emphasis)

Sandra Harding (1991), writing about white American feminists' relation to Black American feminism, says that she

> . . . can be only a white who intends to take responsibility for her racial location; I cannot be a person of Third World descent, seeking to take responsibility for that different social location. (p. 283)

Similarly, adult researchers into children's lives cannot be children. This may be particularly the case in the context of schools where, as I have argued above, the very structures of schooling and age relations more generally compromise an adult researcher's ability to enter into a child role, or to adopt completely a child's standpoint. On the other hand, we can try to start from children's lives, listen to children, and take responsibility for our different social locations. Furthermore, notwithstanding the different ways in which childhood is constituted at different times and in different geographical and social locations,[7] we can draw on our memories of childhood in ways in which white researchers, for example, cannot draw on memories of being black. Moreover, adult researchers may, as Davies and Thorne both indicate, regress during the research process so that, however momentary the regression, there are times when we feel like a child. There are ways in which this is both a strength and a weakness. On the one hand, it gives us a direct point of entry into the children's worlds and an empathetic connection to them. On the other, we may overestimate the degree to which we understand from children's points of view precisely because of resonances with our own past experiences.

Children 'Researching' the Researcher

In my own research, I have been much less invested than Bronwyn Davies appears to have been in almost becoming a child. My adoption of the 'least adult role' lay in allowing children to make the first move in most interactions (at least in the early stages of the research), answering their questions as openly and as honestly as I could, allowing them to draw and write in my field notebook when they wanted to, and joining in their play when invited and in ways which were physically open to me (I could, for example, turn the skipping rope for them, but was mostly too tall to be able to use their skipping ropes myself — as well as being significantly less physically fit than the children). Corsaro (1985, pp. 28–9) records that it was only on his fourth afternoon in the nursery school that any of the children initiated discussion with him. I did not have to wait so long, possibly because the children were older (9–10 rather than 3–4) and more confident about approaching an adult. Not only that, they were also interested in quizzing me about what I was doing, who I was, and where I came from. My research diary for my first day in school records the children's early attempts to find out more about me:

> We had to come in a bit early from dinner break because it was wet play. In the classroom I had the following conversation with Cuneyt and another boy [whom I later identified as Marios]:
>
> *Marios*:   Are you Australian?
> *DE*:   No, I'm South African.
> *Cuneyt*:   (surprised) Oh! I thought you'd be Jewish or Mediterranean!
> *DE*:   Well, I *am* Jewish.
> *Cuneyt*:   (looks puzzled)
> *DE*:   Jewish *and* South African.
>
> I think it's interesting that C is so aware of ethnicity. How on earth did he come to conclusion that I was Jewish or Mediterranean? I am much more used

to questions from children based on my accent (Marios thinking I was Australian — this happens a lot). It must have been based on my appearance — or perhaps my name, but I doubt that. I must ask him some time. (Research diary: 7 September 1995)

This early interchange illustrates graphically the children's interest in trying to establish, for themselves, who I was and what I was doing at the school and in their classroom. They were quite as interested in finding out who I was as I was in finding out about them, and this interest was most vociferously expressed in my early days at the school. Cuneyt's guess seems extraordinarily accurate and, as I say in my diary, surprising.

Other children, including some not in 'my' class also asked about me. The question of my chapter title, 'Are you a girl or are you a teacher?', was asked of me in the playground during my first full week in the school. The girl who asked me this question had spent some time observing me (watching me watching them) and then came up to me with her query. My research diary notes that:

I was standing in the playground chatting to some of the girls when Aysegul ran up to me. Although she is not in 'my' class, it seems like she has been talking to some of the girls who are. She interrupted my conversation with the others:

Aysegul:	Are you a girl or are you a teacher?
DE:	Well, I'm not a teacher here.
Aysegul:	Are you a girl then? Are you a student teacher?
DE:	No, I'm not a student teacher.
Aysegul:	What are you?
DE:	(slowly) We-ell, I'm a researcher.

I expected Aysegul to ask me what that meant, but she went off on another tack:

Aysegul:	How old are you?
DE:	How old do you think I am?
Aysegul:	21
DE:	No, I'm *much* older than that.
Aysegul:	51
DE:	That's right.
Aysegul:	Why haven't you got old hair?

(Research diary: 9 September 1995)

When Aysegul asked me whether I was a girl or a teacher, I was initially thrown, then pleased. It seemed to me that the query indicated that I was managing not to behave like a teacher — I was not disciplining children, nor was I telling them what to do and where to go, nor was I showing them how to do things. Her problem was that I did not fit into any framework that she had for understanding who I was. Adults in schools are usually teachers (or student teachers), or exert authority over the children in some other way (for example, as dinner

supervisors or classroom assistants). It seemed that the word 'researcher' had
no meaning for her and, rather than ask what it did mean, she followed up her
query about whether I was a girl or a teacher by delving into my age (and here,
too, it seemed that I was puzzling, since someone as old as me ought to have
had 'old hair'!). Aysegul's enquiries about my age were, in a way, a logical
follow-up to her first question. Maybe my age would give her a better handle
on who I was, given that she did not understand the concept of 'researcher'.

Informing Children/Informed Consent

It was not really until after I had completed the fieldwork and begun to analyse my data, that I realized that if the children lacked a framework for understanding who I was as a researcher, then the notion that they had given their
informed consent to the research was, at least, questionable. Prior to the research and as it started, I tried to be very careful to abide by ethical guidelines
which demand that the subjects of the research give their 'informed consent' to
being researched. My discussions with Mr Stuart about what the research might
involve took place over a period of weeks; I wrote to Mr Snowden putting in
writing my commitment to retaining the school's anonymity, and met him early
on to discuss the issues that might arise in relation to my work, especially given
its sensitive nature; Mr Stuart wrote, on my behalf, to the parents of children in
his class explaining who I was, what I would be doing and how it would fit in
with the class topic on 'Me, my family and my history'. Mr Stuart told the parents that I was researching the ways that boys and girls related to and thought
about each other. He also pointed out that the project would include sex education and might give rise to questions about sex and sexuality. Parents were
invited to meet with him and me if they had any questions or worries and I
promised that I would not record observations of their children if they preferred me not to (no-one took up this offer).

   I started at the school on the second day of term, and, after assembly, Mr
Stuart asked me to introduce myself to the children. My explanation to the
children of my interests was honest, and as full as I thought would be under-
standable to them, but possibly were not as full as it might have been:

> I took this opportunity to tell them that I was a 'researcher', and I was inter-
> ested in the things they did, the ways they got on with each other, who their
> friends were, and, especially, the ways that girls and boys got on with each
> other and did not get on with each other. I showed them my notebook and
> said that I would be writing down the things that I saw and that they said, but
> that I would not be showing Mr Stuart or any of the other teachers what I
> wrote down. I explained that they could ask me what I had written down
> about them and that if there was stuff that they didn't want written down, they
> should just tell me and I would tear it out if I had already written it. (Research
> diary: 7 September 1995)

This was not the beginning and end of the explanation of my research to the children or of the process of getting and retaining their consent in practice. I always answered questions about what I was doing as honestly as I could, and when, on occasion, they asked me why I was interested in a particular game (for example their version of 'Blind Date'), I told them that I was interested in finding out what they thought about boyfriends, girlfriends and going out.

During my introduction of myself, I also told the children that I was hoping, eventually, to write about them in a book, and that they could choose their own names as I would not use their real names. This has actually caused me some difficulty because the children have often chosen the name of their best friend in the class. It has also, to a significant extent, scuppered my usual practice (and the usual practice, I would think, of many ethnographic researchers) of giving research subjects ethnically similar pseudonyms. I did not specifically ask the children to choose names common to their own ethnic/language group and did not intervene to prevent it. I have been asked whether, if a child had chosen a name of the other gender, I would have allowed it[8] and my honest answer would have to be that I had not thought about it at the time and still do not know what I would do. It would be very unusual for a girl to choose a boys' name, though they might, and sometimes did, choose names with gender ambiguity (Jo, for example, or Amarjit) and even more rare for a boy to choose a girls' name, probably because being a 'tomboy' is much more acceptable than being a 'sissy'. Gender is a very strongly bounded and policed binary and the ethnic differences in naming maybe less strongly marked because, in common sense, the boundaries seem more fluid. However, it is also true that the choice of names across ethnicities was likely to reflect the power dynamics of the wider society, with children from ethnic minority groups tending to choose more English-sounding pseudonyms than their own names when they chose names from across ethnic divides. This is not a problem I have solved: I like giving research subjects the opportunity to choose their own pseudonyms and find that they, especially when they are children, like this too; on the other hand, it may make publication of the research findings misleading in some ways. And I think that I would, probably, resist the use of non-ambiguous boys' names by girls and vice versa — though a judgment in such a situation would always have to be contingent, depending on the context.

The production of a book about the research was a subject of great excitement throughout the time I was at the school and even 18 months later, when I went to a concert at the school, some of the children asked me if I had written my book yet and when I said I had (Epstein and Johnson, 1998), they were happy to have featured in it, although they did not ask to see it. In telling their story, or the story of my time with them, then, it seems on one level that I am doing it with the children's knowledge and consent. But there still seems to be a level at which such knowledge and consent are hollow fictions. Geoffrey Walford (1991), writing about researching somewhat older children at Kingshurst City Technology College comments on the importance of researchers having a long-term involvement with their research subjects:

I believe this is particularly pertinent when attempting to obtain information
on children's (rather than adults') thoughts and experiences. First, it is far
easier to explain confidentiality and the purpose of research to adults than it is
to children. But, second, children also have less reason than adults for believ-
ing that an interviewer is going to be honest with them, and they are often
correct in being cautious about claims from adults about confidentiality. (p. 97)

This is a concern for me in my research. I have always used the chosen pseudonyms (even in my field notes), to the extent that I cannot now always remember the children's real names, but I am sure that the head and other teachers
reading my articles were probably able to identify several of the children. This
is not something that the children themselves were worried about. Indeed, it
was not unusual to hear children going up to Mr Stuart or Mr Snowden and
saying things like 'D'ya know what my name's gonna be in Debbie's book? It's
gonna be_____'. My promises to the children and to the adults involved in the
school were at odds with each other in this respect. I had promised Mr Snowden
that I would show him anything I wrote about the school before publication.
In the light of the potential for adverse publicity for a school which allows
access to researchers in such sensitive areas, I believe that this was an important, and correct, decision. My undertaking was that I would make every effort
to meet any objections he had which were pertinent to protecting the school's
good name, though I did not offer him the power of veto on my analysis of the
data I collected.[9] On the other hand, I had promised the children confidentiality and Mr Snowden would probably be able to identify many of them from
their reported activities and conversations. But perhaps more important than
concerns about confidentiality, is the realization that my explanation of my
role to the children did not, in fact, enable them to give their informed consent
to the research since they had no experience by which to make sense of my
role. Notwithstanding their clear and sophisticated ability to decide how much
to say to me (or any other adult) in reply to my questions, my explanations
about doing research were, to a certain degree, nonsense to them.

Of course, children are regularly put into positions where their consent
is assumed not to be needed or irrelevant. Medical procedures, for instance,
require the consent of parents rather than children and, indeed, in this (and
other) research parental consent overrides that of children; I would not have
been able to note observations of children whose parents objected no matter
how keen the children were to be part of the research. In the case of medical
procedures, one might be able to argue children are unable to make the best
judgments and that it is in their own interests that decisions are taken for them
by others. However, in social research the benefits, if any, are rarely, indeed
almost never, directly to the research subjects.[10] Rather, there may be a more
general gain for, for example, the category 'children in school' if we know
more about schooling processes and about children's cultures in schools. On
the other hand, one might also wish to argue that children should have rights
in relation to issues like medical treatment too and might, in some cases, know

better about their illness than concerned adults. Indeed, there are a whole range of issues over which I would want to argue that children's abilities to make adequate judgments are much greater than we give them credit for and that their ability to give 'informed consent' may be contingent on a number of different factors, just as it is for adults. Some of these, like the form and amount of explanation given, the researcher has the power to deal with. Others, like the degree to which children are accustomed to being consulted about their lives and therefore practised in making decisions, are beyond the researcher's control.

Furthermore, it seems to me that the concept of 'informed consent' is always flawed and is applied inconsistently. First, in any kind of ethnographic work, an inescapable consequence of the presence of an observing outsider is that the practices and relationships of the group being researched will be changed, however subtly. The aim of the ethnographer must be, in part, to cause as little disturbance to the culture of the research subjects as possible. But explaining the research in detail to participants is likely to make more difference to the aspect of the 'local culture' being particularly explored than one would, ideally, like. Thus my explanation that I was especially interested in how girls and boys got on with each other may have made them more conscious than usual of gender relations (at least for a while), even if they did not quite 'get' what being a 'researcher' meant or precisely what aspects of gender relations I was concerned with. Second, very few social scientists would question the ethical status of, for example, covert research on far Right groups (see, for example, Hewitt, 1996) whereas almost everyone now condemns covert research on subordinated groups (for example, Humphreys, 1970). Indeed, in my own research on anti-racist strategies in predominantly white primary schools, I have felt less concerned that I might not have had the fully 'informed consent' of teachers (Epstein, 1991, Chapter 1) than I do about the inadequately informed consent of the children on this occasion.

The judgment being made, then, is an ethical/political one and ethical guidelines need to be read in that context. I am comfortable with this. Feminist researchers have long argued that all research is political and that research always involves power relations (see, for example, Bowles and Klein, 1983; Harding, 1987; Roberts, 1981; Siraj-Blatchford, 1994; Stanley, 1990). I do not believe that fascists or powerful elites necessarily require the same consideration as vulnerable groups. My difficulty, of course, is that children in schools are neither fascist nor powerful. The judgment to be made, then, is a somewhat different one: is the research important enough to justify researching children when their capacity for informed consent may be limited in the ways that I have discussed here? and have I made every effort to explain to the children what I was trying to do in order that their consent might be as informed as possible? In this context, the importance of laying out exactly how one has negotiated this particular minefield of power relations cannot be over-stressed. I am grateful that Geoffrey Walford's request for a chapter for this book has given me the opportunity to do this.

Notes

1   I am grateful to Deborah Lynn Steinberg for discussions about this paper and for her detailed comments on parts of it. I would also like to thank Geoffrey Walford for his careful and interesting editorial comments and the participants at the 1997 *Ethnography and Education* Conference, Oxford, for their constructive discussion of my presentation of an earlier draft of this paper.

2   The school's name and all names of teachers and children have been changed in line with the name changes I have used elsewhere in relation to this work.

3   For example, Walkerdine (1981), Jackson (1982), Lees (1986, 1987, 1993), Wolpe (1988), Thomson and Scott (1991), Davies (1993), Mac an Ghaill (1994), Ray (1994), Epstein (1995), Silin (1995).

4   Proposals to the ERSC are subject to peer review. Reviewers are asked to rate such proposals, with 'alpha' as the highest rating. During the 1990s, approximately 30 per cent of alpha-rated projects have been funded by the ESRC.

5   Methodological debates have formed a significant area of concern within feminist theory and practice. Concerns have ranged from consideration of whether there are specific methods which are inherently more conducive to feminist research to whether research should always be on/with women to ethical questions about the conduct of the research. Other major concerns, especially in engagements between feminism and postmodernism, have been questions of how to represent one's research findings and one's research subjects, the nature of truth claims in research, and the interpretation of 'experience'. For a very small selection of books out of a huge body of literature dealing with one or more of these issues, see Stanley and Wise (1983, 1993), Harding (1987, 1991), Stanley (1990, 1992), Stanley and Morgan (1993), Bell et al. (1993), Gitlin (1994), Maynard and Purvis (1994), Behar and Gordon (1995), Wilkinson and Kitzinger (1996).

6   'Kids' is Thorne's term, chosen on the basis of discussions with the children she was researching about how they would like to be described.

7   This is a matter of intense interest to me as an immigrant from South Africa. In that context, as a white 13-year-old at the time of Sharpeville, I was unusual in being involved in anti-apartheid politics in contrast to those black children who, some 15 years later, were largely responsible for making apartheid South Africa ungovernable and, indeed, making a revolution. In 1961 I was positioned as a precocious schoolgirl while many of my fellow South Africans of the same age were working or responsible for keeping house and childcare while their parents worked.

8   I am grateful to Geoffrey Walford for raising this point with me.

9   On a previous occasion, I had, in fact, withdrawn a chapter from a book because of the fears of the head about potentially adverse publicity, and substituted a two paragraph account of why the chapter had not appeared (Epstein, 1994).

10 I am grateful to Judith Green for discussions about this section of the paper.

References

BEHAR, R. and GORDON, D.A. (eds) (1995) *Women Writing Culture*, Berkeley & Los Angeles, CA: University of California Press.

BELL, D., CAPLAN, P. and KARIM, W.J. (1993) *Gendered Fields: Women, Men and Ethnography*, London: Routledge.

BOWLES, G. and KLEIN, R.D. (eds) (1983) *Theories of Women's Studies*, London: Routledge.

BUTLER, J. (1990) *Gender Trouble: Feminism and the Subversion of Identity*, London: Routledge.

CORSARO, W.A. (1985) *Friendship and Peer Culture in the Early Years*, Norwood, NJ: Ablex Publishing.

DAVIES, B. (1989) *Frogs and Snails and Feminist Tales*, St Leonards, NSW: Allen and Unwin.

DAVIES, B. (1993) *Shards of Glass: Children Reading and Writing Beyond Gendered Identities*, St Leonards, NSW: Allen and Unwin.

EPSTEIN, D. (1991) 'An examination of anti-racist pedagogies, INSET and school change in the context of local and national politics', Unpublished PhD Thesis: University of Birmingham.

EPSTEIN, D. (1993) *Changing Classroom Cultures: Anti-racism Politics and Schools*, Stoke-on-Trent: Trentham Books.

EPSTEIN, D. (1994) 'Lesbian and gay equality within a whole school policy', in EPSTEIN, D. (ed.) *Challenging Lesbian and Gay Inequalities in Education*, Buckingham: Open University Press.

EPSTEIN, D. (1995) ' "Girls Don't Do Bricks." Gender and sexuality in the primary classroom,' in SIRAJ-BLATCHFORD, J. and SIRAJ-BLATCHFORD, I. (eds) *Educating the Whole Child: Cross-curricular Skills, Themes and Dimensions*, Buckingham: Open University Press.

EPSTEIN, D. (1997) 'Cultures of schooling/cultures of sexuality', *International Journal of Inclusive Education*, **1**, 1, pp. 37–53.

EPSTEIN, D. and JOHNSON, R. (1998) *Schooling Sexualities*, Buckingham: Open University Press.

FINE, G.A. and SANDSTROM, K.L. (1988) *Knowing Children: Participant Observation with Minors*, Newbury Park, CA: Sage.

GITLIN, A. (ed.) (1994) *Power and Method: Political Activism and Educational Research*, London: Routledge.

GRIFFIN, C. (1996) ' "See whose face it wears": Difference, otherness and power', *Feminism and Psychology*, **6**, 2, pp. 184–91.

HARDING, S. (ed.) (1987) *Feminism and Methodology: Social Science Issues*, Bloomington, in Milton Keynes: Indiana University Press/Open University Press.

HARDING, S. (1991) *Whose Science? Whose Knowledge? Thinking from Women's Lives*, Milton Keynes: Open University Press.

HEWITT, R. (1996) *Routes of Racism*, Stoke-on-Trent: Trentham Books.

HUMPHREYS, L. (1970) *Tearoom Trade: A Study of Homosexual Encounters in Public Places*, London: Duckworth (originally published, Chicago: Aldine, 1970).

JACKSON, S. (1982) *Childhood and Sexuality*, Oxford: Basil Blackwell.

LEES, S. (1986) *Losing Out: Sexuality and Adolescent Girls*, London: Hutchinson.

LEES, S. (1987) 'The structure of sexual relations in school', in ARNOT, M. and WEINER, G. (eds) *Gender and the Politics of Schooling*, London: Hutchinson/The Open University.

LEES, S. (1993) *Sugar and Spice: Sexuality and Adolescent Girls*, London: Penguin.

MAC AN GHAILL, M. (1994) *The Making of Men: Masculinities Sexualities and Schooling*, Buckingham: Open University Press.

MANDELL, N. (1988) 'The least-adult role in studying children', *Journal of Contemporary Ethnography*, **16**, pp. 433–67.

MAYNARD, M. and PURVIS, J. (eds) (1994) *Researching Women's Lives from a Feminist Perspective*, London: Taylor & Francis.

RAY, C. (1994) *Highlight: Sex Education*, London: National Children's Bureau/Barnardo's.

REDMAN, P. (1994) 'Shifting ground: Rethinking sexuality education', in EPSTEIN, D. (ed.) *Challenging Lesbian and Gay Inequalities in Education*, Buckingham: Open University Press.

RICH, A. (1980) 'Compulsory heterosexuality and lesbian existence', *Signs*, **54**, 4, pp. 631–60.

ROBERTS, H. (ed.) (1981) *Doing Feminist Research*, London: Routledge.

SEALEY, A. (1993) 'Making up stories: The constraints of discourse in research with children', Paper given at *British Sociological Association*, University of Essex.

SILIN, J.G. (1995) *Sex, Death and the Education of Children: Our Passion for Ignorance in the Age of AIDS*, New York: Teachers College Press.

SIRAJ-BLATCHFORD, I. (1994) *Praxis Makes Perfect: Critical Educational Research for Social Justice*, Ticknall, Derbyshire: Education Now Books.

STANLEY, L. (ed.) (1990) *Feminist Praxis: Research, Theory and Epistemology in Feminist Sociology*, London: Routledge.

STANLEY, L. (1992) *The Auto/Biographical I: The Theory and Practice of Feminist Auto/Biography*, Manchester: Manchester University Press.

STANLEY, L. and MORGAN, D. (eds) (1993) *Sociology: Special Issue on Auto/Biography*, **27**, 1.

STANLEY, L. and WISE, S. (eds) (1983) *Breaking Out*, London: Routledge & Kegan Paul.

STANLEY, L. and WISE, S. (eds) (1993) *Breaking Out Again*, (2nd edn) London: Routledge.

STEINBERG, D.L., EPSTEIN, D. and JOHNSON, R. (eds) (1997) *Border Patrols: Policing the Boundaries of Heterosexuality*, London: Cassell.

THOMSON, R. and SCOTT, S. (1991) *Learning about Sex: Young Women and the Social Construction of Sexual Identity*, London: Tufnell Press.

THORNE, B. (1993) *Gender Play: Boys and Girls in School*, Buckingham: Open University Press (published in the US by Rutgers University Press).

WALFORD, G. (1991) 'Researching the City Technology College, Kingshurst', in WALFORD, G. (ed.) *Doing Educational Research*, London: Routledge.

WALKERDINE, V. (1981) 'Sex, power and pedagogy', *Screen Education*, **38**, pp. 14–24.

WILKINSON, S. and KITZINGER, C. (eds) (1996) *Representing the Other: A Feminism and Psychology Reader*, London: Sage.

WOLPE, A. (1988) *Within School Walls: The Role of Discipline, Sexuality and the Curriculum*, London: Routledge.

4   Critical Moments in the *Creative Teaching* Research

Peter Woods

Introduction

We have been researching creative teaching since the mid 1980s (Woods, 1990, 1993a, 1995; Woods and Jeffrey, 1996). I wish to consider here some of the critical moments in this research. Like teaching, research consists of a bedrock of planning and routine. There are many false trails and blockages and unsure directions (Measor and Woods, 1991). In qualitative research in particular it is customary to have long boring periods when the whole research rationale comes under question, and/or the researchers are swamped by the data. The 'creative teaching' research was no different from this. But it did have its critical moments. These can be either positive or negative. It is the former I am concerned with here. Without them, the work would have been much diminished. In some cases, the criticality arose from the conjuncture of chance, accident, or 'near miss' (something that nearly did not happen) on the one hand, and particularly revelatory insight on the other — a phenomenon commonly termed 'serendipity'. Of course, chance occurrences can destroy, as well as create. Fine and Deegan (1996), in their discussion of 'serendipity', comment

> The difference lies in being prepared to turn what seems like the ashen remains of a project into a creative opportunity for scientific discovery. In this way, courting serendipity involves planned insight married to unplanned events. (p. 435)

But critical moments occur not only through chance. They may be the product of a particular decision, or somebody else's key input, or a combination of factors that go uncommonly well. They have three distinguishing characteristics: 1) they lead to exceptional insight; 2) this result is unanticipated; and 3) they are radical in that they lead to new directions for the research. All such instances, as with chance, require a quality of 'recognition' in the researcher — the ability to see and grasp the opportunity. In this paper, I select examples of types of prominent critical moments that have occurred throughout the research. First, I give a brief description of the creative teaching research to date.

Creative Teaching

During many years of observing teachers at work, I have been aware of a special quality which seems to pervade their best work, to inspire teaching and learning, to maximize learning opportunities, and to cope with difficulties. It enables them to devise 'coping' and 'survival strategies', to adapt to the curriculum, and to manage the conflict in the teacher role. My research in primary schools in the 1980s impressed upon me the extent to which a particular quality informs the actual pedagogy of primary school teachers. I characterized the quality 'creative teaching' and studied its nature, manifestations, effectiveness, and attendant conditions (Woods, 1990).

I went on to consider exceptional cases of this kind of work. Analysis of these led to the concept of 'critical event' (Woods, 1993a). In contrast to routine processes and gradual cumulation of learning, critical events bring radical change in both pupils and teachers. The conditions favourable to their development include a supportive school ethos, certain resources such as time and finance, and critical agents. They also require some flexibility within the curriculum and scope within teachers' working conditions. I consequently examined the reactions of primary teachers to the National Curriculum, showing a range of adaptations from 'resistance' and 'appropriation' to 'enrichment' and 're-routeing' (Woods, 1995). A predominant theme throughout, whatever the adaptation, was 'self-determination' — the resolve of teachers to keep faith with their principles and beliefs, to stay true to their own selves, and to seek opportunities for self-renewal and realization in (and in some instances out) of teaching. Subsequently, we have explored the nature of creative teaching in the everyday interaction in the classroom (Woods and Jeffrey, 1996), and work continues on 'creative learning' (Woods, Boyle and Hubbard, 1997). In this article, I draw on methodological experiences across the range of this work to illustrate the impact of critical moments.

'Recovery' — Critical Moments of Access

There is a considerable literature on the problems of negotiating access in qualitative research. These are either to do with problems of 'getting in' and techniques of negotiating (for example, Beynon, 1983; Burgess, 1984), or with trends in society and how they affect attitudes within schools towards research, leading to variable ease of access at different times (Troman, 1996). There is little directly on how researchers themselves can affect access, often in unconscious ways; or on the occasionally surprising impact of others.

Access involves movement on the part of the researcher, but that cannot always be taken for granted. We can set up our own blocks through sloth, ennui, tiredness, failing spirit, bad choices where accepting one line of access stops more promising others. I was reminded of this at various points of the creative teaching research. Sometimes, however, something occurs which not only redeems the situation, but reveals startling new possibilities and provides new inspiration. I have termed the experience 'recovery', since it is to do with, as my dictionary tells me, 'finding again', 'making good', 'recapturing', 'bouncing back', 'getting back on one's feet', 'taking a turn for the better'. Two notable instances were as follows.

On the 'critical events' research, one part of my strategy was to visit the area where the educational event had occurred for two or three days in the first instance and engage in a concentrated period of interviews, observations and documentary inspection during my stay there. This was in order to extract as much data as possible from the situation while I was there. I could analyse and reflect at leisure once I got back home. Every minute of my day there was programmed, and it was very tiring. There were times when I was mentally and physically aching to opt out of part of the programme. I was always glad that I did not.

One of the 'critical events' I covered involved children from two primary schools planning and designing a heritage centre for their city, aided by their teachers and a group of architects and planners (discussed in Woods, 1993a). I experienced two moments of flagging wilt followed by exciting uplift. The first came at the end of a hard day's interviewing when I was recovering in my hotel in the early evening. I had been told that Philip Turner, Assistant County Planning Officer for the environment, who had been a member of the project, would be happy to talk to me that evening on his return from London, but was not available otherwise. I was sitting in the bar with a whisky and ginger in one hand and his card with his telephone number in the other, wondering what on earth he would be able to tell me that I hadn't been told already. It was raining heavily outside, and at the back of my mind, too, was the next day's crowded itinerary. Researchers, I think, must have a streak of masochism. I pulled myself together and phoned his number. That evening, the project came to life in Philip Turner's drawing room. It was a startling interview, full of new data and new insights from somebody with special skills and knowledge, and with a distinctive role in the team. He had folders of exhibits of the pupils' work at various stages. He pointed out aspects of its giftedness and of its deficiencies:

> I think the architects were pretty astounded at some of the results. Looking at some of these early designs, that one [pointing to one that was not actually pursued] is quite extraordinary for a 10–11-year-old, to have got to that stage with the concept of a building of that kind and to be able to draw it in that way almost entirely on his own. . . .

He was also reflexive, putting himself into the situation, looking at the effects on himself as part of the event. He recalled a talk he once gave to some sixth formers:

> They said to me: 'You half hinted that you would really like to see some strong planning control over what the farmers do as they are damaging the

environment, are you pressing for that?' and I said 'I don't think it's realistic in this political situation' and they said 'That's a cop out!' Now I remembered that and that's actually coloured my approach to the whole subject ever since.

In the critical event itself, Philip was what I have termed a 'critical other' (Woods, 1995). These are people who make a significant input into the event, but have no formal role within the institution where it is based. Their function is to enhance the role of the teacher, basically through the provision of a charismatic quality. This derives from three main attributes:

1 qualities emerging from being 'other'. They challenge the taken-for-granted, introduce novelty, present new role-models, make the familiar strange, widen perspectives;
2 personal qualities emerging from self, providing trust, faith and inspiration; they induce new insights, build confidence, strengthen relationships;
3 qualities emerging from 'profession', through their specialist knowledge and expertise contributing toward the authenticity of teachers' work.

Philip was a 'critical other' in these ways in respect of the research also. He contributed his own specialist knowledge and judgment, and his own enthusiasm and inspiration for the project were contagious. Though I had conducted a number of interviews on that day and gathered a great deal of information, it was only that evening that I began to capture some of the charisma that attended the event. The contrast with my earlier lethargy could not have been greater. This marks out 'critical others' as special kinds of 'key informants' — the usual conceptualization for this sort of relationship.

Charismatic input was to come from an even more surprising source. I had had another long day in one of the schools after a poor night's sleep in the hotel. The tough, continuous schedule had been arranged by the headteacher. The day began at 9 am with an hour-and-a-half's discussion with the headteacher. This was followed by a visit to the Teachers' Centre, where the children's work was on exhibition, and where I had another lengthy discussion with the Head of the Centre. Back at the school over a working lunch I continued my talk with the headteacher and studied more examples of the children's work. In the afternoon, I interviewed groups of children non-stop over a two-hour period. As I finished my last scheduled interview at 4 pm, I breathed a sigh of relief. It had been a good day, plenty of rich data. Now the mind, which had had to keep alert for every moment of the seven-hour day, yearned for rest. At this point, however, I was told that 7-year-old Jonathan, who had not been included in the group interviews, 'wanted to talk to me, would I see him, or had I seen enough?' I really thought, quite strongly, that I had 'seen enough'. After all, data collection should leave room for concurrent reflection and analysis. But Jonathan was already at the door. As he came into the room, exhaustion was again taking hold and I was resigned to simply sitting there and going through the formula. However, as he talked on, there was an urgency and insistence in his words and manner that brought me back to full attention. The fact was that Jonathan was different from those I had seen earlier. I was told later that he was described by his teacher as 'a very average pupil', but to the astonishment of all, he had excelled at the project:

> This is exactly what this child needed. He's not a confident boy. He's a very worried child and he loved this project. He thrived on it and got a lot of attention because he came in with his lovely work and everybody praised it up to the hilt because it was quite exceptional for him. It was lovely to see him shine.

Jonathan wanted to convey this to me, and somehow, the brightness in his eye, the eagerness of his tone and his wide-awake body language perched on the edge of his chair brought even this worn out, ancient researcher back to life. It was a key discussion in two major respects. One was in the way it emphasized the charismatic quality that attends critical events, that can only be conveyed by feeling: that a small boy could conjure that effect on me in such circumstances illustrates the power of the charisma. Secondly, it was the key to two important parts of the learning theory that emerged from the research as a whole. The first illustrates understanding which includes 'developing a feel, a sensitivity, a grasp, and a love for a subject, entering creatively into the *spirit* of an area of enquiry' (Best, 1991, p. 269). The second was a key to the population of pupils affected by critical events (all learners, and *particularly* those who had not yet been very successful); and the degree to which they were affected.

These examples of 'serendipity relations' (Fine and Deegan, 1996, p. 440) illustrate the occasional cathartic effects on the researcher of subjects in situations where the opposite seemed prefigured. In the same moment and on the same matter that the research begins to hang heavy, one can experience that sublime excitement that comes with the totally unexpected.

A Critical Situation

Fine and Deegan (1996) talk about 'temporal serendipity' — 'being in the right place at the right time' or 'being exposed to a particularly dramatic event'. I want to concentrate on one such moment here, that again has sloth/exhaustion/bad management as a factor, but which provided access into the heart of another critical event — the Roade School production of 'Godspell' (in Woods, 1993a, 1993b and 1993c).

Roade is my local secondary school. They first produced 'Godspell' at the school for one week during December 1988. I heard that this was an outstanding production, and thought idly that it might qualify as a critical event. But by the time I got round to enquiring about a seat, all tickets had been sold. I didn't feel that I could ask for special privileges, not being in contact with anybody at the school, so it seemed that it was one of those opportunities I had let slip. 'Godspell' was not finished, however. It had been seen by selectors for the National Student Drama Festival, and chosen by them as one of the entries. It duly appeared at Cambridge in March/April 1989, and won a top award. Though all this was reported on the local radio, I made no attempt to go over to Cambridge to monitor events, though in retrospect this would have been a splendid opportunity. Following their success, however, BBC Northampton asked the school to give a final performance to the general public in Northampton to launch their BBC Children in Need appeal. This was given in October. Convinced there would be plenty of room at the spacious Derngate, I turned up at the door only to be told that it was a full house — except for one seat. Being able to get in at all was the first piece of luck, especially as there was a considerable queue behind me.

The second piece of luck was the position of this seat — in a side box almost on the stage itself. This was the reason it was still available — it was too close to appreciate the spectacle. But for a researcher, and especially one who welcomed participant observation, it was ideal. I was indeed almost part of the action. I was caught up in the swirling dances of the performers, singing songs with them, taking part in the interactions, feeling the force of meaningful looks, laughing and suffering with them. A most interesting and revealing sequence that I probably would not otherwise have noticed occurred during the interval. As usual, the audience relaxed, went out for coffee or sat and talked, but the performers stayed on the now dimly lit stage and in role, acting out little impromptu scenarios for their own amusement. I found this fascinating, giving me insights into a kind of 'back region' of the company's culture. The whole performance as I experienced it had a special character not available to professional companies and older actors, being essentially a celebration of youth within the framework of basic humanitarian values. There was something eternal, universal, reassuring and uplifting in this demonstration of the buoyancy of youth and its power and promise to sustain and renew the world on terms that are constantly under attack and often difficult to meet in the real world. I felt that I had visited the heart of the production, therefore. But my position was even better than this, for I was able to look out and see the bulk of the audience in the auditorium, which reminded me that there *was* an audience. I could monitor their reactions, put myself in their position, cultivate a measure of analytic distance, while at the same time entering fully into the spirit of the production.

Later that evening I made extensive fieldnotes on aspects of the production, the ingenious appropriateness of the adaptation, the skills of the players, the many different kinds of games, the blend of moods, tempo, noise, the meaningful minutiae, the camaraderie, the infectious zest, the 'organized chaos' of the choreography, the ecstatic audience who were at one with the players . . . But I also knew, from my analysis of other critical events, that this was the 'celebration' that came at the end of a long and involved educational process. It was a catalytic experience. Looking back, it was the *focal point* of the research on this event.

What such an experience does for the researcher is 1) induce a high state of cognitive and emotional awareness. There is a deep sense that you are witnessing something significant happening, that it is quite profound, and potentially very revealing. Researchers need motivation, too, and this provides it. One is excited by the possibilities, keenly alert in anticipation, and the mind buzzes with ideas. So much is to do with feeling and emotion. 'Observation' here carries wider connotations than just observing. One's whole self conjoins with the performers and audience alike in similar spirit; 2) being part of that celebration in that particular way informed the rest of my enquiry, and put an edge on my 'appreciation' (Eisner, 1985) that enabled me to take the analysis a little further than some of the other events (Woods, 1993b and 1993c). One of the central notions of the analysis, for example, that of 'communitas' (Turner, 1974), began with my 'appreciating' the strong affective bonds which were particularly evident in the 'offstage' moments of the performance; 3) witnessing the event enabled me to triangulate what participants told me later. But, more than this, it enabled me to pick up on some of the fine detail that occurred which participants later referred to in interview — a change in inflection of voice, a slight gesture, a look, a small item of dress — which all contributed to the richness of the experience; 4) It was an integrating experience. The interconnections among the various strands of the later analysis were all demonstrated here. Furthermore it was a defining moment, and a final one. This was what all the preparation over the previous 18 months had been about. Things had never been quite like this before, and, in some senses, never would be again.

A question raised is whether the 'embracement' of the researcher in this way has negative consequences for the research. Is there not even more of a risk of 'going native' (Paul, 1953), and losing one's own perspective? Undoubtedly, the higher the stakes, the higher the dangers. But with respect to 'Godspell' the intensity was tempered by the 'analytic advantage' of my viewing position, and confined to the production. This enabled me to take a full share in their ultimate achievement, and to re-engage with that during later discussions in the attempt to understand fully the educational meaning of the event for participants — for later analysis at comparative leisure.

Critical Agents

Among the prominent factors contributing to 'critical events' were the 'critical agents' that stood at the heart of them. The events were their idea, their inspiration; and their drive, enthusiasm and organizing skills held things together and pushed things on to their successful conclusion. I also benefitted from their abilities and enthusiasm, in this case in organizing the research, a bonus I had not anticipated, though I did see the research in large measure as collaborative. Without prompting, they all volunteered to organize my concentrated visits to my specifications, and they did this extremely well. They managed to cram so many meetings and activities into two or three days, and to pilot me around the various venues with a contagious energy, sufficient to give me a good grounding in the event that I could then follow up with largely documentary (including tapes and videos) analysis. This revealed the need for further discussions in some cases, and a further visit. In reality, I feel, they were still living out the event, and they were offering me honorary membership of the 'communitas' that was such a prominent feature of them. The organizing of the research was all part of the event to which they dedicated the same amount of attention to detail, and the same kind of flair and creativity. Access into these events was in consequence a joy, a sharp contrast to experiences in some other circumstances (see, for example, Troman, 1996).

Critical agents also made a distinctive contribution themselves to understanding and interpretating the event. In long, exploratory conversations, critical agents and I strove to get to the 'heart of things'. Taking 'Godspell' again as an example, in the following exchange Sally (the producer) and I are considering the meaning of the event for her:

Sally: Well, I suppose it's changed my life in that it's taken over a year of my life really, fully, and almost excessively, I suppose, at times so that in that sense obviously it's like dominated a whole year of your life. You can't be the same person after that. If anything takes over your life for years, you're going to change, depending what it is. On this occasion, it's yes, it's difficult to say exactly how. I feel much more vulnerable in some ways as a person because it opened up sort of whole ranges of emotion that I hadn't experienced to such depth before, and it gave me tremendous faith, obviously, in young people. It's given me some very wonderful friendships with some of them, two or three particularly, which I value even though I know young people change, particularly from sort of 18 to 21–22 — they'll change a lot — but it's given me those people to care for and it's made me happier really, I suppose that's the thing I'm getting at — it's made me much happier as a person, just from being through it because it's such a wonderful memory to have, you can look back on it. But it's difficult. It just gave so much more meaning to life. I mean it was so wonderful to see that on stage, and it just made me very, very happy to have thought I'd created that and, of course, very proud; and it's given me much more confidence in myself. I mean I know Sam was saying that — but to feel you can achieve that. There's knock-on effects. Clive Wolfe, the guy who runs the National Students' Drama Festival, has now asked me to direct a production in Edinburgh next year for him, and so there's knock-on effects from that, so inevitably it changes. Practically speaking, it's changed my life because it's led to other things and probably will continue to do so. It's given me an insight into what we see at more professional theatres, the Derngate and places like that. It's just made me feel more relaxed and much happier about life in general, because it does. It gives you so much sort of hope when you see young people working like that, and you see what they get out of it, and it sort of suddenly makes everything worthwhile. Is that the sort of thing you want, or am I being too vague?

Peter: No, no. When you say it gives more meaning to life . . .

Sally: It's not so much the religion thing. It's the essence of the religion that came through — the caring. The whole play is about learning to care for one another, and to be aware of other people's feelings. And that's exactly what was happening in the cast, so it was like a reflection of the play's message within the cast themselves, and that's what I mean by giving more really because I've actually seen that happen now. I've seen that happen in a very big way where a group worked together and achieved something and just sort of loved one another, I suppose. And it's the kind of thing we're striving for all the time in the Arts areas — that feeling of being able to express how you feel, to disregard people's faults and only see the good and work to enhance the good, and that was happening all the time. That was what was so marvellous.

Peter: So it got very close to what you regard as the sort of central meaning of life, that lies at the heart of your educational philosophy?

Sally: Yes, well said, Peter.

Peter: Which, by implication, is rather difficult — well, it's very difficult to get to in ordinary circumstances. We might strive towards it . . .

Sally: Exactly, exactly. You've hit the nail on the head, that's exactly what it's done . . . (Sally expands on the point, to do with relationships between people)

Peter: As teachers and educationalists, we're all striving to get near that all the time, and we get some of the way, but we very rarely get as near to it as this, so when you do I think you get a new conception of what's possible. You might never have thought that possible before, and that might make a difference to the future?

Sally: Yes, you're constantly striving to get that feeling back — not 'back', to get the feeling again in other situations with other productions, in other lessons — and it does seem — yes, you're right — it does seem much more attainable purely because — yes, because of my attitude. I'm much more positive now and I'll go into lessons and expect the best. I suppose in that sense the work actually has improved but I never even thought of it like that, but that's probably exactly what's happened, and that's one of the reasons why I'm so pleased with my teaching over the last few months. It's probably exactly that reason, but I've never even put it down to that. It's only as you say that now that you're right . . . which is interesting, very interesting.

Here we have a creative interchange within the discussion. It is not just a matter of question and answer, seeking, and being given, information. The objective is much more difficult to pin down and describe, because it has not before been put into words, or even thought of. This is clear from the first extract above, where Sally seeks to identify and articulate what the experience has meant to her. Important here, too, is the animated way in which she responds. As with Jonathan, tone, gesture, and facial expression as well as words, help convey the meaning. In the ordinary course of events, teachers do not have time to reflect long on these events. As Lesley, the Music Director, told me, 'I say, "Right! That's over, it's lovely, but let's go now on to something else".' Sally, therefore, was exploring her feelings, or at least seeking to articulate them, for the first time. The researcher was an aid in this. The fact that I had been a participant in the event improved not only my ability to do this, but also my credibility with the teacher. My knowledge of the event was 'hot' rather then 'cold' (Atkinson and Delamont, 1977). I could be a useful sounding board to try ideas out on ('Is that the sort of the thing you want, or am I being too vague?'). I could understand, make reasonable inputs, prompts, summaries, foci. In this way, researcher and teacher jointly construct understanding and meaning. But ultimately, it is the teacher's meaning, the researcher helping to give shape to ideas.

There were many such discussions in the course of the creative teaching research. One series rapidly escalated into a research project in its own right over a further period of two years. This arose from a remarkable set of coincidences. I heard of a critical event in my neighbourhood involving the production of a prize-winning book by a group of primary children assisted by a well-known children's author. On contacting the school, I discovered that the head — the man responsible for the event — had gone to the same schools as me as a student, within the space of two years of each other, and though we had had little contact at the time, we shared from those times many memories, experiences and interests. Curiously, we even shared the same name. This aided rapport, the development of the research, and ultimately the validity of the account. Peter J. Woods felt the need to go deep into his life history to explain the meaning of his event to him. I wrote up aspects of this life history with Peter's assistance in standard academic format under the title 'Managing marginality: Teacher development through grounded life history'. One of the referees for this paper, David Thomas, wrote a commentary to accompany it, raising key questions of validity; and this was answered by Peter. Readers are referred to the discussion in the *British Educational Research Journal*, 19, **5**, 1993, and in Thomas (1993). The points I make here are 1) the rich seam of activity in teaching and learning typical of critical events was visited on the research also; and 2) it gave rise to some interesting methodological discussion. Thomas' critique reflects a nagging problem in life history research:

> Eco distinguished between legitimate interpretation and *over-interpretation.*
> Over-interpretation occurs when the interpreter transgresses by deconstructing

the writer's own 'world knowledge' through imposing the interpreter's own world knowledge and ignoring the writer's intentions. (1995, p. 169)

Here, the interpreter is the person writing the account (me in this instance), and the 'writer' is the person of the account (P.J. Woods). Lather (1991) makes a similar point when she refers to the 'textual staging of knowledge'. She wishes to give the voices of the researched more say in the finished product, and is critical of the rhetorical device ethnographers often use of presenting quotes in the final product, possibly out of context and their original frame of meaning, to suit their own framework (see also Atkinson, 1990).

I sympathize with this point in these particular cases, but I also believe the sociologist has something special to bring to the analysis — a particular form of knowledge that adds comparative dimensions, some theoretical understanding that might suggest explanations, a certain skill in collecting, organizing and analysing data, and in presenting accounts. The aim is to try for the best of both worlds with the aim of a unified validity. The key is the link between what Schutz (1962) described as first order constructs (the participant's expression of reality) and second (the sociologist's analysis). One way of testing for firmness of fit between the two kinds of construct is through respondent validation. Does the sociologist's account ring true to the person involved? Do his constructs keep faith with that person's reality as he sees and feels it? In this particular case, P.J. Woods (in Thomas, 1995, p. 187), in reply to Thomas, states that the interpreter 'has to become attuned to the writer's "inner music"', and quotes William Walsh:

> Civilised man has formed during the whole course of civilisation the habit of seeing first as the photographic camera sees . . . He sees what the Kodak has taught him to see . . . As vision developed towards the Kodak, man's idea of himself developed towards the snapshot . . . each of us has a complete Kodak idea of himself. In literature we have not a snapshot but the total man. And we find him only if we go in to literature as literature. If we can't hear . . . we can look in the real novel and there listen in. Not listen to didactic statements of the author, but to the low calling cries of the characters, as they wander in the dark woods of their destinies.

P.J. Woods (1993) comments, 'I believe that my interpeter has achieved just that, not least because he enjoyed the advantage of having known many of the places and characters of our shared childhood environment.' This is a converse argument to that of 'making the familiar strange' (Delamont and Atkinson, 1995), which has its own research uses, but is not a recipe for all research situations. Strauss and Corbin (1990) point out how 'familiarity' can lead to theoretical sensitivity:

> Throughout years of practice in a field, one acquires an understanding of how things work in that field, and why, and what will happen there under certain conditions. This knowledge, even if implicit, is taken into the research situation and helps you to understand events and actions seen and heard, and to do so more quickly than if you did not bring this background into the research. (p. 42)

Goffman (1989, p. 130) refers to 'deep familiarity', which enables you to 'pick up as a witness — not as an interviewer, not as a listener, but as a witness to how [individuals] react to what gets done to and around them'; and others have described as 'intimate familiarity' the experience of getting 'so physically, socially, and emotionally close to whatever people are under study' (Lofland, 1995, p. 45; see also Altheide and Johnson, 1994). With respect to P.J. Woods, I felt my inner knowledge aided: 1) contextualization — I could in-fill from my own knowledge and experience many of his descriptions, which recalled sights, sounds, smells, tastes; 2) his construction of meanings, as I was able to input some of my own recollections, which stimulated further recall; 3) understanding his feelings, since we came to similar conclusions about many of our childhood experiences, especially at school; 4) the efficiency and thoroughness of data gathering; 5) the relationship, which was one of fellow researchers, looking out at the world together, as Lawrence Stenhouse (1984) was wont to do with his interviewees. However, I think we both had a mind to the dangers of familiarity in blocking other kinds of insights and in taking too many things for granted, and maintained a critical mode toward our own, and each other's, constructions. Some of Peter's sections of his early life history went to six or more drafts as he strove for accuracy of detail and expression ('That was not *quite* what I wanted to say'); and I did not always accept his testimony on his 'critical event' where it was unsupported by evidence.

Conclusion

It would not be right to leave this article without noting some of the bad moments that have occurred in the creative teaching research. One, involving a staff/governors' meeting at a school where an extension of part of my research was under consideration, was, to my astonishment, so disastrous that I have written about it at length in Woods (1996) in an attempt to understand what happened. Another severe moment was when the headteacher of a school at which we were about to begin work on a new extension of the research ('Child-meaningful research in a bilingual school') suffered burnout and took early retirement. There had been excellent chances in this school for researcher–teacher collaboration — the teachers themselves had initiated the research. This all now fell through. When we began work in a replacement school, the one very promising 'collaborative' teacher left after a term for a post in another school. The 'collaborative' side of this research, in consequence, did not occur on the scale we had planned, and the whole research design had to be revised. There were 'critical events' that did not materialize. Many feelers were put out, situations tried, people approached, before settling on the final sample. No doubt there were lost opportunities that I was unaware of and uninvestigated paths, where weariness, misguidedness or lack of ambition won out. There were good opportunities that I *was* aware of which, frustratingly, I could not find ways to take advantage of. One of these concerned a primary school and a school for children with special needs who did some exciting collaborative work, including a week's visit to the Lake District, where they made a film of their own creation, later given a public viewing. This was a splendid 'critical event' with singular properties, given the contributions of the special needs children, but a) I could not find time to accompany them to the Lake District (in hindsight, I should have made time to do this); and b) I could not gain access to the special school (which is perhaps not unrelated to point a). My only consolation for these bad moments is that they are not untypical of qualitative research in general — and, of course, the fact that they were compensated for by the good moments.

We live in creative times, with some dazzling new opportunities for the qualitative researcher. I have discussed elsewhere (Woods, 1996) the matter of seeking new insights through new forms of enquiry and new forms of representation in the wake of the so-called 'postmodernist' or 'literary turn' (Tyler, 1986). I consider there, too, how the researcher's varied use of research implements and the working relationship with others involved in the processing of the paper might aid creativity.

A word might be said for external stimuli, such as the invitation to write this paper. They can inspire new lines of thought, or encourage the marshalling together of a number of hitherto disparate thoughts. They also awaken the reluctant analyst or writer from the cosy contentment of data collection to the more taxing task of doing something with it. This article would not have been written were it not for the invitation. Some of the thoughts that it contains would have been replaced by others, or remained locked within the subconscious, and/or in the hidden depths of the computer's memory. Invitations to give a paper at a conference on 'Pupils, Students and Learning: A Struggle for Empowerment' in 1993, followed by an article in a journal (Woods, 1994), and, three years later, an article in a book collection on 'The Perspectives of Children on Their Curriculum', both rounded off two of the projects in ways that might not otherwise have occurred, and launched a third — the 'creative learning' side of the research. The latter article, for example, gave us an opportunity to consider pupils' responses to creative teaching, and to expand on one of its essential properties, that of 'relevance' (Jeffrey and Woods, 1996). There have been several such instances.

In the end, we have to recognize that the truly creative thought is almost impossible to pin down, and that the attempt to do so might work against it. The moral, perhaps, is to try to cultivate conditions in which creative thoughts might happen; and, in circumstances where exactly the opposite is prefigured, to develop and maintain a state of mind which will enable us to turn apparent adversity to good account.

Acknowledgments

I am grateful to Bob Jeffrey, Geoff Troman, Mari Boyle, Barry Cocklin and Geoffrey Walford for their comments on an earlier draft of this paper.

References

ALTHEIDE, D.L. and JOHNSON, J.M. (1994) 'Criteria for assessing interpretative validity in qualitative research', in DENZIN, N.K. and LINCOLN, Y.S. (eds) *Handbook of Qualitative Research*, Thousand Oaks, CA: Sage.

ATKINSON, P. (1990) *The Ethnographic Imagination: Textual Constructions of Reality*, London: Routledge.

ATKINSON, P. and DELAMONT, S. (1977) 'Mock-ups and cock-ups: The stage-management of guided discovery instruction', in WOODS, P. and HAMMERSLEY, M. (eds) *School Experience*, London: Croom Helm.

BEST, D. (1991) 'Creativity: Education in the spirit of enquiry', *British Journal of Educational Studies*, **34**, 3, pp. 260–78.

BEYNON, J. (1983) 'Ways in and staying in: Fieldwork as problem solving', in HAMMERSLEY, M. (ed.) *The Ethnography of Schooling*, Driffield: Nafferton.

BURGESS, R.G. (ed.) (1984) *The Research Process in Educational Settings: Ten Case Studies*, London: Falmer Press.

DELAMONT, S. and ATKINSON, P. (1995) *Fighting Familiarity*, Cresskill, NJ: Hampton Press.

EISNER, E.W. (1985) *The Art of Educational Evaluation: A Personal View*, London: Falmer Press.

FINE, D.A. and DEEGAN, J.G. (1996) 'Three principles of Serendip: Insight, chance, and discovery in qualitative research', *International Journal of Qualitative Studies in Education*, **9**, 4, pp. 434–47.

GOFFMAN, E. (1989) 'On fieldwork' (transcribed and edited by Lyn H. Lofland), *Journal of Contemporary Ethnography*, **18**, pp. 123–32.

JEFFREY, B. and WOODS, P. (1996) 'The relevance of creative teaching: Pupil's views', in POLLARD, A., THIESSON, D. and FILER, A. (eds) *Children and Their Curriculum*, London: Falmer Press.

LATHER, P. (1991) *Getting Smart: Feminist Research and Pedagogy with/in the Postmodern*, New York: Routledge.

LOFLAND, J. (1995) 'Analytic ethnography: Features, failings and futures', *Journal of Contemporary Ethnography*, **24**, 1, pp. 30–67.

MEASOR, L. and WOODS, P. (1984) *Changing Schools: Pupil Perspectives on Transfer to a Comprehensive*, Milton Keynes: Open University Press.

MEASOR, L. and WOODS, P. (1991) 'Breakthroughs and blockages in ethnographic research: Contrasting experiences during the "Changing Schools" project', in WALFORD, G. (ed.) *Doing Educational Research*, London: Routledge.

PAUL, D. (1953) 'Interview techniques and field relations', in KROEBER, A.L. et al. (eds) *Anthropology Today*, Chicago: University of Chicago Press.

STENHOUSE, L. (1984) 'Library access, library use and user education in academic sixth forms: An autobiographical account', in BURGESS, R.G. (ed.) *The Research Process in Educational Settings: Ten Case Studies*, London: Falmer Press.

STRAUSS, A.L. and CORBIN, J. (1990) *Basics of Qualitative Research: Grounded Theory Procedures and Techniques*, Newbury Park: Sage.

THOMAS, D. (1993) 'Empirical authors, liminal texts and model readers: A response to "managing marginality"', *British Educational Research Journal*, **19**, 5, pp. 467–74.

TROMAN, G. (1996) 'No entry signs: Educational change and some problems encountered in negotiating entry to educational settings', *British Educational Research Journal*, **22**, 1, pp. 71–88.

TURNER, V.W. (1974) *The Ritual Process: Structure and Anti-structure*, Harmondsworth: Penguin Books.

TYLER, S. (1986) 'Post-modern ethnography: From document of the occult to occult document', in CLIFFORD, J. and MARCUS, G. (eds) *Writing Culture*, Berkeley, CA: University of California Press.

WOODS, P. (1990) *Teacher Skills and Strategies*, London: Falmer Press.

WOODS, P. (1993a) *Critical Events in Teaching and Learning*, London: Falmer Press.

WOODS, P. (1993b) 'Towards a theory of aesthetic learning', *Educational Studies*, **19**, 3, pp. 323–38.

WOODS, P. (1993c) 'The magic of "Godspell": The educational significance of a dramatic event', in GOMM, R. and WOODS, P. (eds) *Educational Research in Action*, London: Paul Chapman Publishing.

WOODS, P. (1994) 'Critical students: Breakthroughs in learning', *International Studies in Sociology of Education*, **4**, 2, pp. 123–46.

WOODS, P. (1995) *Creative Teachers in Primary Schools*, Buckingham: Open University Press.

WOODS, P. (1996) *Researching the Art of Teaching: Ethnography for Educational Use*, London: Routledge.

WOODS, P., BOYLE, M. and HUBBARD, N. (1997) 'Child-meaningful learning in a bilingual school', *Final Report to the ESRC*, June.

WOODS, P. and JEFFREY, R. (1996) *Teachable Moments: The Art of Teaching in Primary School*, Buckingham: Open University Press.

WOODS, P.J. (1993) 'Keys to the past–and to the future: The Empirical Author replies', *British Educational Research Journal*, **19**, 5, pp. 475–88.

5 Developing the *Identity and Learning Programme*: Principles and Pragmatism in a Longitudinal Ethnography of Pupil Careers

Ann Filer with Andrew Pollard[1]

Introduction

Setting the Scene: The Identity and Learning Programme (ILP)

The second half of the 1980s saw the conception and early development of a longitudinal ethnography of pupil learning and school careers, contextualized within the period of great educational change in the UK of the late 1900s. In 1987, with a group of 10 4-year-olds in a Reception class at Greenside School, their parents, teachers and peers, Andrew Pollard began research on the social influences on learning. Some 18 months later I approached Andrew to discuss some research I wished to undertake. So, in the Autumn term of 1989 I began researching in Albert Park School for a part-time longitudinal PhD study, which Andrew had agreed to supervise. My interest was in the tracking of the successive classroom assessment experiences of a group of 5-year-olds in the context of newly introduced national assessment procedures.

Though the substantive questions and main focus of the two studies were different, our shared research interest meant that both Andrew and I sought multi-perspective understandings of classroom events, which would include the strategies and perceptions of pupils and teachers and the dynamics of peer group action. The two studies were distinct in those early days of what was, in time, to become the ILP. In due course Andrew and I were to bring them together, informally at first, then later through a formal collaboration.[2] This enabled us to develop comparisons across the schools, which were situated in very different socio-economic communities. We also constructed theories and models of pupil learning and careers through the Greenside study, which we later elaborated with reference to assessment issues. At the time of writing, Andrew and I, with the support of a research student, Anne Malindine, continue to track the young people from Greenside and Albert Park schools through their ten different secondary schools.[3] This latter phase of the programme follows the pupils through to their GCSEs and sees them embarking on their 16+ careers in school, college and work.

The application of a longitudinal design to holistic, multi-perspective approaches of classic ethnography is, we have come to believe, unique to this study. Certainly, in 10 years' experience we have found no methodological guidelines for such work. From Andrew's early conception and design in relation to the Greenside study, through the joining together with my work at Albert Park, and continuing through the secondary phase, we therefore continue to struggle with the many methodological implications that become apparent in the process. In setting out some of the dilemmas and tensions that have arisen, I focus predominantly on the primary years of the Greenside study. However, I also make reference to the Albert Park study for elaborating the collaborative experience as Andrew and I came to work together and the comparative work of the ILP began to emerge.

Greenside School was set in a generally affluent, middle-class suburb of Easthampton, a city in the south of England. Andrew's original design for the Greenside study was aimed at generating understandings of patterned ways in which children shaped and managed their learning strategies, identities and school careers in the context of a matrix of family, school and peer group expectations and evaluations. Year-on-year effects on children of successive classroom learning contexts were to be tracked, together with the ways in which children differentially experienced those contexts. In its early development the research design was that of a classic case-study approach, with associated strategies of observing, participating and developing personal rapport as a means of trying to understand the perspectives and actions of people within the case.

Traditional ethnography usually presents a static picture based on an implicit assumption that there is no change over the research period. The power of a *longitudinal* ethnography, however, is that it adds the dimension of time to the holistic and multi-perspective research design of classic ethnography. In so doing it is more able to distinguish the enduring from the transient in social action, to track conditions for change together with the ways in which change is differentially experienced and acted upon by individuals and groups. Creating a research design for a year-on-year tracking of pupil career presented some dilemmas. A classic ethnographic approach to data collecting and analysis, would, in addition to the above, also need to incorporate methods of progressive focusing and grounded theorizing. In some contradiction to this, however, the study also required a research design that embodied a *theoretically informed, annual* data-gathering schedule. That was essential so that year-on-year comparisons could be made across the changing contexts of classroom experience. Thus, notwithstanding its undoubted potential, the application of a longitudinal dimension to ethnographic study began with the need to resolve a fundamental tension between data gathering and analytic progression.

In the account that follows I set out some of the issues that we have had to address as the programme has progressed. I also explore the principles, commitments and pragmatism that have underpinned the methodological development and progressive integration of the two studies.

The development of these longitudinal ethnographies has often seemed to us to be an uncertain, time-consuming and perplexing business. Necessarily, the intellectual rewards of achieving analytic outcomes and published accounts of each phase have always been a long way down the road from initial plans and proposals. Further, the possibility has always been there of creating a treadmill of data collecting with no guarantee that a satisfactory longitudinal analysis would emerge. Maintaining the interest of families, children and school staff, whose continued support across the years are essential to the study, has needed an enormous investment in time and care. Similarly we have had to work continually to gain and maintain the support and interest of educational institutions, funding bodies and other academics through each successive phase. The year-on-year accumulation and increasing complexity of the data through each new phase continually requires innovation with respect to its management and theoretical analysis. Further, how do you 'hand over' a case-study relationship and knowledge developed over several years to a new research team member, making room for the theoretical interpretations and analysis that they will bring to the study?

What then has kept us going, continuing to follow and develop the career stories of those children who, starting as 4- and 5-year-olds, and now in adolescence as I write? Clearly we must have found our way through most of the above difficulties and kept participants, funding bodies and institutions interested and committed thus far. Through this methodological account, therefore, I want to elaborate the major dilemmas and tensions which seem to be inherent in the longitudinal and collaborative approach to ethnography, as well as our solutions to them. In addition, however, I want to convey the interest, excitement and continual fascination which Andrew and I have derived from our year-on-year exploration of the school, family and friendship experiences of the children of Greenside and Albert Park. It is the powerful insights we think the children's learning and career stories offer, that have continually prompted us to move forward, to collaborate, to plan for the next phase.

There have been some basic principles and commitments which have underpinned our attempt to get close to pupils' experiences. These seem to us to have been fundamental to the relationships we have formed and the responses we have obtained from the children, their families, friends and teachers. Andrew and I both brought to our original Greenside and Albert Park studies a fundamental wish to understand the perspectives of pupils in school and to developing research methodologies which enabled us to access the voices of very young children especially. As we argued in *Children and Their Curriculum* (Pollard, Thiessen and Filer, 1997), one of the reasons why voices of children in their early years of schooling do not feature to any great extent in educational research is because we often question their conceptual and linguistic competencies in addressing our research concerns. Through that publication we brought together the work of researchers in the UK and in the US which reflect diverse approaches to accessing these very young voices. In the following extract from Andrew's research diary can be seen some of his early struggles with just such methodological concerns in attempting to access the perspectives of 4-year-old children on their learning:

> These interviews took place in the Pottery Room. We had to go past the hot kiln and sit in [an inner room]. It's a new situation for the children and I don't think it is good. I took them off individually. (. . .) I felt that the children were not as relaxed as I would like. Is it the [physical] situation? Is it that I have not been in for a few days? Is it the nature of my questions? I felt these were a bit too closed and repetitive. I showed them photos of different activities, paint-ing, maths, mobilo, (etc.) I felt I asked them 'what they like' about these things much too much and got some rather wooden and unreliable answers. (. . .) I have been much more observer than participant in the past few months. This may be an issue. Could I achieve more by *teaching* with the children part of the time. (. . .) I think I should consider this very carefully. There is a quality of data/feel that is only accessible through involvement. The question is whether this also cuts one off from other sources. And how do you handle it if you have to reprimand a child? On the other hand I am going to get very one dimensional if I don't get involved and my relationships could go down too. (. . .) Also I do worry about the quality of my actual knowledge of the children. There is a limit to its depth when it is not first hand. After all, isn't this essentially the argument I'm making — knowledge through social interaction. How then can I sensibly stand back? (Andrew Pollard, research diary, February 1988, Reception)

In this account we observe Andrew's attempts to see his research processes from the perspectives of children as *individuals*, to consider power relations and aspects of children's physical and social comfort, to explore alternative methods and commit time to building relationships, trust and understanding. Of course, such reflectiveness upon interview and observation methods is fun-damental to good ethnographic practice. It is our experience, however, that in order to get close to the perspectives of very young children, we have needed to give very much more explicit and continuously reflective attention to such consideration than is usually found to be necessary with most older children and adults in schools.

In this chapter, the account of the development of the longitudinal and collaborative approaches to ethnography takes the reader chronologically through the primary years at Greenside School and the eventual integration with the Albert Park study. In *Getting Started* I set out some of the implications for designing a data-gathering schedule and methods which Andrew had to consider at the outset of the Greenside study, as well as those relating to an appropriate sample and to the development of field relations for a longitudinal study. When I joined him on the Greenside study,[4] Andrew had been working with parents, children and teachers for four years. The middle section of the chronology thus relates to *Collaborative and Comparative Developments* and the process of handing over responsibility for the development of case studies, with the implications for the different nature of the field relations I would

Figure 5.1: An overview of phases of the Identity and Learning Programme

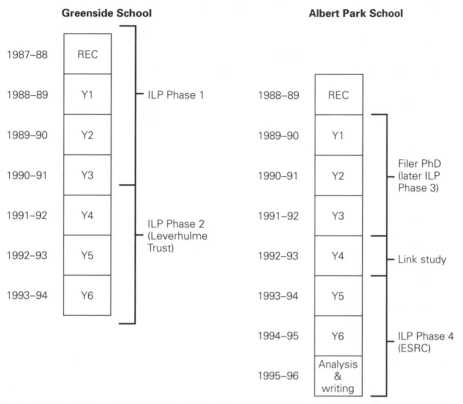

Phase 1: *The Social World of Children's Learning* (Pollard with Filer, 1996)

Phase 2: *The Social World of Pupil Careers* (Pollard and Filer, in press)

Phase 3: *Classroom Contexts of Assessment in a Primary School* (Filer, Unpublished PhD, 1993)

Phase 4: *The Social World of Primary School Assessment* (Filer and Pollard, forthcoming)

Phase 5: 1996–2001 'Identity and Learning in a Secondary School: A Longitudinal Ethnography of Pupil Careers' Directed by Andrew Pollard and Ann Filer. The Economic and Social Research Council.

necessarily develop, and the different data, interpretations and analysis I might bring to the study as we, now jointly, strived to make sense of the accumulation of data. Later phases of the primary years study brought new dilemmas to the fore, as we wrote up and shared the long awaited accounts of the primary school phase. In the third section of the chronology, *Communicating and Reflecting,* I relate the ways in which we navigated the sensitivities of children and their parents and their responses to the stories of their lived experience which we offered. This final section of the chronology also considers some of the questions which most frequently surface in relation to the validity of the study as a whole.

An overview of the phases, funding and main publications of the ILP, to which I refer on page 61 in the following account, is reproduced in Figure 5.1. We begin the account in the year of 1987 when a group of 4-year-old children were about to embark upon their school careers and also upon a process that, as well as addressing our research questions, would give them, in time, a unique record of their childhood school years.

Getting Started — 1987 to 1990

Selecting a School

Greenside Primary School came to Andrew's attention when he heard of some interesting innovations in classroom organization which were being introduced by the new headteacher, Mrs Davison. For a while he had been considering a study of social influences on learning which would span at least a few early primary years. A major factor in selecting a school though, had to be a head-teacher who was supportive of the study and likely to remain in the school over the period. When Andrew got to know Mrs Davison, she seemed to offer the necessary support and stability for such a study. Not only was Mrs Davison new to the school, but this was her second headship and she was confident in her values, educational aims and management style. Andrew established a good relationship with Mrs Davison, who was interested in his research plans and shared his interest in the perspectives of pupils on their learning. She went on to support his access to the school, the staff and parents and remained in post throughout the study.

Selecting the Families and Children for Study

At the start of the Autumn Term 1987, the parents of 26 children in Mrs Powell's Reception class were invited to a meeting to hear about the project and the data which Andrew hoped to gather. He set out the ethical code within which he would work; of particular concern in a longitudinal study which was to accumulate considerable amounts of personal family data (see *The Social World of Children's Learning*). Parents of 22 children were both willing to become involved, and, very importantly, did not expect to move their children from the school during their primary education. Andrew selected the five boys and five girls who were the oldest children in the class, since he was advised (incorrectly as it turned out) they were likely to stay together as a group through the school.

One of the most often occurring questions put to us — from academics through to interested casual acquaintances — concerns the basis on which we chose children for the study. As can be discerned in the above, initial decisions relating to the Greenside school and children were driven largely by pragmatism and opportunism. That is to say, those decisions made the study happen and secured its foreseeable future. Among those early decisions, though, the question of how many children to study was rather more complicated. Through the various phases of the ILP, sample sizes have been finely tuned. Decisions were shaped by the original conception of holistic, multi-perspective case studies, which, if they were to be truly ethnographic demanded a relatively small sample, covered in great depth. Against this we have had to consider that longitudinal studies are particularly vulnerable to losses from their research sample. Moreover, the importance of each case to the overall analysis, together with the long-term investment in time and resources for each, meant that any permanent loss would be acutely felt.

Comparative Issues in Relation to the Sample

Greenside had offered an ideal opportunity which Andrew felt he had to seize, certainly. He was though, at the same time, concerned about the representativeness of the Greenside sample. Whilst the gender balance within the sample provided some interesting contrasts, only one child, Sally, was from a working-class family and all the children were from indigenous, white, English homes. Indeed, Greenside was not typical of Easthampton generally. Most families in the suburb had flourished during the Thatcher Government years. The national pattern of increased affluence of middle-class families such as these contrasted with that of rising unemployment and poverty among poorer areas of Easthampton. At the beginning of 1987, however, Andrew had originally envisaged starting two parallel ethnographies based around schools serving communities with contrasting socio-economic circumstances. The Greenside Primary School case-study had originally been conceived as part of that strategy and an ESRC application was made to fund work on the other case study. Comparative methods (Glaser and Strauss, 1967) could then have been deployed in an integrated analysis. However, at that point funding was not obtained and Andrew had to carry on with just the Greenside study.

Through the various opportunities and difficulties in setting up a longitudinal study, two principles remained clear. First, as I have described above, was the importance of accessing and understanding pupil perspectives on their learning. Second, the holistic and multi-perspective data to be gathered, from home, playground and classrooms should not be compromised or diluted.

As the study progressed some of the early compromises began to seem not quite so important. Despite the apparent relative similarities in their social circumstances, the emergent uniqueness of each individual and the subtle variations in the social influences on them proved to be at least as interesting as the major and more obvious differences which might have been highlighted by a more contrastive sample. Had it been possible for Andrew to develop his initial preference for a comparative ethnography in an inner-city context, the analysis would undoubtedly have developed in different ways and raised different issues. However, as I have described, two years later, I would begin a study with a similar longitudinal design and in a contrasting school as the site for my PhD work, and collaboration and comparisons across the two studies would, in due course, take place.

Data Collecting

As I have described, a research design was needed that embodied methods of progressive focusing and grounded theorizing (Glaser and Strauss, 1967), but which also incorporated a theoretically informed annual data-gathering schedule. I also highlighted the seeming contradiction between the two approaches, as they are classically applied. In the following description of the design and data-gathering methods used at Greenside I show how the two approaches were combined.

The annual data-gathering schedule Andrew devised at the outset of the study drew on a broad range of sources. Parents kept diaries and these were followed by semi-structured interviews in their homes. Pupils were observed on one day per week in the playground and classroom and some video-recordings and photography were also used. Children were interviewed in friendship groups and individually, and examples of their work were collected regularly. In addition to naturally occurring conversation during classroom fieldwork, the teachers were interviewed twice each year, and the headteacher annually. Teacher records of children's attainment, reports to parents and other assessment data were collected. School and classroom observations and documents relating to curricular and extra-curricular events, classroom and school management provided details of the wider structural context within which all the children operated.

Some innovation was needed in data collection methods with regard to family life, which we were not in a position to directly observe. Parents were therefore provided with diaries and asked to complete them twice each year over the space of a week. For the Autumn Term diary entries, parents were asked to record a simple day-by-day narrative of routine family events with particular reference to the child on whom the research was focused. The Summer Term entries were used to provide an overview of the year as a whole, with parents being asked to consider their child's learning progress, social, emotional and physical development and key social relationships and experiences.

Parent interviews were used to follow up each of their diary entries, and these were conducted as informal discussions. Nevertheless, the conversations were structured by the topics which parents were routinely asked to address in the diaries and which parents had responded to a week or so earlier. In addition, as particular concepts emerged in the study and the analysis developed, further topics were introduced for each interview. They were also used to further explore interesting events or issues in the life of the child, to provide contextual information and supplementary accounts.

Alongside these ongoing topics, any other concerns, developed perhaps through analytic notes and sensitizing concepts (Blumer, 1954), could be introduced and developed through the study. By the same token, the conversational, reciprocal style of the semi-structured interview meant that parents also raised concerns. So it was that for different parents particular issues tended to surface. For one it might be their worries about the new teaching methods which Mrs Davison was introducing in the school. For other parents this was not an issue, whereas their child's distress about rough treatment in the playground, or their lack of stable friendship relations might be concerns on which they would elaborate at some length.

The process described here in relation to diaries and interviews demonstrates the way in which data collecting enabled both repeated comparisons within a broadly defined field of action, alongside progressive focusing as certain topics in each child's life story became elaborated. The progressive focusing, however, did not mean that, as in classic ethnography, data was no longer collected around other areas of social action as research questions become more clearly defined (see, for example, Hammersley and Atkinson, 1983); rather it achieved a structured 'snowballing' effect whereby, although increasing amounts of data were collected around particular interests for each case, virtually any issue which might, at some point focus on as important had some 'history' in the data which could be drawn on for comparison. We discuss the management of the huge amount of data that was generated below. As readers may imagine, after five, six, seven years, our research questions widened along with our accumulating knowledge of the children. So it was that as the study lengthened we experienced some problems with controlling the length of interviews. There were more questions that we wanted to ask and more shared knowledge and previous conversations to refer to, make connections with, and to build on.

In the introduction to this account, I highlighted the risk that the longitudinal schedule could become routine and repetitive. From the above, though, I hope I have conveyed something of the way in which, as the study progressed, repeat sampling became simply the unfolding of stories of the lives and the learning development of the children; of their successes and struggles seen in the context of the 'ups and downs' of their school and home relationships and experiences.

Collaborative and Comparative Developments — 1991 to 1993

Collaboration and Field Relations — Handing Over

To pick up again on the chronological development of the research programme, by 1990 it was becoming clear to Andrew that the accumulation and complexity of data and analysis could not continue to be managed alongside his other responsibilities. If the study was to continue he needed help and, fortunately, he succeeded in securing funding from the Leverhulme Trust. By that time, we had known each other for five years, for the latter two as a result of my PhD studies. Funding enabled me to join the Greenside project on a part-time basis alongside my part-time PhD work at Albert Park, which was then halfway to completion.

The process of handing over responsibility for data collection had to be handled with great care. Agreements had been negotiated with Andrew, and trust and relationships had been built over a long period of time. Further, as readers will appreciate from the description of data-collection processes, for each of the children and settings in the study documented evidence was complemented by the detailed knowledge which he carried in his head. Indeed, this supplementary knowledge was drawn on continually in observing, interviewing and ongoing analysis.

As I began to take over the Greenside case studies, we could not let it be thought that school and family relationships, developed over several years, had been abandoned by Andrew. Thus he would pay an occasional visit to the school or to parents in order to maintain relationships and demonstrate his continued and real interest. Similarly, from time to time I would tell the children about his interest in what they were telling me in order to 'keep his memory alive' for them. This approach meant that when Andrew again began working with some of the children for the secondary school phase, he was able to resume trusting relationships very readily.

We were conscious also of the need for the established researcher to 'get out of the way' and make room for me to shape new relationships. In a similar vein, we had to strike a fine line in handing on that accumulated knowledge of individuals and their relationships and social settings on which the longitudinal ethnographer continually draws. Whilst I was, of course, familiar with the analytic concepts that Andrew was working with, the temptation for Andrew to 'explain how it is' was consciously moderated, allowing me to bring a fresh eye to the data and the developing analysis. However, before I could begin any sort of analysis, and particularly as an ethnographer, I needed to recreate for myself something of that immersion and in-depth knowledge of people and situations that had been Andrew's rather than my experience. I had studied his data of course, but I felt I needed a more coherent sense of the children's lives, the connectedness of events in them and the varying perspectives on them offered by participants. I achieved something of that coherence in my mind through the process of drafting some children's 'stories' from the data. This was, of course, a complex process which, I am aware, raises many epistemological questions which I do not have the space to address here. Nevertheless, the following methodological account from that time reflects just a few of the dilemmas I faced in shaping those stories.

> . . . Another problem concerned the fact that I had not collected the data, had not known the children or their families at the time when the data was collected, and had not met the teachers I was to write about as they had since left the school. (. . .) The data which I was handling, as is the case with any data, represented a 'reality' that had been filtered through the questions, perceptions, interpretations of the researcher in the field. What I wanted to avoid as

far as possible was the creation of another layer of interpretation and filtering in my (first draft) of the children's stories. (. . .) In the light of the above, I decided that as faithful and as full a rendering of data as was possible was my first priority, (. . .) irrespective of any interpretation or analysis which would be needed later. My biggest data handling problem, though, was the need to compress a lot of data into relatively few words and still do justice to it. What I found particularly difficult to resist was the urge to 'interpret' the data as a means of compressing it. (Ann Filer, a draft account of the process of analysis and writing from data gathered by Andrew Pollard, July 1992)

Through the drafting of some of the children's stories in this way I began to achieve something of a 'feeling' for the holism of children's experience. I was then able to present my accounts to Andrew for discussion and comparison with his perception of the same people and events. From a basis of the shared understandings we reached, I was then able to go on to bring new perspectives to the developing analysis.

Collaboration, Researcher Identities and Data Gathering

We have frequently considered the implications for the Greenside study of having a different fieldworker for the first and the second phase. Thus my fieldnotes with regard to peer group dynamics of classroom and playgrounds were particularly extensive, reflecting an already established and ongoing research interest. On the other hand, Andrew's career history together with his well-established association with Mrs Davison meant that his accounts yielded more extensive headteacher perspectives on school organization and managerialism at Greenside. As the children got older, my data relating to girls' groups reflected their developing gendered-pupil and sexual identity and awareness. Whether Andrew would have captured corresponding material for boys, or whether boys might be less forthcoming anyway than girls on these topics, whatever the sex of the researcher, are debatable points.

On reading the children's stories in the final publications, however, I do not believe that any reader would consider that the boys' gendered experiences and perspectives were underrepresented compared with those of girls. Parents, teachers, friends and other peers contributed their perceptions of children's gender relationships, emerging body consciousness, styles of self presentation, their opinions of the styles of peers, and so on. These, together with our own observations, enabled us to generate as rounded accounts for boys as for girls, though in some cases, and almost inevitably, there may be less of the immediacy of the subject's own voice on some topics than on others. In such ways, and applied across different topics, the ethnographic principle of generating multi-perspective and multi-dimensional accounts, repeated over time, proved a powerful means of accessing rounded and triangulated (Adelman, 1977; Lever, 1981) pictures of children's sense of identity, as learners and as pupils generally, as members of friendship groups, as a brother or a sister and so on.

Thus, both Andrew and I believe that any differences between us in the data we gathered were, ultimately, not very important when set within the overarching concepts and purposes of the study. As the above suggests, this was in part due to the fact that we were supported by a particular research design and data-collecting methods. Also, alongside the data gathering, lay a continuous process whereby we reviewed and discussed the emerging analysis and generated our ongoing research questions. It was, though, in the area of analysing the data we gathered that perhaps our different perspectives had observable, and positive, effects as we collaborated to variously challenging and supporting one another's emerging perceptions, descriptions and interpretations.

By the summer of 1992, I had been working with Andrew on the Greenside project for a year. Data collecting was coming to an end at Albert Park and the writing-up phase of my PhD beginning. Undoubtedly, both studies benefited from the fact that they were simultaneously undergoing a tremendously creative phase in their development. I moved between the two school contexts of Greenside and Albert Park, further developing my PhD analysis of the latter. Andrew was finalizing his analysis and models relating to the early years case histories for *The Social World of Children's Learning*. Together we were discussing and developing hypotheses around theoretical models of the dynamics of pupil identity and career. Though Andrew was familiar with the Albert Park cohort through my writing, collaboration across the two studies at this stage remained on an informal and ad hoc basis.

By now, however, I had begun to feel that I was going to be reluctant to relinquish the cohort that I had been working with for virtually a day a week for three years at Albert Park School. Moreover, this was the first cohort to experience the new National Curriculum assessment procedures. During my time with them I had studied their experience of SATs at age 7 and in three years' time they were to experience the first 'end of Key Stage 2' tests. To somewhat objectify them, the ethnography of their progression so far made them a valuable and unique resource which I was looking for an opportunity to develop. Following them through to the end of their primary school years would also create the possibility of a comparative study in a different socioeconomic context from Greenside School. Andrew and I began to discuss the possibilities of a collaboration between the two.

Having concluded preliminary discussions with the headteacher at Albert Park School, we submitted a proposal to the Economic and Social Research Council to develop the PhD data set through to Key Stage 2, especially in relation to 10 key pupils. I was, of course, by this time known to most of the parents and had met and chatted with them in classrooms, on school trips, when I attended school concerts, and so on. All parents except three expressed a willingness to take part in the study and to help me develop retrospective accounts of early family life and school life from their perspectives. Our sample for this cohort was therefore selected on the basis of my knowledge of the pupils. As well as both sexes, a range of attainment outcomes, classroom strategies, membership of different peer friendship groups and peer statuses were represented in the final choice. Alongside the development of my PhD data set and analysis, we proposed to develop comparisons with the Greenside study and elaborate our various learning and career models with respect to assessment issues. However, we had to write the proposal and await funding decisions. I also needed to complete the writing of my PhD. For a while therefore, we had to scale down data collecting at Albert Park School, spending a year maintaining relationships and gathering essential data only, whilst hoping that funding would be secured. Fortunately, funding was granted to begin in the autumn of 1993 on what was now Phase 4 of the programme; my PhD having retrospectively been incorporated as Phase 3 (see Figure 5.1).

Interpretation and Analysis

In order to explain the way in which the vast amounts of data would be managed and analytic processes would ultimately be brought to bear on the longitudinal data sets, we need to return to the early days of the study and track the process through. Certainly, during the middle and late 1980s, there were those who had warned Andrew that he was courting trouble in considering the longitudinal and multi-perspective research design, and, for a while, he was beginning to see their point! His early and brief attempt to develop a coding scheme to classify each small element of data very quickly proved itself to be both mechanistic and impractical and there was a period during which he feared that the volume of data could prove unmanageable. However, he felt that the basic research design was fundamentally sound and the longitudinal design, though contributing to some analytical difficulties, also provided time to consider how to solve them. Meanwhile he introduced a way of managing the accumulating data more effectively. Basically, this consisted of 'units of analysis' in terms of each of the children and each of the three main settings in each of seven years. Over the full Greenside study this projected no less than 210 child/setting/year units of analysis, but at least it provided a clear structure within which to attempt to integrate the diverse forms of data.

The data-management system underpinned the construction of a first level, 'descriptive analysis' in which summarizing matrices were developed to become the basis of the children's case studies and identify patterns in the children's learning stories. As I indicated above, the collaboration between us became important now, for when I joined Andrew in 1991 I inevitably brought a fresh perspective to the material when I studied the early data-sets as part of my familiarization process. Although Andrew wrote the case-study accounts for the 'learning' book accounts (Pollard with Filer, 1996) and I drafted the case studies for the 'career' book (Pollard and Filer, in press) we had innumerable discussions, sharing and checking one another's perceptions and analysis to produce the stories for each child which were offered to the parents for respondent validation.

Communicating and Reflecting — 1994 to 1996

Writing and Dissemination

The difficulty of how to write up and communicate the study went in parallel with the struggle for descriptive and theoretical analysis reported above. To return to the beginning again, the project itself imposed three important requirements: that the longitudinal development was shown: that the holistic influence of the social contexts and relationships was demonstrated; and, that the voices and perspectives of the participants could be clearly conveyed. Also, the two themes of children's learning and pupil career, as well as two particularly important variables, the individual children and the social contexts, needed to be represented. We considered various ways of doing this, but eventually the simplicity and meaningfulness of basing the writing-up around 'child stories' won the day.

By 1994, Greenside pupils were coming to the end of their primary school careers, though the children in the parallel study at Albert Park still had another year to go. We made the decision not to release the early years book, *The Social World of Children's Learning* in published form until the children had left Greenside School. This helped protect confidentiality and identities in the local community, as well as reduce our concerns about possible reactivity among participants. Moreover, not all of the children's stories appeared in the early years book, providing another good reason for withholding accounts until we could simultaneously present each of the parents with a draft of their child's story. Andrew's writing of *The Social World of Children's Learning* was well under way, however, and I was drafting the case-study stories for the 'career' book, *The Social World of Pupil Careers*. The time was approaching when we would be able to share drafts with parents, families and school. Each of the families was to be presented with the draft of their child's study. We had agreed that teachers who were still at the school were to be presented with draft accounts of their classroom practice and organization and the headteacher was to see a complete draft of each book before publication.

The construction and refinement of the case-study texts had been the product of many discussions, judgments and dilemmas, especially in relation to material which, though highly relevant, we knew might be of a particularly sensitive nature to the adults or children concerned. At the same time though, we did not wish to sanitize the accounts and, where conflict, misunderstanding, tension or anxiety had been important to the children's experience, we wanted the case-studies to reflect it accurately. In order to allow parents and children time to 'live with' the accounts and to reflect beyond an initial, perhaps very emotional, reaction, we left the drafts with families for about eight weeks over the summer holidays, before contacting them to discuss their responses. Whilst we retained editorial control over the accounts, we wished to be informed of any particularly sensitive issues that families felt we had not handled well, or any factual inaccuracies. Overall, we were very pleased by the responses of parents and children. On reading the accounts, parents generally felt that the texts expressed much of what they already knew, though the patterns that were revealed in their children's responses to events and relationships variously intrigued, saddened, and amused them. Parents conveyed various experiences of emotional upheaval, discomfort, and minor shock when confronted with their lives and those of their children reflected back at them in that way. However, the parents' general satisfaction with the experience must, in the long run, be reflected in the fact that, after a year's break and, in some cases, taking a deep breath, they all agreed to carry on into the secondary phase. One pupil who featured in the early years book and who had transferred to an independent school at age 7, declined to rejoin the study.

Despite the above, we do recognize the problems inherent in any claims to 'truth through respondent validation' (Schutz, 1964; Ball, 1982) and certainly its limitations meant that the more analytic chapters in the book were not presented for respondent validation.

There remains the question of the children's responses to these case-study stories and of how they may feel about them in the longer term. In our discussions, no parent expressed concern about their child's perception of the stories. In most cases they had shared them with their children through the diaries. In pupil eyes, the case-study stories were thus 'history' and often amusing history. For the children at that time, a new world of secondary education was absorbing all their attention. Nevertheless, one can never really tell how the children will respond as adolescents or as adults, and this remains a concern. We hope though, that a wry smile or an occasional laugh will be raised by some memories from the past, that they will understand a little bit more both about themselves and about those who cared for them and, if they are saddened by anything that they read, that they will understand that their experiences have much in common with those of many other children. There are aspects of these stories that in different ways resonate with the childhood experiences of us all and from which we can all learn.

Assessing Validity

The longitudinal and collaborative design of the study raises particular questions concerning validity and reliability. I do not have space here to explore them fully. However, some questions touch closely upon the issues in this account, and I will address those here.

In the context of the longitudinal design, some of the most frequently raised questions concern what can be described as 'ecological validity'. Ecological validity is concerned with the effect that researchers and their methods may have in influencing the actions and responses of participants. Though case studies are less likely to be affected by such reactivity than other research methods (Hammersley, 1992) the effect of 'audience' is an intrinsic aspect of social action and it is the ethnographer's role to interpret action in terms of the social context in which it takes place (Hammersley and Atkinson, 1983).

Overall, the experience of the longitudinal programme suggests that transient reactivity of participants matters less than it does where the time in the field is limited. We would argue that it is precisely that continuity in the field, together with the collaborative perspective, which has enabled us to see enduring patterns of relationships and social action and distinguish them from any transient or context specific reactivity to us as researcher.

However, in a long-term ethnography perhaps we should give greater consideration to the possibility of having had some enduring effect; some effect on routine action, that is, as opposed to a simply transient one. The question of reactivity which is most often raised in relation to the ILP, concerns precisely that issue. It concerns whether long-term continuity in the field could raise awareness and familiarity with research foci, and thus significantly affect them. This is an important consideration, for significant reactivity to such awareness, should it have occurred, might render the case studies unrepresentative of those which we generalize to in constructing models and typologies (Hammersley, 1992, p. 164).

We are sometimes asked whether the children felt 'special' in any way in the classroom as a result of our interest in them. For the children's part, however, they were, almost to the end of their primary years, largely unaware of themselves as a particular focus of interest. All children in the wider class cohort talked from time to time about the book that they would feature in, and indeed, to varying degrees, we probably did feature all. We were careful not to observe or interview key children in ways that would single them out in school. It was part of the research design that we interviewed all children in their friendship groups and we also interviewed other children individually from time to time. In this and in our occasional visits to home, usually at around bedtime, we were simply accepted as part of the scene. We had, after all, always been around, on weekly visits to school, in the playground, talking to parents at school events and on school trips, and so on. Though the key children developed an awareness that some parents were talked to at home as well, who was 'in' the study simply did not arise as an issue of particular interest for them. We believe therefore, that any effects on them in classroom or playground were transient and certainly of no more consequence in the context of their ongoing learning, social strategies, or overall career histories, that they were for any other child in the class. Parents, for their part, occasionally remarked that our discussions gave rise to issues which otherwise they might not have thought about, and which were discussed between them. However, our contact with them occurred only twice a year and all have rejected the notion that we had any significant effect on their parenting decisions. Perhaps the most important factor in our perceptions of this is that our routine enquiries were open and general in nature. For instance we asked parents to write about 'the ups and downs of family life this term', 'any changes in friendships and peer relations', and so on. Any *particular* foci that emerged from this, therefore, tended to reflect their own ongoing concerns as parents, rather than ones that we introduced. As parents ourselves, we often shared the dilemmas addressed in reciprocal ways, though we carefully refrained from forwarding opinions or judgments based on our knowledge of their children in school. Certainly, therefore, whilst we provided regular opportunities for parents to reflect on their children's development and experience, we do not believe that we had an *enduring* effect on their routine *action.*

Conclusion and the Way Forward — 1996 to 2001

In 1994, the Greenside cohort moved on to their secondary schools, followed a year later by the Albert Park cohort. At the same time, and in the context of the interest and support of the wider academic community, our perception of the value in understanding pupil career patterns widened to include issues of, for instance, the development of adolescent identities, a range of gender issues and the influence of wider school organization and youth and community cultural contexts. Our growing recognition of the importance of addressing these factors came together with the fact that our pupil sample moved from two primary schools to no less than ten secondary schools. Hence we were faced by the need to reconfigure the team. In 1996 John Furlong agreed to work with us on the secondary phase of the ILP[4] (Phase 5). We also inducted a PhD student, Anne Malindine, whose study of gender issues in girls' school careers provides a secondary focus within the programme.

As the team has grown and work continues, the need to maintain an analytic overview presents us with challenges, as does the need to address and reconcile the diverse theoretical perspectives which different researchers draw on in interpreting data. We need to hold together the continuity between the past and the future of the programme and across its diverse settings, allowing for the undoubted benefits of fresh perspectives and creativity — our own as well as those of new researchers. This latter is important, for a programme spanning 1987 to 2001 needs to locate its research questions and findings within an evolving political scene, with ever-shifting educational policy issues and debates to be addressed. Further, we cannot assume that we can communicate our findings in 2001 within a theoretical framework derived from the mid-1980s. We have to connect with shifting debates about the changing nature of society and the ways in which sociological research relates to, and describes it (Hollinger, 1994).

The way forward in the secondary phase, and with new team members, is supported by the primary years' experiences of Andrew and myself, some of which I have recounted here. The experience of collaboration, of developing comparisons across parallel studies, together with a solid core of shared understandings and perspectives continues to provide a strong focal point around which perspectives can cohere. The value and strategic principle of a commitment to listening to and understanding pupil perspectives remains central to all our concerns in this.

The necessary commitment of time and resources, as well as of care and trust, from participants, researchers, educational institutions and funding bodies, goes some way towards accounting for the continuing survival of ILP. As throughout, however, alongside our research and personal commitments, we continue also to accept the need for some pragmatism and flexibility in response to new research problems; to live with setbacks to some of our plans and to seize opportunities for others as they came along. Overall, we feel that the insights that are made available through the children's stories, together with our continued fascination in tracking their future outcomes, provide ample justification for continuing to struggle with the dilemmas and perplexities of longitudinal ethnography.

Notes

1   The account of methodology in relation to Andrew Pollard's early years work at Greenside School draws directly on his writing in *The Social World of Children's Learning*, Chapter 10. We also have had numerous discussions around the issues addressed here, not only in the context of this paper, but continuously as part of our ongoing reflection on our work. Thus the chapter speaks for both of us, though through my (Ann Filer's) authorial voice.
2   *Assessment and Career in a Primary School*, 1993–1996. Funded by the Economic and Social Research Council. Directed by Andrew Pollard and Ann Filer.
3   *Child Careers in a Primary School: An Ethnographic Study*, 1991–1994. Funded by the Leverhulme Trust. Directed by Andrew Pollard.
4   Identity and Secondary Schooling: A Longitudinal Ethnography, 1996–2001. Funded by the Economic and Social Research Council. Directed by Andrew Pollard and Ann Filer. John Furlong worked with us as a co-director in the initial stages but, because of work pressure, subsequently withdrew to a consultancy role.

References

ADELMAN, C. (1977) 'On first hearing', in ADELMAN, C. (ed.) *Uttering, Muttering: Collecting, Using and Reporting Talk for Social and Educational Research*, London: Grant McIntyre.

BALL, S.J. (1982) 'Beachside reconsidered: Reflections on a methodological apprenticeship', in BURGESS, R. (ed.) *The Research Process in Educational Settings: Ten Case Studies*, Contributions originally published at a workshop on the ethnography of educational settings, Whitelands College, March 1982.

BLUMER, H. (1954) 'What is wrong with social theory', *American Sociological Review*, **19**, pp. 3–10.

FILER, A. and POLLARD, A. (forthcoming) *The Social World of Primary School Assessment*, London: Cassell.

GLASER, B. and STRAUSS, A. (1967) *The Discovery of Grounded Theory*, Chicago: Aldine.

HAMMERSLEY, M. (1992) *What's Wrong with Ethnogrpahy?* London: Routledge.

HAMMERSLEY, M. and ATKINSON, P. (1983) *Ethnography: Principles into Practice*, London: Tavistock.

HOLLINGER, R. (1994) *Postmodernism and the Social Sciences: A Thematic Approach*, London: Sage.

LEVER, J. (1981) 'Multiple methods of data collection: A note on divergence', *Urban Life*, **10**, 2, pp. 199–213.

POLLARD, A. and FILER, A. (in press) *The Social World of Pupil Careers: Case Studies of Children Aged 4 through to 11*, London: Cassell.

POLLARD, A. with FILER, A. (1996) *The Social World of Children's Learning*, London: Cassell.

POLLARD, A., THIESSEN, D. and FILER, A. (eds) (1997) *Children and Their Curriculum: The Perspectives of Primary and Elementary School Children*, London: Falmer Press.

6 Using Ethnographic Methods in a Study of Students' Secondary School and Post-school Careers

Gwen Wallace, Jean Rudduck and Julia Flutter with Susan Harris

Ethnography is usually seen as either a process (a method of working 'in the field') or as a finished narrative account of research findings. In this paper we challenge such a dichotomy, arguing that methodological issues in ethnographic research are not simply a discussion of the merits of techniques but an inextricable part of the final narrative account. This was particularly so in our longitudinal study where methodological and theoretical issues interconnected with the way the relationships between the members of a (changing) research team, school staff and students developed over time *in the context of events*. In this chapter we recount something of the story of our research project. The story is inevitably partial. Our aim is to demonstrate the value of ethnographic methods for educational research; to answer Silverman's (1985) question, 'What is going on here?'

The project began in September, 1991 and was based at Sheffield University. Jean Rudduck, Jon Nixon and David Gillborn drew up the proposal as a bid for one of 10 programmes in the major ESRC funded initiative, 'Innovation and Change in Education: The Quality of Teaching and Learning'. The programme initiative was coordinated under the leadership of Martin Hughes and members of all 10 programmes met occasionally to discuss progress and share their ideas. As Martin Hughes points out elsewhere (Hughes, 1996, p. xiv), the aim was to illuminate and inform (education policy and practice), not criticize and condemn.

Our project was called 'Making Your Way Through Secondary School: Students' experiences of teaching and learning', and was designed as a longitudinal study to track students through their last four years of secondary education from 1991 to 1995. This proved to be a period marked not only by changes in the students as they grew up, but also by changes in the schools as they responded to government policy; notably the 1988 and 1993 Education Acts.

There were also changes in the membership of the research team and changes in the focus and concerns of the educational and academic debates of which they were part. Jean Rudduck became Project Director and proved the only constant. Susan Harris was recruited as the first Post-Doctoral Research Officer but she was partly replaced by Julia Flutter (then Day) when Jean moved to Homerton College during the third year of the project. Secretarial support remained at Sheffield until almost the end. David Gillborn contributed to the first two terms of fieldwork in one of the schools. When he left to take up a tenured post elsewhere, Gwen Wallace joined the team and stayed with it until all the fieldwork was completed.

As the team changed, spreading first beyond Sheffield to Derby and then across to Homerton College, Cambridge, a formal day's conference at least three times a year kept everyone in touch. The telephone, correspondence and e-mails filled the gaps in between. The fieldwork needed constant reflection and discussion in order that decisions could be agreed and understood collectively, although the hub of activity was inevitably the 'home' institution: first Sheffield and later Homerton.

Jean's first academic subject discipline was English literature. Her interests in educational research and particularly students' perspectives had their roots in the curriculum development movement. She was aware that although teachers were given extensive support to manage new approaches to teaching, the impact of change on students was neglected (Rudduck, 1984 and 1991). In her work on group work, gender and achievement, she had a long record of trying to represent pupils' views (and also in her work training students to teach).

Susan came into research through an academic study of education. At the start of the project she had just completed her PhD and her major interest was in careers' education. As a sociologist, she had an interest in schooling and social class and was looking forward to seeing how changing policies might relate to changing practices. However, after three years with the project, she decided to remain at Sheffield when Jean moved to Cambridge.

David's influence, with his particular expertise in ethnic issues, turned out to be short-lived. He did two terms of fieldwork in one of the schools before moving to a tenured post at the London Institute. The transcripts evoke a deep sense of shared understandings with the boys and his grasp of the intricacies of football remained a legend long after he had left the scene. Gwen joined the team as David's replacement in the summer of 1992 without such an advantage. A sociologist of education with a keen interest in the relationship between educational policies and teachers' beliefs and practices, she had embarked on her research career in 1979 after more than 13 years as a secondary school teacher. She was more convinced than Jean that structural and management issues were of considerable importance in understanding what happened in schools, and had become keenly interested in the local management of schools.

Julia came in as the project's Research Assistant in November 1994, taking over some of Susan's work. However, it was decided not to use her as an interviewer because she could not possibly get to grips with the mountain of existing data in time. Her first task was to familiarize herself with 700 taped interviews and an extensive collection of notes and reports from the schools — a task she says she found 'painstaking but absorbing'! As a relative 'outsider' with a teenage son she was nonetheless well tuned into student perspectives and brought a fresh set of ideas to the analysis.

Clearly, even amongst the team, there was plenty of scope for different, even conflicting perspectives and priorities in the collection and interpretation of evidence. The key to cooperation lay in their shared belief in the value of the project's focus on students' testimonies.

For the first four years of the project, we followed the fortunes of around 85 students in three very different schools administered by three different local authorities stretching from the north east of England to the East Midlands. Subsequently (following a successful bid for some additional money), a small sample of 24 students (eight from each school) were selected for follow-up interviews to see how they were faring post-16.

All available students were interviewed three times a year, usually alone, but on two occasions in small friendship groups. As a research team, we also had access to key documents, including student reports and records of achievement. We also interviewed form tutors, year tutors, subject staff, heads and deputies on a regular basis, and attended key parents' meetings such as those when students chose their options (at age 13) in Year 9. All the interviews were transcribed and the transcripts of the students' school interviews were coded for analysis using Text-based Alpha. Many results from the substantive, four-year study have already been published (see for example, Rudduck, Chaplain and Wallace, 1995; Wallace, Rudduck and Harris, 1994; Harris, Rudduck and Wallace, 1996).

We begin with a general statement on our approach to research and then describe our original research design. We show how we set out to establish early relationships with heads and school staff, and demonstrate how the institutional and professional perspectives they provided gave us a sense of their changing expectations of the students over four years of secondary schooling. The major part of the chapter is about the students. Who did the students think we were? How did we interact with them and they with us? How far did we establish and sustain rapport? What happened as the research progressed? What were the effects of race, gender, age and class? How did the relationships students had with us change over time? We conclude by discussing what makes a valid ethnographic account and we argue that such accounts may contribute theoretical insights that go beyond the descriptive narrative of the case study.

Methodological Issues: Aims, Methods and Ethics

Hammersley (1994) points out that ethnographic research in education has 'mainly been addressed to those on the ground: to teachers, above all, but also to local authority advisers, governors, etc.'. He offers three models: social policy, social criticism and the theoretical model that contributes to disciplinary knowledge (pp. 140–41). Yet, in practice, as he notes in his subsequent review of educational research, and we found in our fieldwork, the different goals of all three models can be combined in any particular programme. His case is, that, in spite of the theoretical distinctions, in practice simple dichotomies always beg a great many questions. Furthermore, in discussing the distinctions between qualitative and quantitative approaches, he has shown how dichotomies often come to represent 'good' and 'bad' practice (Hammersley, 1992, p. 159) and concludes that, in setting up dichotomies, we 'obscure the range of options open to us'.

In a longitudinal research programme, covering more than four years of turbulence in educational policy and practice, we had two pragmatic essentials: first we had to sustain good relationships with everyone we worked with over a long period; secondly, we could not design a rigid research agenda because we needed to be able to react to unanticipated events in a period of flux and change. We were particularly conscious that we were working in a 'climate of moving perspectives' as far as educational policy was concerned (Wallace et al., 1994).

Jean had conceived of the project as a survey of students' views of their schooling as they made their way through their final four years of compulsory education. Whilst this remained the enduring strand of enquiry, to accommodate the changes in the schools, and the changes in the demands made on the project by changing educational priorities and concerns, we had not only to combine different goals and different ethnographic approaches but also to juggle and change them over time. What we seek to do here is to show how our work unfolded, recognizing that both the context and the subjects of the research were interconnected in a dynamic interplay of events, processes, changing personnel and developing relationships. As the work proceeded, so the options, the team and our thinking about the project changed.

Career: An Organizing Concept

The problem of 'making sense' of what would become a huge archive of material stretching over time and space, required an overarching concept capable of relating to what Giddens (1981) termed 'agency' and 'structure'. We opted for Goffman's concept of 'career' and continue to vouch for its enduring analytical power in our subsequent papers. Its value is its 'two-sidedness'; one side linked to the development of image, of self, self-identity, and sense of future, while the other concerns the progress of the individual through institutional time as well as her or his movement within the hierarchical structure of the institution (Goffman, 1959, p. 119; Harris and Rudduck, 1993, p. 230; Wallace et al., 1994, p. 170). Evetts (1992) has offered a critical review of the way the concept has been used in the literature. Drawing on Giddens (1981 and 1984) and Harré (1981), she stresses the importance of avoiding reification. Although she was referring to adult careers, she argues that in acknowledging the relationship between agency and structure, we can account for both stability and change. As a team, the weight given to structural changes varied with the individual, but, in general, we concur with her claim that:

> ... structures and systems do have properties which confront individuals in such a way that individuals are presented with a series of limited choices. In respect of careers, the implications are clear. In so far as individuals in organisations and professions develop their careers in particular ways, using the rules and resources which organisations have devised, the intended (and unintended) consequences of such actions are the career patterns that emerge. (Evetts, 1992, p. 15)

We wanted to know how students experienced their four final years of post-compulsory schooling and how they responded to events as they went through the personal and social turmoil of adolescence. Rather than attempt to select a stratified sample which, in theory, we might claim to represent young people of different genders, ethnic origins or socio-economic background, but, in practice, would obscure the contextual events we felt were crucial to interpreting the data, we negotiated access to three very different schools, in each of which we could follow a single, mixed-ability class from Year 8, when they were 12, to Year 11, when they formally completed their compulsory schooling at age 16. This was administratively more convenient than dealing with different form teachers and we also reasoned that the young people we interviewed would understand the rationale and would not be left to speculate on why they had been chosen.

Most importantly, we had to consider the effect of our presence on the students. We were not seeking to standardize the interviewing process but to get their side of the story. We had to see ourselves as 'outsiders', who needed to gain students' confidence. Initially, we reasoned, our approach would be aimed at gaining trust and maximizing rapport.

We planned to interview everyone twice in Year 8; first towards the end of the autumn term and then around half-term in the summer. We also hoped to get the whole group together for about 40 minutes in term two. In practice, the idea of meeting form groups was largely abandoned on logistical grounds, except towards the end of the project when we were taking our leave.

We also needed to understand how the schools were being affected by government and local authority policies and how, in turn, these were affecting the organizational context in which students experienced their schooling and gave meaning to their experiences. Understanding the perspectives of heads, senior management teams, pastoral and subject teachers was part of this, so they too would need to be interviewed. Negotiating with heads and staff on the basis that there would be mutual benefits was crucial to gaining access to students. We also needed to bear in mind how we would honour such a commitment.

Our record of early papers sent out to schools reminds us that we told them we wanted to 'explore what it is like to be a pupil in the 1990s — learning in the framework of a new curriculum and new assessment procedures, and in a climate that stresses the importance of continuing education and training'. There was sufficient interest in the idea to open up the access we needed.

Negotiating Relationships with School Staff:
To Establish, Maintain and 'Give Back'

We used our local knowledge to find three very different schools scattered over three local education authorities. At the time, schools were somewhat circumspect about getting involved in research. The dawn of 'parental choice' and league tables, following the 1988 Education Act, had evoked a sense of vulnerability. Much work went into the early discussions on the project and staff were invited to presentations. The schools finally selected had shown that the headteachers and staff were confident enough to agree to a long-term partnership and were genuinely interested in working with us.

We were being invited into schools at some cost to staff in terms of time and inconvenience and our aim was to work with the teachers in ways that would not jeopardize the rapport we needed to establish with students. We had a folder for each school that set out in detail the terms of our contract with them. We talked through the way we might get student agreement to the research, and accepted the principle that heads acted in *loco parentis*. By and large, heads were more concerned about getting parental approval than approval from students. We therefore left them to approach parents in their preferred style. This meant that they either told parents, in a reassuring way, that their children would be involved in a national project but that no individuals would be identified; or, alternatively, they asked parents, more directly, for permission to involve their children.

With form-tutor agreement, each head identified a mixed-ability form group of students as they entered Year 8 (at age 12). As all classes were mixed ability at this stage, the choice reflected the head's faith in the form tutor to work cooperatively with the project. A volunteer member of staff from each school (the form or year tutor) agreed to liaise directly with the research team. These staff arranged times and rooms for the interviews and generally smoothed our paths with other staff. We gave them our home, as well as our work telephone numbers so they could contact us easily. We needed their goodwill and support, and, in spite of their considerable workloads, they responded with enthusiasm for the project. Aware of the costs to the school, we provided some funds for supply teachers to cover the time we took interviewing staff and as a *quid pro quo* we also offered to help any teachers engaged in their own research with problems such as research design.

All our requests and agreements went to the schools as written material, and were followed up in meetings. Our focus was on the students' experiences of learning. We told heads and staff we were interested in the kinds of teaching and learning their students enjoyed and found worthwhile (or not); what 'shared understandings' of the principles and purposes of learning existed between teachers and students; the status of different kinds of learning in students' eyes and what counted as 'work' for them. We also wanted to know about their expectations and aspirations about life after school. We built in the idea of regular meetings, when teachers involved in the research could meet the research team twice a year to discuss issues. We promised confidentiality for schools and for individuals. We offered to feed back our findings and share our papers with heads before final publication. More controversially, in respect both for their expressed feelings of vulnerability and their expressed interest in the project, we agreed that, in the event of sustained and irresolvable differences of interpretation, we would ensure that their views, as well as ours, together with the grounds for the differences, would be included in the publications. In our view, such an inclusion would broaden the interpretative debate, rather than compromise the evidence. In the event, although we often discussed the work with heads, and talked about its implications with staff on staff development days, none of the heads raised significant objections to our interpretations of data.

Each member of the fieldwork team was associated with a particular school and had a specific, named member of staff to liaise with. Jean went into an 11–16 comprehensive in the North East, situated in an economically disadvantaged area with high unemployment where the headteacher was a man. Susan's school was an 11–18, split-site comprehensive, also with a male headteacher. It was situated in a relatively prosperous area. Formerly a boys' grammar school, it now drew its mixed gender, multi-ethnic students from a range of social and economic backgrounds across the city. Gwen followed David Gillborn into a community school in an East Midlands city where about a quarter of the students were from ethnic minority backgrounds and the headteacher was a woman. The council-built estate that had once formed its catchment area had been refurbished and much of it sold privately. New private developments were springing up in the area. Nevertheless, the number on roll was falling because the school competed for students with a new City Technology College and a neighbouring comprehensive with aspirations to go grant-maintained.

Numbers on roll ranged from David/Gwen's 700 (and dropping) to Susan's 1400 students. All heads had a general commitment to mixed-ability teaching in the early years, with variable degrees of setting for some subjects, beginning in Year 7 in Susan's school, but not until Year 9 in Gwen's. In spite of its growing diversity, Susan's school had a relatively homogeneous community skewed towards the more affluent. This could leave young people from ethnic minority backgrounds or from lower socio-economic groups feeling alienated. Jean and Gwen had changing school populations skewed towards families of lower socio-economic status. Jean's was traditional, white, working class. Gwen's school had a significant range of ethnic diversity.

We established a pattern of interviewing the students and their form tutors every term as well as headteachers and deputies. With rare exceptions (see below), we kept to the schedule. Year tutors and subject staff were interviewed annually at least once and sometimes twice. These interviews gave us our context material. Staff philosophies, their views of each student's particular pattern of development (and staff frequently disagreed about particular students), together with school reports and our experiences of parents' evenings, gave us insight into the way students were perceived and helped us locate the students' own perspectives in a wider pattern.

Over the four years (1991–95), the programme of formal meetings declined in number and importance and, as trust was established, we became part of the less formal networks and our routine visits were institutionalized. Nonetheless, tensions in the schools could arise at times when interviews were scheduled with students. These reflected some staff concerns about loss of lesson time and occasionally about loss of the tutorial room or similar, where we were interviewing. These problems became most acute in Years 10 and 11, when some subject staff expressed their anxieties at losing students from class during important GCSE lessons. Paradoxically, students never voiced such anxieties; they were more likely to express their relief at the opportunity to escape the classroom! Even so we abandoned the winter interviews in Year 11 in favour of written comments from students, so as not to disrupt the period leading up to 'mock' GCSE examinations; possibly at some loss to the data on work placements which we would have liked to probe more deeply.

Controversially, we started to write up the research at the end of the first year. Whilst our overall aim was to get a longitudinal perspective on student careers, we felt there was much in the interviews worth reporting that fitted with prevailing educational research interests. We also found our work well suited to contribute to the growing movement on school improvement. At the end of four years of the project, we celebrated the publication of a book on this subject with key staff who had worked with us throughout, together with volunteers from the students (see below).

Establishing and Maintaining Rapport with Students

Whilst our cordial relationships with teachers were open and obvious and crucial to the establishment and maintenance of a workable project, it was important that students saw us as people they could talk to without their confidences being passed on to staff. In seeking to represent students' views, we took the view that their interests were often very different from those of the teachers but they had very little power to bring them into the official discourses.

We opted to do conversational-style (Powney and Watts, 1987) in-depth interviews three times a year towards the end of each term. We reasoned that the interval was sufficiently long to allow changes and events to occur, without being so long that significant memories would have faded. We reasoned that in-depth interviewing allowed everyone more scope for participation in developing the agenda than a questionnaire could do. Although the students constituted a 'captive' audience, we planned to ask them each time, as individuals, if they were willing to answer our questions and have their answers taped. If they did not like us or our questions they had a variety of strategies at their disposal including returning to their class or not answering specific questions.

The students were not part of the preparatory negotiations because our access to school was dependent on the willingness of headteachers to co-operate with the project in ways that were meaningful and logistically viable to them. We also had to rely on form tutors to provide students with an initial explanation of what was going to happen; hence the importance we gave to our relationships with headteachers and other staff.

For our first encounters with students, we believed that we might establish better relationships with friendship pairs than by talking to each student individually, so for the first set of interviews we asked for 25–30 minutes; each to involve a pair of Year 8 students, and each interview to be separated by a ten minute 'break' for us to complete our notes. Subsequently, we interviewed everyone in most years every term, except in Year 11 (see later). In Year 9, the time given for interviews was substantially reduced to around 15 minutes, as we found this averaged out as sufficient for most students. Girls tended to have more to say than boys and the time allowed for some flexibility without either creating a queue or leaving long waits between students. We also abandoned the idea of using school space and time for our own note-making as this extended the amount of time in which we were likely to disrupt the school day, interrupt student learning time and alienate teachers. Additional notes were made using normal school breaks and at the end of sessions.

Before each individual interview began, we explained the project briefly, reminded the student of its longitudinal design (and, following the first visit, recalled when we had last talked with them). We told them we were writing a book about them. We also said that we wanted to use our findings more generally to help teachers understand students' better. We explained that we were looking for general patterns and assured them that nothing they said would be attributable to them and that individual identities would be kept strictly confidential. We then asked each student for permission to put our questions and tape record their answers.

No-one refused at the start of the interviews, although we found we had to be sensitive to students' feelings as we talked, and we sometimes shifted the ground of the conversation if we felt (through their verbal or non-verbal communication) they were uncomfortable with the way it was going. Questions about options and setting in Year 10, for example, could evoke either anger or embarrassment when students felt they had not been given a fair deal (see below). Some students were keen to hear themselves on tape and playing some of the interview back to them helped rapport.

We took the view that school students aged 12 and upwards were not children and could be expected to participate knowingly and competently, within the bounds of their experiences (see, for example, Morrow and Richards, 1996). Apart from assuring everyone of confidentiality, we were aided in our wish *not* to be seen as authority figures *in alliance with* the schools' authorities by the way students saw the interviews as opportunities to escape the classroom; albeit for limited periods.

In the event, the first group interviews did not take place until March 1992, when the students had been in Year 8 for six months and were aged 12+. Looking back over the transcripts, the evidence is that rapport was not difficult to establish. Difficulties, were more apparent in Year 9. This may have been because for these first interviews we interviewed students in friendship groups of twos and threes, which encouraged dialogue particularly amongst the boys; but it may also have been because many of the questions we asked in Year 8 invited students to look back at the memorable novelties inherent in the experience of changing schools. Another possibility is that in Year 8 the students were at a less self-conscious age than they were the following year. The differences are particularly marked with the boys who talked to David. In terms reminiscent of the 'lads' in Willis' (1977) study, they egged one another on to express feelings about teachers, events, sex and football in ways they may well have felt they could not do with any of the women interviewers. Jean, Gwen and Susan, on the other hand, were very successful in getting responses from the girls. This suggests that work with young people is likely to be more insightful with same-sex interviewers, although it is also possible that group interviews with boys encourage some exaggerated claims, particularly when they are aged around 13.

Transition from primary school had clearly been an exciting and (sometimes) frightening time. Although much has been done recently through preliminary visits and so on to ease the strangeness described by Measor and Woods (1984), the problems of making new friendships, the size of the building (and of the fifth years), new impressions of staff and some horror stories about fights and bullying were recalled and retold with some relish. In the summer interviews, students also talked avidly of recent school camps and outings. Such outings provided significant and long-enduring memories of relatively uninhibited out-of-school experiences, and were to be recalled as highlights even in the final interviews at the end of the project.

Nonetheless, discontents in school were building up over rules and regulations in what may be seen as the common adolescent challenge to authority but may also be a symptom of a wider malaise. Young people, many of whom could not be described as anti-school, were irritated by and resented restrictions on their time, space and movement (Harris, 1994). They illustrated their frustrations by observations on the controls staff exerted over such things as how, what and where they ate at lunchtime (particularly the queues), rules about movement in corridors and stairways, and by criticizing the smoke emanating from the school staffroom at a time when they were subject to severe sanctions for even possessing cigarettes. (It is worth noting that, by the end of the project, there were very strict controls on smoking by staff.) In spite of significant exceptions, and considerable dedication from some staff, lessons were often dismissed as 'boring' and could be difficult to recall at all. A common complaint from students was that they wanted to be treated as more 'grown up' (Harris, 1994). We were also finding that the school organization could exacerbate problems. For example, where there were staffing problems, it was the Year 8s who tended to get the less experienced, temporary staff; and these were often a target for disruptive behaviour. In learning terms, we identified Year 8 as a relatively 'fallow' year (Harris et al., 1996).

In Susan's school which setted students by ability early on, the form class was predominantly middle class and white. The setting policy reinforced differences and rivalries, particularly the separation of a small number of Asian girls from the rest. Susan was finding it difficult to maintain an objective, 'outsider' stance on several issues. For example, the Asian girls saw her as an authoritative but sympathetic 'other'. They feared (rightly) that they were to be separated and hoped (wrongly) that Susan could intervene on their behalf to prevent it happening. Susan felt the best she could do was to encourage the girls to talk to their tutor about their fears. She also considered (but did not pursue) the idea of offering personal help to a working-class girl who was having problems at home.

In the other schools where mixed-ability work predominated, the sense of disorientation engendered by change of school soon cemented into a new sense of collective, rebellious peer identity. Students in all the schools often talked on behalf of the whole form as 'We're the worst class'; an epithet echoed and reinforced by some teachers (Harris, 1994; Wallace, 1996). In Susan's school this became 'we're thick' when students referred to being in a low set. There were also clear gender differences which led our interview 'conversations' down different routes. Girls resented the degree of disruption generated by the boys and, as David's data in particular indicated, there was strong peer pressure amongst the boys to compete for physical superiority and show enthusiasm for football. We all found moments when we were moved by students' problems and in one instance (which must remain obscure) came close to formally reporting some extremely dubious behaviour on the part of at least one member of staff about which we were told during the interviews. To our relief, the school became aware of the problem through parents and instituted disciplinary proceedings without our intervention. The dilemma of what to do about confidential information that suggests adult intervention may (or may not) be required to prevent young people being misused or even abused, was resolved for us. This is an area of ethical concern on which researchers talking to children and young people need to formulate a clear policy before the research begins.

Our general impression at this stage was summed up in the student view, 'School's great apart from the lessons!' (Harris and Rudduck, 1993). Overall, we had been reinforced in our earlier belief that student comments had to be interpreted in a broad context.

By the end of the first year David had moved on, Gwen had joined the team and all three interviewers were women. Although students wanted to know what had happened to their former interviewer (recalled his football interests and allegiances, and expressed regret at not seeing him again), Gwen found no obvious difficulty in establishing rapport. However, getting students to talk about their learning in any reflective way was much harder than talking about their other interests and concerns. Indeed, students often said they looked forward to our visits (and the associated opportunity to escape lessons).

Although some of the boys returned to recount the 'laddish' views and experiences they had shared with David, it is nonetheless likely that they were less inclined to talk in the same way about their more personal feelings to Gwen than they had to David. Gender, as well as the different interests, and age of the new team member played some part both in the kinds of evidence obtained and in the way the data were interpreted.

Year 9 provided something of a fresh start. Faced with a new timetable and new teachers, efforts were being made by staff to make the students more future-oriented. When we asked students what had changed, they responded that they were being treated 'more like adults', although restrictions on time, space and movement still irritated them. Most importantly in terms of their encounters with school work, this was the year both of the new Standard Assessment Tasks (SATs) and the more well-established practice of choosing GCSE and other options for Years 10 and 11. The practice of setting by ability (already well established in Susan's school) was either in evidence or clearly anticipated. Although the SATs were ultimately abandoned shortly before they were due in early summer, because of NUT opposition, all the schools carried out internal tests across the year and provided parents with the results. The methodological point we are making here is that the personal circumstances of individual development and the structural changes were now closely inter-related in the interview responses.

For many students it was their first experience of this kind of formal testing and we picked up responses ranging from the deeply worried (more often than not those with parents who were aware of the implications) to the totally mystified (those who had no experience of setted groups and little or no idea what it was all about). As differentiation increased, identities based on the form group were breaking down. Within the form group, this was more apparent initially as gender differentiation, when the girls, who were more likely to want to do their work well and were more work-oriented than many boys, identified the boys as disruptive (Wallace, 1996). In spite of the sense that Year 9 marked a turning point in the career of students, our attempts to use the Year 9 interviews to get them to articulate their long-term goals were largely a failure. There was no evidence that most students had any. Apart from some, often vague, career aspirations, the long-term agenda was a mystery and not under their control. They were largely ignorant of its ramifications. Students' school concerns remained broadly grounded in the regularity of the day-to-day procedures and routines (Rudduck, Harris and Wallace, 1994). Their significant life events occurred outside.

However, by this time, we had found we had some reliably articulate 'key informants' who were not necessarily pro-school and who had begun to reflect, as individuals, on their work. These students spanned the socio-economic spectrum but they were more often girls than boys (Rudduck et al., 1996, pp. 32–33, 59, 62). The idea of being the subject of a book intrigued them and helped generate trust. We were asked repeatedly how the book was coming along and some students requested copies (some boys suggested they should get it at half price). Such requests stimulated us to reflect on possible ways of satisfying their requests.

Yet, whilst many of the Year 9 interview transcripts showed evidence of extended, conversational responses, there were some (particularly but not exclusively from some of the boys) where we had little but monosyllabic answers. In an attempt to recover some of the spontaneity of the Year 8 interviews, we began Year 10 by repeating the paired group formula. Students were now in their sets and option groups for GCSE and non-examination options and no longer spent much time with their form groups. Broadly, we wanted to know if they had got the options they wanted, what was going well for them (or badly), what was happening in their relationships with friends and family and how they were planning their futures.

The attempt at group interviews worked very differently this time. The boys seemed much more willing to carry on an extended conversation in the group interviews where they reinforced and added to one another's accounts (although we also recognize that they were growing up fast). Two Asian boys, for example, gave graphic, mutually supportive accounts of a recent visit to the neighbourhood of a group they called the 'Ku Klux Klan'. In contrast, two girls, who had previously worked together in a form group, and came to be interviewed as 'friends', appeared estranged. One dominated the conversation and the other conveyed silent hostility. It turned out that the dominant partner had been placed in a relatively high set for mathematics and her friend had been placed in the lowest one, a situation that required some sensitivity on the part of the interviewer. Sometimes friends took alternative perspectives on our questions and debated them in heated disagreement (see also Burgess, 1984). Overall, the diversity of responses was increasingly evident as students perceived their specific sets and options as indications of their personal futures (see Wallace et al., 1994). Where sets were a relatively new experience, the *meaning* of setting by ability (often conceived as the ability to 'work fast') was often openly explored in conversation. The pattern reflected the growing differences between students, their changing relationships with their peers, their teachers, and us, and the different patterns of progress they were finding as they changed their status in the school and began to recognize what was at stake for them as individuals. Even so the interview conversations continued to reflect more of the passion of immediate events, than future aspirations.

Our interviews were now reflecting the growing diversity of experience as the institutional procedures made students more conscious of themselves as individuals and competition between some of them for good grades heightened. On the other hand, the incidence of missed schooling through truancy, sickness or exclusion increased, particularly amongst boys with a reputation for 'dossing around'. A few boys were lost to the project altogether; one from Year 9 onwards because he was ill and needed home tuition; several because they were persistent truants; a couple of girls found themselves pregnant. One student left to change schools in Year 8 and returned a year or two later. A few moved away altogether. Overall, for one reason or another about 12 of the cohort missed so many interviews they were effectively lost to the project.

Worries about the coursework grades needed for post-16 study became a dominant issue in some interview conversations. In Gwen's area, the City Technology College and another school with a sixth form were prepared to recruit only the best students from 11–16 schools. Conditional places were offered to some students, after interview. These sixth forms were seen by some students as higher status places than the Further Education College for A level studies; a perception that enhanced their motivation for high grades but added to their worries. Relationships with teachers changed. Teachers who were working lunchtimes and after school to help individuals with problems gained high praise. Others were seen as less helpful. Sometimes, a teacher was condemned for providing inadequate, even wrong, information.

Interviews with these students became opportunities for them to reveal the pressures they were under; the problems they were having with time-management and the problems they had in getting to grips with 'revision' and formal examinations, often for the first time. We learned how mothers and older sisters (rarely fathers and never brothers) would often help, but did not always understand, particularly where their own experiences were limited (Rudduck et al., 1996, pp. 134–8).

The tensions were relieved as the end of Year 10 and the start of Year 11 took them into work placements. Reluctantly, we abandoned the autumn term's interviewing and resorted to written accounts. Gwen was still recovering from a broken leg and we had lost Susan (although she found time to undertake the late spring round of interviews). Mock GCSEs were imminent and teachers were reluctant to allow students out of class. Written accounts could be done in form tutor time. The switch could not be avoided. It relieved pressures on the team and helped us to retain good relations with staff who believed every teaching moment to be precious. Because of the timing, our early data on work placements came through the written reports (which we followed up later in interview). Importantly, work placement data confirmed the students' sense of individual difference and reinforced their belief in the competitive nature of post-school life.

Ranging from a prestigious placement in journalism to local jobs which offered little more than shelf-filling, work placements hardened students' feelings towards school. Some returned determined to get the grades they needed. Others dropped out permanently, convinced school had little to offer them. By now Julia had taken on much of Susan's work and was developing a major interest in analysing the data in this area (Day, 1996).

The climax to the year came with the GCSE results. We returned to the schools and recorded reactions. We found some who had good results and felt the effort had all been worthwhile. For others, the results were concrete evidence they were 'rubbish'. Some did not bother to find out one way or the other. Some were working and could not get in anyway.

With the benefit of a successful bid for a small amount of money for follow-up interviews, we embarked on two further sets of post-school interviews with eight students from each school. Our sample was chosen using what Glaser and Strauss (1967) call 'theoretical sampling'. This is a reasoned process, rather than a statistical formula. From each school we selected small groups of two or three key informants whose school careers and future plans suggested they would take very different post-school career paths. Much of this data still requires scrutiny and analysis. What we can say, at this stage, is that these members of our cohort, with the benefit of experience, were able to reflect on their school careers and look forward into their uncertain futures with considerable insight. Yet the responses reflect the different cultures and show how the shared experiences of school finally give way to the competitive individualistic world of the young adult, even where it had been resisted. Regrets across the board, from prospective A-level students to those labouring in unskilled manual work, were that they wished they had worked harder, understood better where their school careers were taking them.

Giving Back

As our cohort frequently enquired about the progress of the book and showed interest in the final result, we decided to attempt to give something back in two ways. Firstly, we produced a glossy leaflet for everyone — much of the credit for which goes to Julia and her teenage son. It had the title of the project and included jokes and drawings related to some selected quotes from each year's data. We took the leaflets into schools on the final day and gave them out with our thanks. Three months later, we launched the book. Jean negotiated with the publishers for a book launch in Cambridge to which we invited all the students, by personal letter. From the names of those wanted to come we drew lots and chose around six from each school. At the launch, they received free copies, read extracts from the book and joined teachers, researchers and publishers for lunch. It symbolized a worthwhile conclusion to our long-standing relationship. Julia, who had known the students only from the transcripts, said she could recognize them all from the tapes!

Many of the responses from students indicated that they valued the chance to talk about themselves and their lives to a sympathetic listener. Some teachers believed that the students in the classes engaged with the project were, to some extent, changed by it because it asked them to reflect on their experiences and became a topic of discussion amongst their peers. In this sense, being a part of the project became an aspect of the schooling context and may well have influenced their career paths, but we can never know this.

Ethnography and Educational Research

So what of validity and reliability? We now have around 750 transcribed interviews which reflect the way we responded to students as much as they reflect the way students responded to their schooling. We have used them to provide selective accounts of what happened to our cohort as they moved from Year 8 to Year 11 and (in some cases) beyond. There are many stories we have not yet told and very many that may never be told. Other researchers may well have evoked different responses, recorded events differently and selected different material for different stories. Yet, whilst we stand by the importance of understanding the context for interpreting data, we would argue for more than mere relativism and lay some claims to 'know' what schools are like for students. The students' perceptions evoke recognition in our teacher audiences as we ask them to examine the implications of our data for their practices. The teachers we talk to and those of us who have taught in schools recognize the enduring nature of the boys who, whilst embracing competition in the peer group and on the football field, reject competitive individualism in the classroom. The students' experiences of examination pressure in Years 10 and 11 evoke recognition in parents and could have been found in any school over many years. The detail varies but the themes and issues are far from new.

At a general level, our work challenges much that happens in schools. If we accept that schooling is an important aspect of growing up, how might young people be given a sense of involvement in an active, participative social, political and economic future without generating disaffection? Is the present age-related form group, with its annual ritual of 'moving up' (whether or not it is seen as mixed ability), the best framework for teaching and learning? Is motivation to learn best linked to competition? Is it then, inevitably, divisive? How might motivation to learn be developed through tutoring in a school community that values cooperation and social cohesion? These questions arise from the insights derived from our ethnographic data. Attempts to answer them will require evaluation by ethnographic methods; a project that needs to be undertaken in the light of Hall's (1997) argument that apparently conflicting dichotomies, such as subject and object, may only be understood when we examine one as a part of the context of the other (Copeland, 1997; Hall, 1997).

What this research has done is helped to raise the importance of including students' experiences in attempts to find a way forward for schooling policy and professional practices; whether the initiators of change are in schools, classrooms, local authorities or government.

References

COPELAND, I. (1997) 'Book Review of J. HOLMWOOD (1996), *Talcott Parsons and the Idea of General Theory*', *British Educational Research Journal*, **23**, 4, pp. 558–9.

DAY, J. (1996) 'Confronting the world of work', in RUDDUCK, J., CHAPLAIN, R. and WALLACE, G. (eds) *School Improvement: What Can Pupils Tell Us?* London: David Fulton Publishers.

EVETTS, J. (1992) 'Dimensions of career: Avoiding reification in the analysis of change', *Sociology*, **26**, 1, pp. 1–21.

GIDDENS, A. (1981) 'Agency, institution and time-space analysis', in KNORR-CORTINA, K. and CICOUREL, A.V. (eds) *Advances in Social Theory and Methodology*, London: Routledge and Kegan Paul.

GIDDENS, A. (1984) *The Constitution of Society*, Cambridge: Polity Press.

GLASER, B. and STRAUSS, A. (1967) *The Discovery of Grounded Theory*, Chicago: Aldine Publishing.

GOFFMAN, E. (1959) 'The moral career of the mental patient', *Psychiatry*, **22**, May.

HALL, S. (1997) Presidential Address to the Annual Conference of the British Sociological Association, April.

HAMMERSLEY, M. (1992) *What's Wrong With Ethnography?* London: Routledge.

HAMMERSLEY, M. (1994) 'Ethnography, policy making and practice in education', in HALPIN, D. and TROYNA, B. (eds) *Researching Educational Policy and Practice: Ethical and Methodological Issues*, London: Falmer Press.

HARRÉ, R. (1981) 'Philosophical aspects of the micro-macro problem', in KNORR-CORTINA, K. and CICOUREL, A.V. (eds) *Advances in Social Theory and Methodology*, London: RKP.

HARRIS, S. (1994) 'Entitled to what? Control and autonomy in school: A student perspective', *International Studies in Sociology of Education*, **4**, 1, pp. 57–76.

HARRIS, S. and RUDDUCK, J. (1993) 'Establishing the seriousness of learning in the early years of secondary school', *British Journal of Educational Psychology*, **63**, pp. 322–36.

HARRIS, S., RUDDUCK, J. and WALLACE, G. (1996) 'Political contexts and school careers', in HUGHES, M. (ed.) *Teaching and Learning in Changing Times*, Oxford: Blackwell.

HUGHES, M. (1996) 'Introduction', in HUGHES, M. (ed.) *Teaching and Learning in Changing Times*, Oxford: Blackwell.

MEASOR, L. and WOODS, P. (1984) *Changing Schools*, Milton Keynes: Open University Press.

MORROW, V. and RICHARDS, R. (1996) 'The ethics of social research with children', *Children and Society*, **10**, pp. 90–105.

POWNEY, J. and WATTS, M. (1987) *Interviewing in Educational Research*, London: RKP.

RUDDUCK, J. (1984) 'Introducing innovation to pupils', in HOPKINS, D. and WIDEEN, M. (eds) *Alternative Perspectives on School Improvement*, London: Falmer Press, pp. 53–60.

RUDDUCK, J., CHAPLAIN, R. and WALLACE, G. (ed.) (1996) *School Improvement: What Can Pupils Tell Us?* London: David Fulton Publishers.

SILVERMAN, D. (1985) *Qualitative Methodology and Sociology*, Aldershot: Gower.

SILVERMAN, D. (1993) *Interpreting Qualitative Data: Methods for Analysing Talk, Text and Interaction*, London: Sage.

WALLACE, G., RUDDUCK, J. and HARRIS, S. (1994) 'Students' secondary school careers: Research in a climate of moving perspectives', in HALPIN, D. and TROYNA, B. (eds) *Researching Education Policy: Ethical and Methodological Issues*, London, Falmer Press.

WALLACE, G. (1996) 'Engaging with learning', in RUDDUCK, J., CHAPLAIN, R. and WALLACE, G. (eds) *School Improvement: What Can Pupils Tell Us?* London: David Fulton Publishers.

WILLIS, P. (1977) *Learning to Labour*, Farnborough: Saxon House.

7 More than the Sum of Its Parts? Coordinating the ESRC Research Programme on *Innovation and Change in Education*

Martin Hughes

Introduction

Between 1991 and 1996 I acted as coordinator of the research programme on 'Innovation and Change in Education: The Quality of Teaching and Learning', which was funded by the Economic and Social Research Council (ESRC). This was a major programme of educational research which aimed to increase our understanding of teaching and learning in the context of the reforms introduced by the 1988 Education Reform Act. The programme consisted of 10 projects, based at various centres in England and Scotland, and involved many of the UK's leading educational researchers. My role as coordinator was to ensure that the programme achieved its full potential, in terms of both its contribution to academic knowledge and its value for non-academic users. As Howard Newby, then Chief Executive of ESRC, put it at our first programme meeting: my role was to ensure that the programme amounted to 'more than the sum of its parts'.

This chapter provides a first-hand account of my experiences as programme coordinator. My aim in the chapter is to provide some insights into the issues raised by programmatic research, and to describe how these issues were addressed within the 'Innovation and Change' programme. In this respect, the chapter is adding to what is virtually a non-existent literature. Despite the growing importance of research programmes in the social sciences, there are surprisingly few published accounts which focus on the nature and problems of this way of organizing research (two notable exceptions are Kushner, 1991, and Martin, 1995).

The chapter starts by describing how the 'Innovation and Change' programme was set up and how I came to act as coordinator. It then focuses on some of the main aspects of the coordinator's role and how these were addressed: these include working with projects and with the ESRC, creating coherence across a disparate set of projects, and disseminating through the media. The chapter concludes with some implications for research programmes in general. Throughout, the focus is on the coordination process, rather than on the academic output from the programme. Readers wishing to know more about the latter are referred to three edited books (Hughes, 1994, 1995 and 1996) and two special issues of the journal *Research Papers in Education* (vol. 9, no. 2, 1994 and vol. 10, no. 2, 1995) which contain some of the main findings of the programme.

First, though, a brief point about terminology. The programme started life in 1991 as an ESRC 'Initiative'. In 1992, however, ESRC decided to standardize its portfolio of programmes and initiatives, and renamed them all 'Programmes'. Similarly, my own role was initially described as that of 'Coordinator'. In 1995, however, ESRC decided to standardize again, and all its coordinators and directors were retitled as 'Programme Directors'. In this chapter I will use the terms 'programme' and 'coordinator', as these were the ones which were in operation for most of the period under discussion. They are also the terms which provide the most appropriate description of what actually took place.

The Origins of the Programme

The programme originated in a paper drafted in 1988 by an *ad hoc* working party of the ESRC's Human Behaviour and Development Group. The paper noted that education was 'living through a decade of unparalleled change in almost every aspect', and called for a new research programme around the question 'What constitutes effective teaching and learning in a curriculum?'. This paper was widely circulated in February 1989 amongst the academic and educational community, and responses were welcomed. As a result of this consultation exercise, a more formal proposal was prepared by the Human Development and Behaviour Group and submitted to ESRC Council in July 1989. This proposal, which carried the full title of 'Innovation and Change in Education: The Quality of Teaching and Learning', noted that the educational reforms currently underway provided 'both a powerful impetus to, and an exceptional opportunity for, fundamental research into the quality of teaching and learning in a variety of settings and curricular contexts'. In particular, the proposal suggested that the programme would address the following 'five over-arching questions':

(i) How is the diversity of teaching and learning processes best characterized?

(ii) To what extent are different forms of teaching and learning associated with quantitatively and qualitatively different learning outcomes?

(iii) How may the outcomes of teaching and learning best be evaluated and assessed? How does the process of assessment influence teaching and learning?

(iv) How can the 'natural experiments' created by externally imposed policy changes be used to illustrate these issues?

(v) More generally, in what ways are teaching and learning being reshaped (and/or perceived as being reshaped) by the reforming of educational provision?

This proposal was approved by ESRC Council, and in January 1990 a further paper was circulated calling for outline proposals from the educational research community. The paper made clear that the programme would 'focus directly on the quality of teaching and learning in the context of radical changes in educational policy . . . in a variety of educational settings and curricular contexts.' This call for proposals generated a huge response. Over 250 outline proposals were submitted, many of which were of excellent quality, and the commissioning panel had the difficult task of reducing this to a shortlist of 25. Those on the shortlist were contacted in May 1990 and asked to submit a full proposal. On the strength of these expanded proposals, an initial group of five projects was funded in summer 1990, and a further five projects chosen later in 1990. A full list of the 10 projects funded under the programme is provided in Appendix 1 (pp. 109–10).

Two aspects of this process are worth noting. The first is that there was a time interval of well over two years between the original conception of the programme in 1988 and the completion of the commissioning process at the end of 1990. During this period, the membership of the various groups involved with the programme inevitably underwent changes: some of those who served on the original working party moved on, while others arrived with new ideas. In addition, the widespread consultation process undertaken in 1989 inevitably introduced fresh ideas into the programme, while further ideas emerged during the commissioning process itself. Thus by the time the 10 projects were in place, the programme had already moved on from its original conception. As I shall argue later in the chapter, this dynamic, changing process was also a feature of the programme after the projects had been commissioned.

The second point is that the lengthy consultation and commissioning process resulted in a small number of 'winners' (the 10 successful projects) and a much larger number of 'losers' (the remaining 240 applicants). These 'losers' — and particularly those who were shortlisted but not funded — had invested a considerable amount of time and energy in generating proposals. In many cases, their proposals were of fundable quality, but simply did not fit into the overall shape of the programme as it emerged. A commonly expressed view at the time was that the programme had raised expectations among many researchers, but had only rewarded a few. Moreover, there was a general perception that the commissioning panel had favoured proposals from experienced educational researchers, who had a strong track record of 'delivering the goods' (as Kushner, 1991, has noted, this is a common feature of many commissioned programmes). While it was rare for hostility towards the 10 projects to be expressed openly, it certainly created a climate in which projects funded under the programme were seen by other researchers as having some kind of 'favoured status', and this in turn created further pressure on the programme. Ironically, several of the 'losers' subsequently re-submitted their proposals to the standard ESRC research grants scheme, and some of these were funded to a greater extent than would have been possible under the financial limits imposed on the 'Innovation and Change' programme.

Martin Hughes

Appointment of Coordinator

The position of coordinator for the programme was advertised in November 1990, shortly after the last of 10 projects had been commissioned. This was normal ESRC practice at the time. Nowadays it is more customary for programme directors to be appointed before the commissioning process has started, so they can play a greater role in selecting the projects with which they will be working. I would certainly have welcomed being appointed at an earlier stage in the process. This was not because I was unhappy with the projects which were actually chosen — far from it. Rather, it was because being appointed at a relatively late stage gave the impression — both to the projects and to the outside world — that the coordinator was something of an afterthought who had been grafted on to an enterprise that was already underway. Indeed, by the time my appointment was confirmed in February 1991, several of the projects had already started work.

One implication of appointing the coordinator after the projects had been commissioned was that the directors of projects within the programme could also apply for the role of coordinator (when the coordinator or programme director is appointed first, they are automatically disqualified by ESRC from applying for a project within their programme). I was already co-director of one of the 10 projects in the programme, and so I was in the unusual situation of being both the programme coordinator and the director of a project within the programme. In practice, there were surprisingly few problems in this dual position, as the two roles were quite distinct. It was important to me, however, that my own project was not seen to be favoured in any way by this dual role; for example, any major decisions about allocating resources to projects were taken by the programme's Steering Committee (see p. 101) and not by myself. If anything, I suspect that my own project may have been disadvantaged rather than favoured by my dual role as coordinator, in that I probably put less energy into integrating it into the programme than I did with the other nine projects.

My own motives for taking on the role of coordinator were somewhat mixed. In some ways, the job was not particularly attractive: I had been warned when I applied that coordinating a major programme involved a lot of hard work for little personal reward. However, I was at the time somewhat dissatisfied with my position in Exeter, and was looking for a new challenge. For personal reasons I was committed to living in Exeter for the foreseeable future, and so moving to another part of the country was out of the question. One of the attractions of the coordinator's job, then, was that it enabled me to take on a fresh challenge whilst at the same time keeping my base in Exeter. Moreover, I was genuinely interested in the management of educational research (I had been research coordinator at the School of Education in Exeter from 1984–90) and I was attracted by the prospect of using whatever expertise I had acquired in this area on a national and international stage. In addition, I thought it would be stimulating — if a little daunting — to be working closely with some of the country's leading educational researchers. Overall, it was the right move for me at the time, and one which I never seriously regretted.

The Role of Coordinator

The role of programme coordinator is often defined as one of 'adding value' to a collection of projects. Thus, the original job specification for the 'Innovation and Change' programme stated that 'the principal task of the coordinator will be to ensure that the Initiative realises its full potential, conceptually, theoretically and methodologically, as well as being of relevance to policy-makers'. In practice, the activities I carried out as coordinator fell into three main (and overlapping) areas. These were:

1 **Networking** — with project directors, ESRC, other academics and policy-makers (etc.).
2 **Creating coherence** — identifying and developing common themes within the programme.
3 **Dissemination** — communicating programme findings to academic and non-academic audiences.

Not surprisingly, the priority given to these activities changed during the lifetime of the programme. In the early days, the main emphasis was on networking — getting to know the various participants and setting up a common agenda. During the middle years of the programme, more emphasis was placed on creating coherence, as initial findings started to emerge and could be discussed at programme seminars. In the later stages of the programme, the emphasis was inevitably on the dissemination of findings.

This changing emphasis also reflected a major shift in ESRC priorities which took place during the period of the programme. This was brought about by the 1993 White Paper 'Realising Our Potential', which argued that publicly funded research should be of greater benefit to non-academic users than had previously been the case. The White Paper called on ESRC to develop a new mission statement making this commitment, and to be more proactive in developing user-relevant research. This development in fact fitted in very well with the timetable of the 'Innovation and Change' programme, as by 1993–94 we were starting to move into the dissemination phase of the programme.

While the main activities of the coordinator can be described in fairly clear-cut categories, in practice I was faced on a day-to-day basis with a sometimes bewildering variety of tasks. Thus in a typical week I might be responding to a request from ESRC for some information about the programme's relationships with 'users', trying to help a project with the problems of moving from one location to another, preparing the agenda for a forthcoming meeting of the Steering Committee, reading a draft chapter written by one of the project teams, organizing a symposium at an international conference, writing an article about the programme for the newsletter of an international organization, and phoning a contact at the Scottish Office to discuss the relevance of particular programme findings to the Scottish education system. I had always considered myself to be reasonably well organized, but the demands of being a programme coordinator constantly tested my limits in this area. A well-organized secretary who was familiar with the people involved was essential, and in Margaret Bown I was fortunate to have such a person.

Throughout the period 1991–96, I was funded on the assumption that 20 per cent of my time would be spent coordinating the programme. In practice, it was virtually impossible to carry out this role on such a limited time allocation: indeed, most ESRC programme directors are nowadays funded at around 80 per cent of their time. A rough log of how I spent my time during this period revealed that I was spending an average of between 1.5 and 2 days a week on coordination activities. There was, however, considerable variation from week to week in how much time I spent on the programme. There were some weeks — particularly when I was travelling around the country visiting projects or meeting policy-makers — when I spent almost all my time on programme activities. At other times, the programme was virtually ignored while I attended to my other duties.

Working with Projects

At the heart of any research programme lies the work of the project teams. It is therefore essential that the coordinator establishes good relationships with these teams from as early a stage as possible. While much of this can be done by phone, post or e-mail — particularly once relationships have been established — there is no substitute for face-to-face meetings with project teams, preferably on their own territory.

For me, visiting project teams was one of the best parts of the job. It was a real privilege to spend two or three hours in the company of an enthusiastic project team, discussing how their research might develop, how it might fit with that of other projects, and how their findings might be disseminated. I was working with some of the best educational researchers in the country, whose work was at the cutting edge of their respective fields, and I was very fortunate to be seeing at close quarters how they went about their business. These visits often revealed interesting differences in personal style. One team, for example, would book a meeting room and have word-processed agendas ready for our meetings, while another team would simply take me off to the nearest pub for free-ranging discussions. The visits also provided useful insights into the internal dynamics of project teams: this was where I discovered, for example, who the 'real' project director was, what role the research fellows actually played in project decision-making, or whether someone named on the proposal as a 'consultant' had any involvement in the project or not. I always found visiting projects stimulating and thought-provoking, and would often tape-record the discussions and listen to them again on the journey back to Exeter.

It took me some time, however, to realize the value of visiting projects. This was partly because, when I first took on the job of coordinator, I was advised that it was essentially a 'desk job'. I was told that project directors were busy and eminent people, and that they would not take kindly to my 'popping in' to see them at regular intervals. I was therefore reluctant, at the start of the programme, to arrange visits with project teams, and by the end of my first year as coordinator I had only just completed my first round of visits. With hindsight, I should have started these visits much earlier than I did.

As Kushner (1991) points out, one of the problems facing all coordinators — and particularly those of large multi-disciplinary programmes — is that they cannot hope to be an expert in all the disciplines and methodologies represented by their project teams. I was no exception in this respect. I came from a psychological background and most of my previous work had been concerned with children's learning in the early years. It therefore took me some time to get an understanding of projects whose work, for example, focused on the secondary curriculum or which built on sociological or linguistic theory. For the most part, the other project directors were fairly tolerant of my ignorance: indeed, several directors commented that it was quite useful having to explain what they were doing to a relative novice like myself. Nevertheless, I did not find it particularly enjoyable when a researcher on one project accused me of being 'theoretically naive' about his area of expertise, although I tried hard not to show my feelings at the time.

One of the most difficult problems faced by programme coordinators is that of negotiating with their project teams a mutually acceptable understanding of what it means to be part of a programme. In particular, everyone needs to be clear about exactly what demands the coordinator can reasonably make of the project teams, and what benefits might accrue to the teams through being part of the programme. Essentially, it is a matter of getting the right balance between programme priorities and project priorities. If the programme coordinator makes too many demands on the project teams, then he/she is likely to lose their cooperation, and the programme will collapse. On the other hand, if the programme coordinator simply allows the project teams to 'do their own thing', then the programme may not achieve its overall aims and objectives.

I was confronted with this problem right at the start of the 'Innovation and Change' programme. At our first two programme meetings, in March and November 1991, three or four project directors made it clear that they did not feel part of a programme, and that they intended to treat their projects as if they had obtained a standard (i.e. non-programmatic) ESRC grant. In particular, they disliked the notion of being 'managed' by an outsider (the coordinator) and/or a group of outsiders (the Steering Committee), and they regarded this as a potential intrusion on their academic freedom. Some project directors also remarked that they saw little common ground between their projects and others in the programme, and that they did not think it would be useful to spend time with them at programme meetings.

While these views were only expressed by a minority of project directors, I still found them very disturbing, and potentially undermining to the whole programme. I therefore set about developing more positive working relationships with and between projects. I set up (somewhat belatedly) my first round of project visits, during which I tried to make it clear that I had no intention of getting involved in the internal management of individual projects. I also persuaded the Steering Committee to co-opt individual project directors on to the Committee, in rotation, in order to break down some of the suspicion with which the Steering Committee was held. I temporarily abandoned my intended programme of holding further large-scale meetings which all project teams were expected to attend, and instead organized a series of smaller meetings on topics of common interest. As the programme proceeded, I set up a wide range of dissemination opportunities for the projects: these included (with the Research Assessment Exercise in mind), two special issues of an international refereed journal. Finally, with the help of the Steering Committee, I was able to find small amounts of funding to support specific project activities, such as travel to overseas conferences. In short, I tried to persuade project teams that being in a programme did not mean that their research was going to be managed from outside, and that sufficient benefits would accrue to them to offset the demands which I inevitably had to make.

While I cannot claim that I was uniformly successful in all that I did, I was extremely pleased with the levels of cooperation and support which I received from the project teams for the rest of the programme. Nevertheless, there was a continual tension throughout the programme between the demands that were being made on the project teams and the benefits which the teams obtained from being part of the programme. This tension was expressed very clearly by two project directors in their End-of-Award reports:

> Involvement in a Research Programme led to requests from the coordinator to participate in seminars and symposia, and to write papers for publications associated with the Programme. Whilst these seemed like additional work at the time, they were invaluable in setting deadlines for writing, and resulted in earlier dissemination of findings than would otherwise have occurred.

> We found it a very positive experience to have a systematic relationship with educational researchers from a variety of disciplines, to share data with colleagues, and to participate with them in discussing work in progress, in conference symposia and in planning publications . . . An unforeseen 'cost', however was the added pressure involved in fitting the additional collaborative activities of the Initiative into the busy schedule of the project itself. Retrospectively, we wish ESRC had encouraged us to build 'windows' for collective activity into the original proposal.

This tension between programme priorities and project priorities seems to be an inevitable part of a research programme, and perhaps needs to be made much more explicit to all those embarking on such an enterprise.

Working with ESRC

As coordinator of an ESRC research programme, I was essentially working on a part-time basis for ESRC for the duration of the programme. An important part of my role was to liaise with ESRC staff, to understand and implement ESRC priorities, and to ensure as far as possible that the programme furthered ESRC's aims and objectives. In practice, this meant working with several different groups of people in and around ESRC.

The first group consisted of the full-time professional officers of ESRC who were based at Swindon. These officers managed the ongoing administration of the programme, dealt with queries about projects, helped me develop and implement a dissemination strategy, and sent me on two courses — a media training course and a presentation training course — which provided me with important skills for my coordinating role. In addition, at any given time there was one particular officer — the programme officer — whose responsibilities included looking after the 'Innovation and Change' programme. These Swindon-based officers were almost invariably helpful and supportive, especially if there was some sort of crisis or difficulty in the programme. However, the ESRC office experienced a considerable degree of staff turnover during the period of the programme, as well as a number of internal re-organizations, and this inevitably led to a loss of continuity: for example, I had to work with a succession of six different programme officers during the lifetime of the programme.

The second group consisted of an ESRC-appointed Steering Committee which was responsible for the overall direction of the programme. This Committee consisted of two experienced educational researchers (one of whom chaired the Committee), two headteachers (one primary and one secondary), one HMI, one educational journalist, and up to three co-opted project directors. The Steering Committee met in London two or three times a year to review the progress of the programme and to suggest future developments. These meetings were extremely valuable, particularly in the early stages, when there was a great deal of enthusiasm about what the programme might accomplish. I usually left each meeting with several pages of suggestions about activities which I might undertake, and usually arrived at the next meeting very aware that I had only been able to put into practice a small proportion of what had been suggested at the previous meeting. This, of course, did not prevent the Steering Committee from generating several more pages of suggestions. In addition, the Chair of the Steering Committee (John Gray) did a considerable amount of work between meetings on behalf of the programme, and provided a valued source of support when the programme encountered difficulties.

The third group within ESRC with whom I had dealings was the ESRC Research Programmes Board. This Board was set up in 1992 to provide coordination and coherence across all existing ESRC programmes, and to set up and develop new research programmes. Its membership was wide-ranging, drawing from both the academic and non-academic communities. Compared with the programme's own Steering Committee, the Research Programmes Board was a more distant and less visible group, and it was sometimes hard to know what the Board's concerns and priorities were. Indeed, virtually my only contact with the Board was to prepare an annual report, on which I received a small amount of written feedback some months later.

The final group of individuals with whom I had contact under the overall ESRC umbrella were the directors and coordinators of other ESRC programmes. These programme directors met two or three times a year to discuss common problems and provide mutual support. I found this group extremely useful, particularly in the early stages, when I was new to the job and trying to discover what it was all about. Indeed, these discussions with other programme directors constituted one of the main forms of training and support for the job.

As I indicated earlier, the ESRC underwent a major shift in its priorities during the course of the programme, as a direct result of the 1993 White Paper 'Realising our Potential'. This shift in priorities was relayed through all the groups described above, and I was left in no doubt that ESRC wanted the programme not only to generate research of high academic quality, but also to communicate its findings to non-academic users and beneficiaries. At the same time, it is important to stress that at no time did ESRC officers or members of ESRC boards attempt to interfere with the academic content of the programme, or to suggest that some findings were politically more acceptable than others — and this despite the fact that our work was impinging on highly political aspects of educational policy. As a programme coordinator, I greatly appreciated the respect which ESRC showed for the academic integrity of the research which it was funding.

Creating Coherence within the Programme

One of the main tasks of a programme coordinator is to generate as much internal coherence as possible within the programme. That is, the coordinator has to ensure that the programme is more than an unrelated collection of projects, and that there are some genuine common purposes and synergies within the programme.

I realized from the start that creating coherence within the 'Innovation and Change' programme would not be an easy task. It was clear that the commissioning panel had chosen to fund projects which spanned a wide range of theoretical approaches, methodologies, research questions, age phases and curricula contexts. In my view, they were quite justified in doing this: they were, after all, trying to bring different perspectives to bear on some central issues in teaching and learning. At the same time, it meant that I was left with the task of generating coherence within what was — on the surface at least — a rather disparate group of projects.

My first approach to this problem was essentially a 'top–down' one. I started from the 'five over-arching questions' which had formed part of the initial programme proposal to ESRC (see p. 94). I then used the project teams' own original proposals, together with what I knew about each project, to draw up a two-dimensional matrix. This matrix indicated which of the five questions I felt each project would contribute to answering, and suggested that projects might 'cluster' around their positions on the matrix.

I presented this matrix in a paper at an early meeting of all the project teams. The ensuing discussion revealed that the projects did not find this approach helpful. In part, their response seemed to reflect a strong rejection of the idea of being 'managed' from the outside (see p. 99). However, it also indicated that the projects did not identify strongly with the five over-arching questions, or feel that they recognized themselves as an item on a two-dimensional matrix. As one project director put it at the time:

> Well, I know what the five questions are, of course, but I don't exactly have them pinned over my desk, or look at them every night before I go to bed.

I therefore decided on an alternative approach. With the agreement of the Steering Committee, the five over-arching questions were put to one side, and a more flexible and mutually acceptable statement of the aims and objectives of the programme was generated. I also asked projects to identify which other projects in the programme they had some affinity with, and suggest areas of common interest. I then used these statements to identify some common themes across different groupings of projects, and I set up a series of internal meetings and seminars around these themes. Some of these meetings were also attended by other ESRC projects, which had not been funded through the programme, but whose work was felt to be relevant to that particular theme. These internal seminars fostered discussion on a range of issues, including methodological problems, theoretical frameworks, shared findings and dissemination strategies. In several cases, the themes were developed further through symposia at national and international conferences. Publications were also generated which encapsulated work within particular themes. The five main themes were as follows:

- Progression in learning;
- Coherence in the curriculum;
- The nature of effective teaching and learning;
- Understanding innovation and change;
- Differentiation and equal opportunities.

While these themes did not by any means encompass the totality of work done within the programme, they served their purpose of creating common ground between different projects. They also provided a focus for involving other researchers from outside the programme, and a framework for joint dissemination. In addition, they demonstrated that, for this programme at least, it was more fruitful to create coherence by starting with the projects' own interests and working outwards, then by starting with a set of questions with which the projects found it hard to identify. At the same time, the five themes which were generated in this way did in fact show a considerable overlap with the initial 'five over-arching questions', and suggest that the work of the programme did indeed proceed broadly along the tracks which had been laid down at the start.

Dissemination

The other main aspect of my role as coordinator was to organize and facilitate the dissemination of programme findings to as wide an audience as possible. While it was clear at the start of the programme that this would be a priority, it became even more important after the 1993 White Paper and its impact on ESRC priorities.

In many ways, this increasing emphasis on dissemination to non-academic audiences fitted in well with what we were already doing. Like many educational researchers, the project directors were used to communicating their findings to a range of non-academic audiences. Most project directors, for example, talked regularly about their research to teachers on INSET courses, or addressed meetings of national teachers' organizations, or wrote articles in the *Times Educational Supplement* or *Education*. We therefore needed to augment this substantial project-centred dissemination activity with some centrally organized activities which would promote the programme as a whole. Essentially our strategy had three main elements:

1 **Identification of target audiences:** the main ones were academics, educational policy-makers, practitioners, the public, business and industry, and international educationalists.
2 **Development of dissemination products:** the main ones were an edited book with contributions from each of the ten projects (Hughes, 1996); an ESRC Research Briefing which described the findings of six projects in clear language; a Findings Pack which contained an information sheet on each of the 10 projects; the development of pages on the World Wide Web; and the production of various leaflets and information sheets.
3 **Delivery of products to targets:** we used a variety of different methods to communicate our findings to these different audiences. Thus we communicated to academics by convening symposia at national and international conferences, writing articles for special issues of the journal *Research Papers in Education* and for the newsletter of the British Educational Research Association (BERA), and mailing the Findings Pack directly to all BERA members. We communicated to policy-makers and politicians by direct mailing of the Research Briefing to MPs, Chief Education Officers, and a range of organizations concerned with education; by running seminars for organizations such as the

School Curriculum and Assessment Authority (SCAA); and by personal briefings to selected individuals. We attempted to reach teachers by writing articles in practitioner journals such as the *Times Educational Supplement, Child Education* and *Education 3–13*; by sending the Research Briefing to over 2,500 secondary schools and 500 Teachers Centres; and by sending leaflets about the programme to over 25,000 primary schools. We also attempted to reach international audiences by presenting symposia at international conferences such as the American Educational Research Association (AERA) and the European Association for Research on Learning and Instruction (EARLI), by writing articles in the newsletter of the European Educational Research Association (EERA), and by mailing the Findings Pack to all EARLI members.

In short, we did all we could to bring the main findings of the programme to the attention of as wide an audience as possible. What is harder to gauge, however, is the impact our efforts had on those whom we were hoping to reach. We had certainly had a number of identifiable successes. For example, we know that findings from the King's and Durham/York projects had a clear effect on the Dearing revision of the National Curriculum for maths and science in 1993–94, and that work from the Oxford and Cambridge projects was taken up by a large number of schools and LEAs who wanted to incorporate pupils' perspectives in the school improvement process. For the most part, however, it seems likely that our work was only one of many influences acting on policy and practice during an extremely turbulent period in education.

Experiences with the Media

The relationship between academic researchers and the media is not an easy one. Many academics have reported the frustrating experience of seeing their research seriously misrepresented in the media, and it is not surprising that many researchers have become extremely wary of having anything to do with the press, radio and TV (see Mortimore, 1991, for further discussion of these issues in the context of educational research). Being part of a high-profile programme, however, meant that such reticence was not an option for us: we had to engage with the media.

Overall, our experiences with the media were decidedly mixed. On the one hand, we had a good deal of positive coverage. For example, we presented a symposium at the 1994 meeting of the British Association for the Advancement of Science, and accompanied this with a number of press releases and a press conference. This resulted in considerable media attention, most of which was fair and reasonably accurate. We also obtained some good coverage through a collaboration with an educational journalist, Maureen O'Connor, who wrote positive and informative articles about the programme in the *Independent* and the *TES*. The *Independent* article in particular generated widespread interest in the programme, and led to a large number of requests for further details about the research.

On the other hand, we had the extremely unpleasant experience of being publicly criticised in an article by the education correspondent of the *Daily Telegraph*. The main theme of the article, entitled 'Teach us what we don't know', was that the findings generated by the programme were already 'widely known' or 'blindingly obvious', and hence that the programme was a waste of public money. In order to make his point, the writer systematically distorted and parodied our work. For example, the Strathclyde project had generated novel and important findings about children's understandings of literacy and numeracy before they started school: these findings were dismissed as merely showing that 'pre-school children can learn quite a lot in a year about reading and counting if they are taught properly'. I naturally felt angry and upset by this unprovoked attack on our research. In addition, senior staff at ESRC were annoyed at this criticism of one of their programmes, and felt there should be a quick response on my part. However, the editor of the *Daily Telegraph* did not respond to my request for an opportunity to reply, and did not publish a letter I wrote in response to the article.

In the summer of 1996, and partly as a response to the *Daily Telegraph* article, we hired a media consultant to obtain some more positive press coverage for us. This media consultant drafted some press releases which focused on the work of two or three projects which had previously received less attention than the others. One of the press releases focused on the issue of 'grammar', and reported some interesting findings from the Southampton project on this issue. The findings attracted considerable media attention, and formed the main education story in the media for two or three days. In particular, they were commented on favourably by Gillian Shepard, then Secretary of State for Education, who used them to support a policy decision to increase the emphasis on grammar in the national SATs for 14-year-olds. The findings also sparked a lively public debate on the role of grammar in the curriculum (including, ironically enough, a series of articles in the *Daily Telegraph*) in the course of which they were quoted approvingly by both the (Conservative) Secretary of State for Education and the (Labour) Shadow Secretary. However, the project team whose work was being quoted felt unhappy about the way their research had been handled, both by the media and by the media consultant, and expressed their concern in public. In particular, they felt that their relationships with local teachers — and with national organizations such as SCAA — had been damaged, and that the Secretary of State misused their research to justify a decision she had been intending to make anyway.

Taken together, these experiences revealed both the benefits and the pitfalls of working with the media. They demonstrated that the media can be an extremely powerful and effective method of communicating research findings to a very large audience. At the same time, they showed that a media story can very quickly get out of control, and that research findings can be used by those who are more experienced with the media — such as journalists and politicians

— for purposes other than those intended by the researchers. At such times, researchers can suddenly find that they have very little control over the way in which their research is being handled in the media.

Conclusions

Coordinating the ESRC programme on 'Innovation and Change in Education' was a novel and challenging experience. It made me acquire new skills in diverse areas such as networking, writing about other academics' research and dealing with the media. I had to become more knowledgeable about ongoing policy issues, about innovative research methodologies and about unfamiliar fields of enquiry. I had to learn when I could reasonably make demands on people and when they were best left alone. I also had to give far more time and energy to the programme than I ever expected to, or was being officially reimbursed for. It was not a task to be undertaken lightly, but at the end of the day it was one I was glad to have undertaken.

My experiences of coordinating the 'Innovation and Change' programme raised a number of issues about research programmes in general, which those who are involved in funding, coordinating or participating in such programmes might wish to consider. They include the following:

1 **The nature of a programme.** There are several different ways in which research programmes can be conceptualized. According to one model, the research agenda is clearly and definitively laid down in advance by the funding agency, and this agenda is then implemented unproblematically — even mechanistically — by the project teams. While there may be some programmes which follow this model, it was not the case in the 'Innovation and Change' programme. As I have tried to demonstrate in this chapter, the programme was a much more dynamic and creative enterprise. While the initial research agenda was undoubtedly important, the programme itself had to be responsive to a wide range of events and influences, many of which could not have been foreseen at the time it was conceived: these included the particular interests and personalities of the project directors, the actual findings which emerged, the rapidly changing educational policy context, and, not least, the shift in ESRC's own priorities midway through the programme. It seems likely that this more flexible, responsive model is in fact a better description of the way most programmes operate in practice, and it might be helpful for those embarking on such an enterprise if this was recognized from the start.

2 **The management of projects.** A second issue, which is no doubt related to the first, is the way in which a programme coordinator or director attempts to 'manage' the projects within their programme. In the case of the 'Innovation and Change' programme, I had no alternative but to adopt a fairly light 'hands off' style: I was dealing with very

experienced and competent researchers, several of whom made it clear at the start of the programme that they would resist having their projects managed from outside. My approach to working with projects was therefore a collaborative one, based as far as possible on openness, inclusion in decision-making and negotiation. While such an approach was appropriate for the 'Innovation and Change' programme, it might not be appropriate for all programmes: for example, I did not have to face the problem, experienced by other programme directors, of having to intervene in a project which was clearly failing in achieving its objectives. Whatever management style is adopted, it needs to be made explicit right at the start of a programme as to what is expected of all those involved.

3 **Communication with users.** There is a clear expectation on all programmes funded by ESRC that they should identify the potential users of their research and devise appropriate methods for communicating research findings to those users. This is an important part of the work of a programme coordinator or director; however, my experience on the 'Innovation and Change' programme suggests that it is by no means straightforward. Users, whether they be practitioners, policy-makers or even members of the public, have their own priorities and agendas, and research findings will inevitably be interpreted in the light of those agendas. Policy-makers, for example, are unlikely to make a policy decision purely on the basis of a single piece of research: however, they may well use (or misuse) the research to justify a decision for which there are other pressures or arguments. The implication is not that researchers should therefore refuse to engage with users, but rather that such engagement is more likely to be satisfactory if it takes place in a context where the intentions and assumptions of both users and researchers can be explored more fully — for example, through personal briefings or small invitational seminars.

4 **The notion of 'added value'.** The final issue is perhaps the most fundamental, and concerns the extent to which a research programme can indeed amount to 'more than the sum of its parts'. My experience as coordinator suggests that a programme can do this in several ways. First, it can provide a **focus** on an issue, or set of issues, which are timely and important from a scientific, policy or practical point of view. Secondly, it can provide greater **visibility** for those issues, and for the research being done on them, through enhanced levels of dissemination and other activities. Thirdly, it can provide **synergy** for those carrying out the research, by bringing together project teams in seminars and workshops, and generating new ideas and developments. Finally, it can turn research into a more **open and collaborative process**, where the centre of activity is located less within individual and isolated projects, and more within an interacting network of researchers and users.

Whether or not the 'Innovation and Change' programme succeeded on these counts is, of course, up to others to say. My own view is that the programme was indeed successful — the projects carried out high quality research on a range of timely and important issues; there was a good deal of creative interaction between project teams; the findings were disseminated widely; and there were some clear influences on policy and practice. I cannot be certain that the whole came to 'more than the sum of its parts', but I know that the attempt to make it so was thoroughly worthwhile.

Acknowledgments

I am very grateful to Chris Brumfit, John Gray, Peter Linthwaite and Geoffrey Walford for their helpful comments on an earlier draft of this chapter.

References

HUGHES, M. (1994) (ed.) *Perceptions of Teaching and Learning*, Clevedon: Multilingual Matters.

HUGHES, M. (1995) (ed.) *Progression in Learning*, Clevedon: Multilingual Matters.

HUGHES, M. (1996) (ed.) *Teaching and Learning in Changing Times*, Oxford: Blackwell.

KUSHNER, S. (1991) *ESRC Initiatives and Their Coordinators: Organising for Innovation in the Social Sciences*, University of East Anglia: Centre for Applied Research in Education.

MARTIN, R. (1995) 'Plus ca change . . . ? The Social Change and Economic Life Initiative', *Work, Employment and Society*, **9**, 1, pp. 165–81.

MORTIMORE, P. (1991) 'The front page or yesterday's news: The reception of educational research', in WALFORD, G. (ed.) *Doing Educational Research*, London: Routledge.

Appendix 1: Full List of Projects in the ESRC Research Programme on 'Innovation and Change in Education'

Project Title: Knowledge about Language, Language Learning and the National Curriculum

Investigators: Christopher Brumfit, Rosamond Mitchell, Janet Hooper

Institution: School of Education, University of Southampton

Project Title: Assessing Quality in Cross Curricular Contexts

Investigators: Geoff Whitty, Peter Aggleton, Gabrielle Rowe

Institution: Institute of Education, University of London

Project Title: Investigation of the Notion of Progression in Learning Mathematics and Science

Investigators: Paul Black, Margaret Brown, Shirley Simon, Ezra Blondel

Institution: King's College, University of London

Project Title: The Interaction of Children's Conceptual and Procedural Knowledge in Science

Investigators: Richard Gott, Sandra Duggan, Robin Millar, Fred Lubben

Institutions: University of Durham, University of York

Project Title: The Interactive Context of Teaching and Learning at the Pre-school Level.

Investigators: Rudolph Schaffer and Penny Munn

Institution: Department of Psychology, University of Strathclyde

Project Title: Parents and Assessment at Key Stage 1

Investigators: Charles Desforges, Martin Hughes, Cathie Holden

Institution: School of Education, University of Exeter

Project Title: Changes in the Classroom Experiences of Inner London Infant Pupils, 1984–93

Investigators: Ian Plewis and Marijcke Veltman

Institution: Thomas Coram Research Unit, Institute of Education, University of London

Project Title: Effective Teaching and Learning at Key Stage 3

Investigators: Donald McIntyre and Paul Cooper

Institution: Department of Educational Studies, University of Oxford

Project Title: Making Your Way Through Secondary School: Pupils' Experiences of Teaching and Learning

Investigators: Jean Rudduck, Julia Flutter, Gwen Wallace, Susan Harris

Institutions: Homerton College, Cambridge, University of Derby, University of Sheffield

Project Title: Concepts of History and Teaching Approaches at Key Stages 2 and 3

Investigators: Peter Lee, Alaric Dickinson, Rosalyn Ashby

Institution: Institute of Education, University of London

8 Climbing an Educational Mountain: Conducting the International School Effectiveness Research Project (ISERP)

David Reynolds, Bert Creemers, Sam Stringfield, Charles Teddlie and the ISERP Team[1]

Introduction

The last 20 years have seen an explosion of research in the field of school effectiveness. From a position of considerable marginality within the educational research communities of most societies, what has been called the school effectiveness 'movement' is now increasingly recognized as an educational subdiscipline, with its own professional association (The International Congress for School Effectiveness and Improvement), its own journal and own annual meeting. Also, the findings of the discipline have achieved very ready acceptance and take up within the political system of the UK, and also more generally within schools themselves, where the notion of being given 'good practice' on which to build has been enthusiastically supported (see Reynolds, 1996, for a survey of these developments, and Reynolds, Creemers, Hopkins, Stoll and Bollen, 1996, for an overview of the field currently).

It would be wrong to portray the school effectiveness discipline as being universally uncritically accepted, however. There have been arguments from many within the sociology of education (Angus, 1993) that school effectiveness research takes too much 'for granted' in its definitions of effectiveness, which are usually argued to be the same as those of governments and more conservative educational philosophers. There have also been arguments (Hamilton, 1996) that it is concerned with simplistic, often managerially based, policies to improve the inevitably highly complex world of schools and classrooms. There have also been arguments (Elliott, 1996) that it has neglected to concern itself with the long-term developmental needs of teachers, and that indeed it neglects to add the 'voice' of the teacher to its many sources of ideas, preferring instead to give primacy and in some cases exclusivity to the voice of the school effectiveness researcher in understanding schools and classrooms.

[1] Asbjorn Birkemo, Shin-Jen Chang, Yin Cheong Cheng, John Clarke, Barbara Dundas, Juanita Epp, Walter Epp, Barry Green, Marit Groterud, Vivian Hajnal, Trond Eiliv Hauge, Jen-jye Hwang, Peggy Kirby, Astrid Eggen Knutsen, Yong-yin Lee, Bjorn Nilsen, Hui-Ling Pan, Desmond Swan, Frans Swint.

Criticism of school effectiveness research has not been confined to the UK. In the US, indeed, school effectiveness research reached a position of centrality in educational discourse in the early 1980s, based upon the research of Brookover, Beady, Flood, Schweitzer and Wisenbaker (1979) and the insights and advocacy of Edmonds (1979). Yet in the US there was a considerable volume of criticism (see summary in Teddlie and Stringfield, 1993), mostly concerning the overly simplistic beliefs reflected in school effectiveness research, which held that the links between certain educational features of schools and certain outcomes were causal, and that school effectiveness research could be used as some cure all 'potion' or 'snake oil' to improve schools simply by dropping it into schools through inservice days.

There is no doubt that, by the early 1990s, many of us in the discipline saw these criticisms as partially justified, and also recognized the quite simplistic nature of much of the research base, and the quite simplistic nature of the educational remedies associated with it (Reynolds and Packer, 1992). It was also the case then, and still is the case now, that the number of reviews of the research base exceeded the number of empirical studies by a factor of perhaps 10 to one, and that more empirical research was urgently needed to develop the field. The fact that the school effectiveness research paradigm was by the early 1990s gaining considerable influence upon governments and practitioners was itself another reason for some of us wanting a new 'second wave' of research to be undertaken that might justify some of this attention. For a group of us, the second wave research was planned to be the International School Effectiveness Research Project (ISERP).

The Disciplinary Context

Three sets of factors also had an influence upon those of us in the discipline who chose to go the 'international route' in school effectiveness. Firstly, the early 1990s saw for the first time research findings that suggested that the effective schools 'correlates' or 'factors' may be somewhat different in different geographical contexts, with the Dutch educational research community particularly being unable to replicate more than a handful of the 'classic' school or classroom factors from the American 'five factor' theories of educational effectiveness (see Bosker and Scheerens, 1997, for a summary). Particularly interesting and potentially important was the failure of some Dutch empirical research to show the importance of the principal/headteacher in creating effective schools (van de Grift, 1990), in marked contrast to the importance of this role and of the role occupants shown from American research (Levine and Lezotte, 1990).

The apparent 'context specificity' of school effectiveness factors and the existence of this phenomenon even *within* countries was shown in the American Louisiana School Effectiveness Study (LSES) where findings of *different* effectiveness factors were associated with effectiveness in different socio-economic contexts (Teddlie and Stringfield, 1993). This suggested an interesting future direction for research which would involve varying social context systematically both within and between countries to see which factors universally 'travelled' and which factors did not, but required particular cultural and social contexts to be potentiated in their effects.

Celebrating contextual difference would, some of us thought, present a more complex picture of effectiveness findings than the early simplistic 'snake oil' that was the subject of the robust criticisms from around the world noted earlier. It would also increase the chances of our being able to generate theory, since the variation in 'what worked' if it could be explained and modelled would force the field towards the development of more complex and multi-faceted accounts than the 'one size fits all' mentality that had hitherto existed in the field. Useful contributions were already being made in the area of theory (Creemers and Scheerens, 1989; Creemers, 1992) — we wanted to take them further.

The final set of considerations and motivations that prompted our attempted climbing of what was to become a school effectiveness mountain concerned our awareness of the frankly lamentable state of the existing research that had emerged from international school effectiveness research hitherto. Reviews of this can be found elsewhere (Reynolds, Creemers, Stringfield, Teddlies, Schaffer and Nesselrodt, 1994; Reynolds and Farrell, 1996; Creemers and Reynolds, 1996) but, briefly, existing research exhibited numerous defects:

- a concentration upon a very restricted range of outcomes, usually academic achievement which was measured only by tests of basic skills;
- a focus upon a very restricted range of factors measured at school and classroom levels, usually of a simple 'resource based' variety that was easier to measure than the potentially more important variables such as climate etc.;
- an almost complete absence of practitioner-friendly, fine-grained pictures of school and classroom life that might have explained how educational processes in the differential cultural contexts might have had their effects;
- a total inability to spell out in any detail the nature of the cultural contexts within which schools were situated in different countries, contexts which would have had considerable implications for the nature of schooling that was 'effective';
- a highly variable quality of the research enterprise as implemented in the different countries contributing samples to these international studies, because central control over the large number of participating countries was not strong enough to reduce variation in response rates, data collection procedures and the general quality of the research procedures.

Setting Up the International School Effectiveness Project (ISERP)

This, then, was the intellectual background which formed the foundations for the design of the International School Effectiveness Research Project (ISERP). The initial suggestion of doing some internationally based research had come from the American effectiveness researchers Sam Stringfield and Charles Teddlie, who had directed the Louisiana School Effectiveness Project noted above. David Reynolds and Bert Creemers were approached to represent the European traditions in the field, a natural request since all four of us had collaborated together and helped to organize the founding of the International Congress for School Effectiveness and Improvement, the professional organization of the discipline.

Early discussions, snatched at the American Educational Research Association in Boston in 1991, were followed by a planning meeting in The Hague, in late 1991, at which it rapidly became clear what both the intellectual and the practical problems of international school effectiveness research were to be. Indeed, after participating in the series of planning meetings that were to follow, it became starkly obvious why comparative education as a discipline, and international school effectiveness as a subdiscipline, had made so little intellectual progress in the last 30 years!

The problems were twofold. Firstly, simply understanding the nature of other countries' educational systems was itself a major intellectual task. The variation in starting ages for junior school (6 in the US, 5 in the UK) was a simple, descriptive factor that was at the beginning unknown to us. The large variation in per capita expenditure characteristic of the US educational system, because of its reliance on property or sales taxes for over 90 per cent of total expenditure, again was unknown to non-Americans. The difference in national educational histories, cultures, assessment systems (public examination or continuous assessment based) was also substantial for the three countries (US, UK, The Netherlands) involved in the study at that stage.

Secondly, the intellectual variation between the four co-founders of ISERP was also marked a rather surprising factor given the apparently small amount of intellectual territory covered by school effectiveness. Two of the four were intellectually more centred upon teacher effectiveness than school effectiveness (Creemers and Stringfield), one of the four knew both areas (Teddlie) and one of the four (Reynolds) was primarily a school-level researcher who had very rarely entered into observation or work in classrooms. Superimposed upon the basic intellectual variation within the team was a further variation in the national traditions of school effectiveness research, with the UK representative for example being committed to the use of multiple outcomes in social/affective as well as academic areas, whilst the representative of The Netherlands school effectiveness community regarded social outcomes of any kind with profound scepticism.

To ensure that all persons in the core team understood the knowledge bases that were only partially understood by individual members of the ISERP team, a large-scale literature review of the world's school effectiveness knowledge was undertaken, with sections focusing on the literature from the (eventually) nine participating countries, the lessons of existing studies in the field and the observation systems of classroom settings and teacher behaviours that were already in existence. This was eventually published for wider circulation (Reynolds et al., 1994) and did have a very positive effect in ensuring a degree of mutual understanding between members of the core team.

It took at least a year from 1991 for all persons in the core team to understand where the others were 'coming from' intellectually, but before there were these 'taken for granteds' the decision had been taken to expand the number of countries involved in order to expand the variation in context, school factors and, we believed, in outcomes. The three initial countries of the United States, the United Kingdom and The Netherlands were joined, then, by a further six countries between 1991 and 1993, with researchers either being approached by or approaching the project in different ways. Norway came in after the Ministry of Education approached the core team, wanting to educate their new and up and coming researchers in the techniques of international comparisons. Australia came in through pre-existing contacts between the core team and educational researchers. Canada came in after some Canadian researchers attended a presentation made by the core team. Taiwan came in after contacts were generated by a visit by three of the core team to give a series of public lectures in Universities and Training Colleges in that country. Hong Kong came in through pre-existing contracts. Finally, Ireland came in because of a desire to participate on behalf of their Ministry of Education, who contacted researchers in the country who were known to them, inviting them to take part.

The sheer speed of expansion in the number of countries, with new countries appearing at virtually every new planning meeting, combined with the time it took for the core team to understand each other, let alone understand the task of constructing an international project, led to inevitable problems. Countries coming in needed to have the design of the project explained, which took time from the more important task of instrument design and the proper consideration of research strategy. Further intellectual variation was superimposed on that already existing with the arrival of persons from the fields of school improvement, educational evaluation and instructional effectiveness, to name but a few of the myriad specialities that team members ultimately exhibited. The final source of variation was seen in the research experience of the new team members, which ranged from those who had directed major projects in the field of school effectiveness to those who had conducted more small-scale school improvement or 'action research' projects undertaken by small groups of teachers.

It is important to note at this stage that the ISERP project was viewed as part of a programme of studies that in the long term would encompass literature reviews of existing projects as well as the comparative study of educational systems and schools. The ISERP project reported here was in fact a pilot for a larger, more informed project which would be built, as is all the best research, on the designs of previous models that have crashed. As time went on, as this chapter shows clearly, the value of regarding the present study as a forerunner of a larger study became more and more obvious.

Designing the ISERP

The quality of research design inevitably suffered from these time pressures (data collection was scheduled to start in Autumn 1992) and from the pressures upon time caused by the need to bring new entrants 'up to speed'. The intensely political needs to ensure that everyone felt a degree of ownership of the project also contributed to an ever-lengthening list of core areas in which research was to take place. Unlike studies from the IEA or the IAEP, studies organized by ETS in the United States, where participating research teams bought into a pre-existing core research plan (see for example Lapointe, Mead and Phillips, 1989, and Robitaille and Garden, 1989) for which national governments gave agreed financial resources, the fact that country research teams had to raise all their own financial resources to undertake the research necessitated them being given something of a voice in the research design, which in the view of the core team would generate a commitment not being bought with money.

Needless to say, the interaction of very large numbers of persons, from a very large number of intellectual backgrounds, with a very wide range of research experience, being given partial design rights over the nature of the research did not necessarily lead to a high-quality research design. Most of the key conceptual decisions were soundly based, partly because they virtually took themselves, given the state of the discipline in 1992 (Reynolds and Cuttance, 1992). These included:

- the decision to focus on young children (because there was no chance of school effects masquerading as intake effects, as might happen with older children);
- the decision to look at contextual variation within countries (axiomatic given the direction of school effectiveness research) as well as between countries;
- the decision to use mathematics as the basic outcome variable (inevitable given the impossibility of designing tests in other areas);
- the decision to gather data from classroom, school and district levels (inevitable given the findings about the importance of the learning at classroom level emerging within school effectiveness, see Creemers, 1994);
- the decision to take a variety of affective and social outcome measures as measures of effectiveness (important since the possibly different levels of performance by the schools and the countries would necessitate the generation of more fine-grained and middle-range theoretical analyses);

- the decision to sample only 'outlier' and 'average' schools (inevitable since we didn't have the resources to generate large sample sizes and then simply select the effective, ineffective and average schools from the larger group, but had to maximize our contrasts initially).

The pressure to generate instrumentation in the areas of school processes, teacher experiential and biographical variables, teacher behaviours, principal or headteacher factors, and pupils' year by year transitions, as well as to find outcome measures in the areas of mathematics, reading, social attitudes of pupils, the social attitudes to teachers of pupils and the attitudes to self of pupils (self-esteem), all meant that there was a tendency to use pre-existing instruments in cases where team members had used them before. Thus, the key outcome measures of mathematics and also reading (for the restricted number of countries that used it as a measure) were the Comprehensive Test of Basic Skills (CTBS) tests from the United States and the measure of class-room behaviour was taken directly from the Special Strategies Observation System (SSOS), itself devised to measure the impact of various American school improvement programmes (Schaffer, 1994). The measures of teachers' 'locus of control' and 'perception of personal power' were also taken from past work in Hong Kong.

Inevitably, there were problems with these procedures. As instruments were translated from their original language to another, there were difficulties when the meaning of words changed too. The mathematics tests measured children's performance in what can be loosely termed 'basic skills', but did not necessarily pick up performance in the 'investigative' areas of maths that have become a feature of the American and British primary school experience. Concepts in the measurement scales for pupils' social attitudes were clearly much closer to the educational discourse of some countries than of others, as in the case of the 'democratic social attitudes' that were measured in all countries because of the justifiable insistence of the Norwegian team, who rightly pointed to the key importance of this area of pupil outcomes in their own country.

There were also further problems caused by the selection of the samples of schools in different countries. The need to find samples of 'outlier' and 'average' schools to maximize the variance without using large samples of schools initially (forced on the project because of cost considerations) necessitated access to data with which to choose these schools. Unfortunately, only certain countries had such datasets already in existence. The United Kingdom team had access to a large dataset from Gloucestershire local education authority, which included information on the free school meal rates of whole school populations (used as a surrogate for the intake quality of schools) and on the outcomes of the schools in the Key Stage 2 tests at age 11 outcomes. It was easy to simply choose a range of schools, and then ensure that the range of different social conditions was also covered. The United States team likewise was able to use schools that had already participated in the Louisiana School Effectiveness Study, chosen from pre-existing high-quality empirical data.

However, some countries only had access to more impressionistic forms of data, lacking totally the means of access to empirical datasets. Choice of schools in those countries was based upon the nominations of 'key informants', who were usually inspectors in the local education services or in some cases government inspectors from the national education services. Whilst in the long term it was intended that schools' effectiveness classifications reflected their gain scores and performance over time rather than their initially assigned performance, there was a concern about the possible biases to the study introduced by some countries using clear value-added methods of school choice whilst other countries were probably inevitably using informants who might have found utilizing value-added formulations rather difficult.

The last concern that was generated by the contingencies of group membership, the pace of the enterprise and the inevitable difficulties of conducting work spread across multiple continents, was that there was insufficient time to train observers in the standardized use of techniques of classroom observation. This observation of teachers' behaviours in their classes and the related observation of pupils' levels of time on task was a key part of the ISERP design, since the intention was to see whether the same teaching behaviours were associated with effectiveness within the different cultural contexts of various countries and whether the behaviours that were effective were the same across countries. The problem was that the observation instrument was partially one of *high* inference measures, and partially one of *low* inference. The measurement of pupils' time on task was an extremely low inference measure in which observers simply looked around a class every 8 minutes or so and judged what proportion of the class were 'on task', defined as working, listening or in other ways concentrating upon their class task. However, the measurement of such aspects of the classroom as the teacher's behaviour proved more difficult, since it required the gradation of teachers in terms of aspects such as their 'classroom control' techniques, their 'exhibiting of personal enthusiasm', or their 'skill in utilization of questioning', all areas in which their behaviour had to be judged by 'high inference'. In Taiwan, for example, it is clear that the concepts of 'positive academic feedback' and 'negative academic feedback' caused particular problems given Taiwanese definitions of 'positive' and 'negative'. The scale item had been chosen with an Anglo Saxon or European conception in mind, in which positive feedback would be a statement by the teacher such as 'well done — keep it up!' and negative feedback would be evidenced by a teacher saying something such as 'that's poor work — you need to improve'. In Taiwan, and to an extent in Hong Kong, such judgments proved more difficult since it would have been possible within the culture to see extreme negativity from a teacher as being 'positive', and likewise an attempt to shield the child from criticism by saying something pleasant about their work as 'negative academic feedback' in the culture, given the need for all children to achieve high achievement levels in the Pacific Rim. To give an example, in one Taiwanese classroom during the filming of a *Panorama* programme related to the publication of a review of literature on England's performance in international achievement surveys (Reynolds and Farrell, 1996), a child stood up to answer a question from their teacher, broadly smiling and full of self-belief that they were about to give the right answer. On clearly being given the *wrong* answer, the teacher let fly a torrent of abuse at the child, clearly what one would have wanted to call 'negative academic feedback'. This was not perceived as such by the child, who continued to exhibit enthusiasm and a still smiling face as he sat down, or the teacher (who on questioning said that her reaction was a positive one), or by an accompanying Taiwanese educational researcher (who also saw the teacher's reaction as 'positive').

Data Collection and Analysis

The problems that had marred the designing of ISERP were much less in evidence in the data collection, where the project structure that had finally been adopted was followed virtually comprehensively by all countries' teams. What happened was that the experience of actually getting out into 'the field' and observing real classroom situations nested within real schools, acted to divert emotional and personal energy away from any investment in micropolitical battles concerning research design, towards an understanding of what was going on in classrooms. Simply, people focused on their sample and their data collection.

Positive rewards started coming through also, which acted to motivate those who had expended large quantities of effort in the selection of schools and trialling of instruments. Conference papers were delivered at national educational research associations (the 1994 and 1995 British Educational Research Associations and American Educational Research Associations) and at international conferences, that began to give tangible rewards (publications) and, more intangibly, esteem to the project. Early analyses (Reynolds and Teddlie, 1996) were widely reported in the British educational press in 1996, and data from the study suggesting the unreliability of, or wide variation between, British schools formed one of the key explanations for British system underperformance that was attached to the review of literature entitled *Worlds Apart?* (that also features as the backcloth to the *Panorama* programme mentioned above, see Reynolds and Farrell, 1996). The Norwegian team also concentrated upon publication of their early literature reviews, their project organization and their preliminary findings in their own country, gaining considerable esteem.

Inevitably, given the huge volume of data being collected from 9 countries, with 6 or 12 schools per country, with 1 to 12 classes per school, and between 20 and 45 pupils per class, the process of analysis has taken some time from the finish of data collection in the Winter of 1995 when Australia finished their school year, which is of course 6 months later in Southern Hemisphere countries. Cleaning the data, checking upon missing data and ensuring that, for example, methods of analysis could handle the tendency for the cohorts of children to lose some existing members whilst all the while gaining new members with incomplete data, all took considerable time. The huge geographical distances between teams in participating countries was particularly difficult at times like this, when personal face to face contact to explain what problems existed with the data that would have saved countless hours of the writing up of the problem for transmission to another country.

The final writing up, appropriately enough by the group of four who formed the initial core team and planned the study originally, is taking place at the time of writing, for publication under the title *World Class Schools: The Findings of the International School Effectiveness Research Project*, in Spring 1998.

Doing Comparative Research: The Lessons Learned

ISERP was a relatively small-scale pilot project, in preparation for the major study beginning in 1999 that is being planned currently. The purpose of a pilot is precisely to ensure that conceptualization, operationalization, measurement and analytic techniques and procedures are appropriate to the nature of the problem being investigated. The purpose of the ISERP pilot was also to see what were the problems involved in putting together a multi-national, multi-site, multi-level project spread around the globe. What are the lessons, of both organization and conceptualization, that have been learnt?

Looking at organizational matters first, it is clear that for projects of this kind to maximize their own outcomes:

- the range of the intellectual backgrounds of individuals in the project needs to be constrained, so that there is greater communality of interests and pre-existing 'taken for granted', which otherwise costs valuable time to create;
- the range of prior research experience likewise needs to be constrained, otherwise the carrying through of the research will progressively differentiate the group as the leading-edge researchers advance intellectually at a considerably faster pace than do the average;
- there should be sufficient time to ensure that instrumentation appropriate for the multiple country contexts is developed, without the need to cannibalize and utilize existing instrumentation that may have been designed for another context and purpose;
- there should be attention given to the problem of the different 'meanings' that apparently similar words convey in different cultural contexts, so that there is enhanced cross-cultural reliability;
- there should be a 'core' research design which is developed prior to the coming together of the project personnel, which would prevent energy and emotion going into design issues (where competencies are not necessarily evenly spread) and channel these instead into implementation, where reliability needs to be high;

- there needs to be enhanced control over the intellectual and practical enterprise generated at the 'centre' of any project, which would
  ideally be enhanced by the presence of permanent personnel in addition to the 'core' team, which itself would of course be enhanced by
  core funding for the 'centre'.

Doing Comparative Research: The Potential Benefits

All the 'lessons learned' that we noted above are precisely the reasons why
piloting of projects that attempt new or innovative research approaches should
be axiomatic within the fields of educational and social research. It is precisely
because of the need to make the as yet 'unknown' a 'known' that collections of
essays like those in this volume and in the prior collection *Doing Educational
Research* (Walford, 1991) are invaluable in preventing any need for the rein-
vention of the research wheel that is occasionally so obvious.

In spite of the numerous problems of methodology, personnel and research
design and implementation that we noted above, of those who planned and
implemented the ISERP pilot there are none that would not do it again, because
the increments in our understandings singly and jointly, have been major.
Indeed, after the ISERP experiment in comparative research one can see quite
clearly why comparative research has such promise. One can also see why
the present near demise of the field is so damaging and costly, both in terms
of broad intellectual matters and more applied, policy-related understandings.
What has ISERP taught us about the importance of a comparative approach?

Firstly, we have simply seen in other societies a variety of educational
practices at classroom and school levels that would not have been seen had
the core research team stayed within their own societies. In the Pacific-rim
societies, for example, the majority of lesson time is filled with what has been
called 'whole class interactive' instruction, in which relatively short lessons of
40 minutes are filled with fast, emotionally intense presentations from teachers,
with accompanying very high levels of involvement from pupils. This model of
teaching, which is also found within a European context in societies such as
Switzerland, is now the subject of considerable debate within United Kingdom
schools. In Norway, as a contrast, there is no formal assessment of children
through the entire phase of their elementary/primary education from the age
of 7, a marked contrast to the United Kingdom practice of formal assessment
and associated publication of results. In the Pacific-rim societies again, one can
see micro-level educational practices such as teachers teaching from a stage at
the front of the class some 6 inches high (to help those at the back of the class
to see), pupils marching to assembly through corridors in which loudspeakers
play music (to ensure a relaxed attitude), and pupils starting the afternoon ses-
sion of school with a 'sleeping' lesson (to deal with the fatigue brought about
by the frantic pace of the school and the heat/humidity of the climate). Put
simply, comparative investigation shows an enhanced range of what appears
to be educationally possible.

The benefits to comparative investigation are more than simply a knowledge of educational factors that might be utilized in programmes of experimentation in one's own country. They are, secondly, that one is made aware of educational philosophies that are radically different from one's own, or those of the government of one's own country. In Norway, for example, there is a strong commitment to the child as an 'active citizen', and to what are called 'democratic values' that have no British or American equivalents. In Pacific-rim societies like Taiwan there is a philosophy that the role of the school is to ensure that all children learn, and that a strong 'technology' of practice should be employed to ensure that children are not dependent on their family background. Such societies are very concerned about the use of practices to improve the achievement of their trailing-edge of pupils, therefore, and are rather less concerned with the education of the 'gifted and talented' than are the societies of the United Kingdom and United States.

There are a third series of benefits to comparative investigation that are even more important than the two above, concerning the possibility that within the right kind of comparative framework one can move beyond looking at the practices of other societies and actually so empathize with other societies that one can look back at one's own society with the benefit of their perspective. Such 'acculturation' is what happened to many of us in the ISERP pilot when we were confronted with, and may have identified with, Pacific-rim educational systems. Looking back at the British system through their 'lens', one wonders at utility of the combination of the very complex technology of practice that is evident in British primary practice, for example, with methods of teacher education that are premised on the importance of teachers 'discovering', or at the least playing an active role in learning about, the appropriate methods to use. To a Taiwanese educationist, this celebrates the desires of teachers for their long-term developmental needs above the needs of children to receive a reliable, consistent, predictable and competently provided experience as they pass through their schools.

The use of another culture's 'lens' to better understand the limitations and strengths of one's own educational practice also applies at the level of educational philosophy as well as educational practice. As an example, those of us involved in the British ISERP team would have historically viewed our primary education practice as loosely 'progressive' and indeed would have thought that in many senses it was the envy of the world. The encouragement of children to learn on their own rather than simply being instructed, the new sets of social outcomes that the system is widely argued to concentrate upon (Alexander, 1996), and the reduced emphasis upon the testing of knowledge acquisition are widely argued to be the hallmarks of progressive practice in the British system. Seen from a Pacific-rim perspective, however, the characteristics of the British system would be seen as regressive, not progressive. Transferring the burden of learning to pupils would be argued as maximizing both social class influences and variation between pupils in Taiwanese culture, since pupils' learning gains would depend on what they brought to the learning situation in terms of achievement levels and backgrounds. Removing the constant of the teacher would be seen as further maximizing individual variation in knowledge gain. Avoiding the testing of basic skills could be seen as maximizing the chances of children who have missed acquiring particular knowledge bases being left without them, through the absence of short-term feedback loops that alert school authorities.

Finally, the last benefit of comparative study and comparative reflection is that it makes possible an appreciation of the complex interaction between the cultures of different countries and their educational systems. In all available educational research upon educational outcomes it is clear that cultural and social factors explain much more of the variation in children's achievement than educational factors (Reynolds and Farrell, 1996). It is impossible to understand the nature of the Pacific Rim's educational experience by only looking at educational factors to explain its high levels of achievement — cultural factors also need study. Indeed, one's understanding of the culture within which different systems are nested is essential if one is to understand issues of context specificity, of the cultural factors that potentiate schools and of the interaction of children with their schools more generally. Through comparative investigation one can indeed advance rapidly in the appreciation of the effects of classrooms, nested in schools which are in turn nested in societies. This is indeed the central core of the educational research enterprise. By gaining variation in contexts and in all that flows from that variation, comparative research like ISERP is indeed engaged with the central task of educational research — the elucidation of what it is to be educated.

References

ALEXANDER, R. (1996) *Versions of Primary Education*, London: Routledge.

ANGUS, L. (1993) 'The sociology of school effectiveness', *British Journal of Sociology of Education*, **4**, 3, pp. 333–45.

BOSKER, R. and SCHEERENS, J. (1997) *The Foundations of School Effectiveness*, Oxford: Pergamon Press.

BROOKOVER, W.B., BEADY, C., FLOOD, P., SCHWEITZER, J. and WISENBAKER, J. (1979) *Schools, Social Systems and Student Achievement: Schools Can Make a Difference*, New York: Praeger.

CREEMERS, B. (1992) 'School effectiveness and effective instruction — the need for a further relationship', in BASHI, J. and SASS, Z. (eds) *School Effectiveness and Improvement*, Jerusalem: Hebrew University Press.

CREEMERS, B. (1994) *The Effective Classroom*, London: Cassell.

CREEMERS, B.P.M. and REYNOLDS, D. (1996) 'Issues and implications of international effectiveness research', *International Journal of Educational Research*, **25**, 3, pp. 257–66.

CREEMERS, B. and SCHEERENS, J. (eds) (1989) 'Developments in school effectiveness research', *International Journal of Educational Research* (special issue), **13**, 7, pp. 685–825.

EDMONDS, R.R. (1979) 'Effective schools for the urban poor', *Educational Leadership*, **36**, 15–18, pp. 20–24.

ELLIOTT, J. (1996) 'School effectiveness research and its critics: Alternative visions of schooling', *Cambridge Journal of Education*, **26**, 2, pp. 199–223.

HAMILTON, D. (1996) 'Peddling feel good factors', *Forum*, **38**, 2, pp. 54–6.

LAPOINTE, A.E., MEAD, N. and PHILLIPS, G. (1989) *A World of Differences: An International Assessment of Mathematics and Science*, New Jersey: Educational Testing Services.

LEVINE, D. and LEZOTTE, L. (1990) *Unusually Effective Schools: A Review and Analysis of Research and Practice*, Madison: NCESRD Publications.

REYNOLDS, D. (1996) 'The effective school: An inaugural lecture', *Evaluation and Research in Education*, **9**, 2, pp. 57–73.

REYNOLDS, D. and CUTTANCE, P. (1992) *School Effectiveness: Research, Policy and Practice*, London: Cassell.

REYNOLDS, D. and FARRELL, S. (1996) *Worlds Apart? — A Review of International Studies of Educational Achievement Involving England*, London: HMSO for OFSTED.

REYNOLDS, D. and PACKER, A. (1992) 'School effectiveness and school improvement in the 1990's', in REYNOLDS, D. and CUTTANCE, P. (eds) *School Effectiveness*, London: Cassell.

REYNOLDS, D. and TEDDLIE, C. (1996) 'World class schools: Some further findings', Paper presented to the Annual Meeting of the American Educational Research Association, New York.

REYNOLDS, D., CREEMERS, B., HOPKINS, D., STOLL, L. and BOLLEN, R. (1996) *Making Good Schools*, London: Routledge.

REYNOLDS, D., CREEMERS, B.P.M., STRINGFIELD, S., TEDDLIE, C., SCHAFFER, E. and NESSELRODT, P. (1994) *Advances in School Effectiveness Research and Practice*, Oxford: Pergamon Press.

ROBITAILLE, D.F. and GARDEN, R.A. (1989) *The IEA Study of Mathematics II: Contexts and Outcomes of School Mathematics*, Oxford: Pergamon Press.

SCHAFFER, E. (1994) 'The contributions of classroom observation to school effectiveness research', in REYNOLDS, D., CREEMERS, B.P.M., NESSELRODT, P., SCHAFFER, E., STRINGFIELD, S. and TEDDLIE, C. (eds) *Advances in School Effectiveness Research and Practice*, Oxford: Pergamon Press.

TEDDLIE, C. and STRINGFIELD, S. (1993) *Schools Make a Difference: Lessons Learned from a Ten Year Study of School Effects*, New York: Teachers College Press.

WALFORD, G. (ed.) (1991) *Doing Educational Research*, London: Routledge and Kegan Paul.

9   The Making of Men: Theorizing Methodology in 'Uncertain Times'

Chris Haywood and Máirtín Mac an Ghaill

Introduction

Sociologists of education have long established how educational research is highly influenced by the social and political context in which it is produced (Waller, 1967; Raab, 1994). As a result, the research design, the resources made available and the conclusions reached are circumscribed by such a context. This chapter focuses upon a closely connected issue. It concerns the impact of new theories that educational researchers are beginning to draw upon to explain social processes of schooling. The paper explores the methodological implications of these new approaches, in examining the production of sex/gender identities within school contexts. We place ourselves within the conditions of rapid social and cultural change in the mid-1990s, arguing that it is useful when carrying out research, to hold onto a range of earlier and recently developed theoretical frameworks.

The Making of Men (Mac an Ghaill, 1994) consisted of a research project that was carried out over a period of five years in a mixed sex secondary school, Parnell Comprehensive. The book presents the findings of a three-year ethnographic study between 1990 and 1992, with much of the material coming from a cohort, of male and female students, who were Year 11 students during the 1990–91 school year. There is also an earlier study of gay students' schooling experiences, some of whom attended Parnell School. Detailed notes were taken and written up each evening. In order to build up student case-histories, they were interviewed individually and in groups. In addition, they kept diaries and they helped to construct questionnaires that they also completed. Participant observation was the core methodology of *The Making of Men*, in exploring the interplay of schooling, sexuality and masculinity. Much of the material was collected from observation, informal discussions and recorded semi-structured interviews with the students and their teachers. Presenting a paper on Willis' (1977) work *Learning to Labour*, Finn (1979) explains that the choice of qualitative methods used in the research was determined by the nature of the interest in the 'cultural'. He claims that:

> The techniques used were particularly suited to record this level and have a sensitivity to subjective meanings and values as well as an ability to represent and interpret symbolic articulations, practices and forms of cultural production.

> In particular the ethnographic account, without always knowing how, can allow
> a degree of activity, creativity and agency within the object of study to come
> through in the analysis.

This research approach, of inferring meanings by understanding the context, through participation in the life of the students and teachers at Parnell School was very productive in *The Making of Men*. More particularly, critical participant observation contributed to making sense of how schooling generated student masculinities and heterosexualities.

During the last four years, while working on a number of research projects, we have been developing our understanding of this area (Haywood and Mac an Ghaill, 1995 and 1996). It is from this perspective that we are evaluating questions of methodology and epistemology with reference to *The Making of Men* (Mac an Ghaill, 1994). There is an emerging uncertainty for critical education researchers concerning the relationship between new theoretical frameworks and the relationship to methodology. Hammersley (1994) has cogently outlined the different trends of educational research and its changing relationship to the discipline of sociology. He suggests that from the 1970s with the impact of the 'new sociology of education', research methodologies are being informed by theoretical perspectives in a range of ways. One methodological response to the 'new sociology of education' was the collapse of the division between theory and methodology. Unlike sociological perspectives that held onto traditional social science conceptions of objectivity and neutrality, critical educational researchers, from certain strands of Marxism, feminism and anti-racism, have argued for a mutually informing interdependency between theory and methodology. This theory-informing research has been productive in rethinking the dynamics of methodology. For instance, it has promoted discussion about knowledge production, notions of objectivity, and the question of reflexivity around power relations within the research process (Ramazanoglu, 1992; Williams, 1993). More recently, post-modernism and post-structuralism, that contests established critical educational research, has offered alternative ways to examine the social relations of schooling. We explain below how *The Making of Men* was a research project where tensions in critical research between an earlier position (identity politics) and a more recent position (the new politics of cultural difference), emerged at both a theoretical and methodological level. More specifically, within the context of theory-led qualitative research, the study highlights, without resolving, the messiness of the eclecticism involved in this methodological transition in the politics of critical educational research. Before exploring the methodological tensions in *The Making of Men*, it is necessary to outline the theoretical background from which it has emerged.

Identity Politics and the New Politics of Cultural Difference: Questions of Epistemology

Locating schooling within developing social and cultural theory, we have found it important to hold onto a distinction between an earlier period in the development of social theory known as *identity politics* and a later period, called the *new politics of cultural difference*. This is not to suggest a linear development from one to the other. On the contrary, the distinction between these periods emphasizes a highly contested and complex tension between accounts. Identity politics refers to social movements, including certain strands of feminism, anti-racism or gay rights that are often politically mobilized around a shared identity. Such social movements assume that identities are placed within relations of power. These power relations are seen to work logically and pre-dictably and it is argued that people who share collective identities such as women, gays or blacks have fixed subordinated positions in social hierarchies. *The Making of Men* was being written at a time when identity politics provided a dominant understanding of gender and schooling. This approach suggests that subordinated gender identities have access to particular experiences of social reality and should inform empirical research. In doing so, a standpoint epistemology is developed, in which an individual is positioned as a privileged knower, possessing a *real* understanding of social relations. As a consequence, research in education often concentrates on giving subordinated groups a voice (Stanley, 1994).

However, *The Making of Men* was a piece of research that actively resisted attempts to produce an account of the gender and sexual processes of school-ing that were reducible to male and female voices. Rather, during the research, theoretical frameworks found in post-structuralist and post-modernist texts became more salient. These frameworks can broadly be identified as part of the new politics of cultural difference. This position argues for greater critical engagement with the notion of a shared identity. For example, it is suggested that the categories of 'woman', 'black' or 'gay' offer limited explanatory power. Rather the new politics of cultural difference examines the regulative and normalizing power within identity categories. In this way, identity is constituted through a range of subjectivities that can not be contained within a singular category. This conceptualization of identity has key methodological implications. The new politics of cultural difference, instead of arguing within a binary of a true/false paradigm, suggests the need to consider a multiplicity of truths at one time. As a result, social relationships do not inherently contain meanings and we are unable simply to read off a resulting analysis from such relations.

Tensions between Older and Newer Critical Theory: The Autonomy of Methodology

Although recognizing the analytical power of particular versions of post-structur-alism and post-modernism, *The Making of Men* at the same time continued to draw upon earlier accounts of feminist methodology (Stanley and Wise, 1983; Bhavnani, 1991; Skeggs, 1991). In carrying out the research, there was an aware-ness of the complex theoretical and political questions involved, if the study was to be located in a standpoint epistemology. As Skeggs (1994) explains:

> Feminism operates within a standpoint epistemology: Human activity not only structures but sets limits on understanding. If social activity is structured in fundamentally opposing ways for different groups, one can expect that the vision of each will represent an inversion of the other, and in systems of domination the vision available to the rulers will be both partial and perverse. (p. 80)

The research in *The Making of Men* attempted to operationalize an emancipatory research method, as advocated by such critical theorists as Lather (1986), with its emphasis on collaboration, reciprocity and reflexivity. Traditional critical ethnographical techniques employed in the analysis involved the use of ideal types as a heuristic device. These were used to illustrate how schooling as a masculinizing agency provided the conditions for the construction of male student styles. These included a number of working-class heterosexual peer groups: The Macho Lads, The Academic Achievers, the New Enterprisers and the new middle-class Real Englishmen. The case-study approach enabled a critical exploration of their values, self-representations and social practices. A real tension that remained throughout the fieldwork and in the book was the use of ideal types that suggest a fixity of male student styles, and the accompanying use of the new politics of cultural difference, to argue that heterosexual masculinities could not be understood as unitary wholes or be seen as static or unchangeable since they are always in the process of production and reproduction.

One of the dangers of these more recent debates between identity politics and the new politics of cultural difference is that increasingly, there is a gap between rather abstract theorizing on research methodology and its relation to the dynamic process of *doing the research* (Walford, 1991; Halpin and Troyna, 1994). For example, one of the key areas of debate in critical social and cultural research is that concerning the explanatory status of experience. Within the context of arguing for the need to develop more sophisticated accounts of ethnographies, it is suggested that subordinated minorities do not speak any simple truth. These debates are often not grounded in empirical work and tend to adopt highly polarized abstracted positions. In *The Making of Men*, theory-led grounded methodology was of vital significance in the generation of theory, that challenges these limiting dichotomies. The fieldwork was involved in a constant mutual interrogation with different theoretical frameworks. For instance, from within an anti-oppressive framework, the accounts of subordinated groups such as female students and gay students, served to make problematic the institutionalized and normalized forms of heterosexuality operating within Parnell School. In fieldwork situations there is the possibility of members of subordinated groups, in this case gay students, sensitizing the researcher to alternative perceptions to those of the dominant institutional explanations of *what is going on*. However, it does not necessarily follow that there is a need to argue that as a result of their subordinated position, groups speak a truth. The gay students' accounts cannot be represented as *telling it as it really is*. There is no simple 'reading off' from the experience to a specific subject position;

rather, as with all accounts, such representations involve complex interpretations of social reality (Spivak, 1988).

The use of the methodological imagination, that acknowledges the relative autonomy of methodology from interrelated theoretical and substantive
issues and the dialectical relationship between these elements, was a major
breakthrough in redefining the research problem. The initial intention of the
study was to examine, from a phenomenological perspective, how male students' experiences of secondary schooling helped to produce a range of masculine styles that they came to take up. The original starting point was influenced
by the need to move away from partial accounts of gender and schooling that
only focus on girls, to a more rounded sociological examination of gender
relations in contemporary schooling. Hence, it drew upon concepts of gender
ideological formations, patriarchal divisions, social reproduction and dominant
cultural capital, in exploring male students' orientation to schooling, and future
occupational and domestic destinies. Critical participant observation, with meaning as its central concern, challenged this theoretical starting point. The shift in
understanding of the research problem arose form interviewing gay male students, who provided a critical account of heterosexuality. Focusing on their
perspectives of the meanings of English schooling, a different focus emerged
around the issue of the cultural production of young heterosexual men (Caplan,
1987; Brittan, 1989; Middleton, 1992).

> *Joseph*: Sexuality is very difficult to talk about. It is difficult to know what it
> really is, when it's present and when it's not. I think that is why it is seen as
> dangerous. Men and women have different positions in the world, with men
> who are supposed to be the rulers. Then we [gays] come along. I suppose we
> are seen as a threat to that power. If there are different ways of being men,
> then it may mean that there's different ways of being women that are equal.
> Then there are no set roles to justify why men rule are there?

> *Rajinder*: At school there's no such thing as sexuality, so it seems. Then one
> day you come out and say you're gay and then you find out that it's the most
> important thing in the world.

In turn, these discussions led to an exploration of the complex interplay of
shifting boundaries between minority and majority gendered cultural forms,
ethnic belonging, class cultural identity and masculine sexual politics (see
Parker, Russo, Sommer and Yaegar, 1992).

The gay students' intervention prevented the study from simply reproduc-
ing inadequate data from dominant theoretical perspectives on gender, such
as sex-role theory. Most specifically, it highlighted the relatively few sociological studies on sexuality and schooling. This work points to the difficulty of
researching the issue of sexuality that is marked by complexity, elusiveness
and fluidity. A major methodological flaw in work that has been carried out in
this area, albeit unintended, is the construction of minorities as 'social problems' or 'victims'. For example, in relation to sexuality, this can be seen in terms

of the ubiquitous search for the pathological origins of homosexuality — that is, the obsessive quest to establish if gays are born or made. Most recently, this has manifested itself in the media's response to research carried out in America that was reported as claiming a genetic basis for homosexuality (Connor, 1993; McKie, 1993). There has been little critical discussion in Britain of this claim, as liberal perspectives remain within a biological determinist framework. In this dominant academic approach to sexuality, sexual majorities remain invisible. For example, when teachers were asked if their students could be interviewed about masculinity, they often claimed that either there were no gays in their tutor groups or that they did not think it appropriate to talk about homosexuality, particularly in the light of Section 28. Interestingly, this section of the Local Government Act, that precludes the promotion of homosexuality by local authorities, does not apply to schools. Such self-surveillance has been the specific and frequently misunderstood hidden state agenda developed during the last decade with the emergence of the New Right and New Right moralism (Weeks, 1989). Implicit in the teachers' responses was the assumption that dominant forms of heterosexuality were unproblematic. They assumed that any research in this area implied a critique of masculinity, which for them could only mean a focus on gayness.

The reconceptualized focus of the book gave high epistemological status to the gay students' accounts, from their position as sexual outsiders, without ascribing a simple truth to them. Within this new focus, in which masculinity was rethought as both a sexual and gender cultural form, the school's institutional practices are all salient features in the making of student subjectivities: including student selection, subject allocation and stratification, disciplinary modes of authority, instruments of surveillance and control, and the web of gendered and sexual student–teacher and student–student social relations (Wolpe, 1988; Connell, 1989).

Understanding Power Relations

Another key aspect to emerge from the interplay of exploring the impact of the tension between identity politics and the new politics of cultural difference on methodology, concerned the question of understanding power relations in operation at Parnell School. Currently, there is a theoretical concern with the interrelationships between different forms of social power, such as the relationships between gender, 'race'/ethnicity, sexuality and class. This is still a largely under-theorized area, while at the same time there is little empirical work available to map out how these interrelationships are lived out within local institutional sites (see McCarthy, 1990).

At an early stage in the research in *The Making of Men*, the critical ethnographic concern with the research subjects' meanings illustrated the need to move beyond accounts of social reproduction and institutional differentiation, that tend to underplay the question of subjectivity, cultural difference and the unconscious. In other words, heterosexuality could not be understood simply as an institutionalized cultural form, circumscribed by state discourses of legislative control, such as Section 28 and the discriminatory age of consent of gays (18 for gays, 16 for heterosexuals), that attempt to codify a way of life by prescribing and proscribing how people should live their lives. As the students made clear, heterosexuality is also a lived category that at a subjective level is marked by contradictions, ambivalences and fluidities.

> *Graham*: I think kissing and hugging [between men] is okay but not anything more, no caressing or getting too close.
> *Mairtin*: Why?
> *Graham*: Because only girls should do that. What if you get aroused? Then you might get used to a bloke doing it and you might not be able to do it with a girl.
> *William*: We [a friend] wanked each other one night when we were really drunk. Then later on when I saw him, he said he had a girlfriend. I knew he hadn't. We just had to move apart because we got too close.
> *Mairtin*: How do you feel about that?
> *William*: Oh fuck it, it was ridiculous. I don't know. I'm not a 'bender' or anything. I don't give a fuck about the sex. I know some girls now and that. But I wish we were still mates. It's great to be close, you know what I mean, really close just to one person and just the two of you know.

By the 1990s, we have been provided with theoretical frameworks, from post-structuralism with useful psychoanalytic emphases, that enables us to analyse systematically and document coherently the multi-dimensional nature of subjectivities (Walkerdine, 1990; Butler, 1993; Davies, 1993; Frosh, 1994; Cohen, 1997). However, much of this work remains at a very abstract level, failing to connect with the lived realities at the local level of institutional and personal life. As indicated above, in *The Making of Men* a multi-layered approach was adopted, in which empirical material from the field and new and old theoretical frameworks interrogated each other. For instance, moving beyond simple models of gender reproduction to the active local production of sex/gendered identity formations within schooling, it emerged that different heterosexual masculinities were highly relational and contradictory in terms of how different groups of male students identified with and against other groups. At Parnell School there were shifting inter-ethnic tensions and alliances in a changing situation. For example, there was no fixed pattern of white or black inter-ethnic response in the different year groups. Rather, different student sub-groups assigned high status to particular individuals or peer groups in which different hierarchies of maculinity were competitively negotiated and acted out. Student inter-ethnic relations were a mixture of 'race'-specific elements and a broader range of social and psychic phenomena located within the school and linked to other social arenas. They involved specific emotional investments and cultural attachments around popular cultural forms, such as music and sport. This is a

long way from the fixed ethnic categories of much conventional equal opportunities discourse on the racialization of British schools. Below, two black
sixth-form students explain the inter-ethnic student complexity and ambiguity
at Parnell School.

> *Carlton*:   Like all the stuff we read on blacks in schools don't even begin
> to get at what is going on. They talk of blacks, Asians and whites and then
> ask them what they think of each other. It's crazy. Like here with black
> culture, the kids' language, cussing and that, their cool movement, the
> hairstyles, the music and clothes, you see the Asians and the white kids
> really getting in to it, deeply into it, right. But at the same time some of
> these Asians and whites will have racist views about blacks. And it's the
> same with the blacks about the others. It's really a mix up and difficult to
> work out, you know what I mean?

> *Rajinder*:   You see there's a lot of sexuality in there. The African Carib-
> beans are seen as better at football and that's really important in this school
> for making a reputation. And it's the same with dancing, again the black
> kids are seen as the best. And the white kids and the Asians are jealous
> because they think that the girls will prefer the black kids. So, the 'race'
> thing gets all mixed up with other things that are important to young kids.

This proved to be particularly helpful in examining the interconnections between
external social relations and internal psychic relations. The students negotiated
their subjectivities through relations of similarity with and opposition to other
groups within their social environment. Dominant modes of heterosexual subjectivity were seen to be constituted by cultural elements which consisted of
contradictory forms of compulsory heterosexuality, misogyny and homophobia.
These were marked by contextual ambivalence, contingency and fluidity. Significantly, the complex interplay of these cultural elements, as institutionally
specific forms of gendered and sexual power, operationalized as key defining processes in sexual boundary maintenance, policing and legitimizing male
heterosexual identities. What emerged of particular salience was the way in
which heterosexual men were involved in a double relationship: of dispar-
aging the 'other', including women and gays (external relations); at the same
time as expelling femininity and homosexuality from within themselves (internal relations). Of key interest here were the ways in which the reproduction
and production of social relations of subordination and resistance, and the
accompanying discourses around gender, sexuality, class, and ethnicity combined and interacted. In trying to work through how young men and women
made sense of their own identities, psychic interconnections became visible.
In this way whilst examining 'race', for the young people it simultaneously
'spoke' gender and sexuality in often unpredictable ways: to be a 'paki' was also
to be a 'poof' was also to be a 'non-proper' boy.

There is a danger in examining the schooling of young gays that by implicitly viewing them as passive and subject to oppressive power relations, the account becomes over-deterministic (Walkerdine, 1990). The students' isolation from other gays at school precluded them from adopting collective coping and survival strategies of sub-cultural affirmation and resistance. Nevertheless, there was evidence from the young men of their contradictory position within schools that actively proscribed sexuality. As a consequence, the gay students articulated the isolation, confusion, marginalization and alienation they experienced in secondary schools that privileged a heterosexuality that was socially constructed as 'natural' and 'inevitable'. However, this account became more complex because their marginalized institutional location, also contained a positive and creative experience. In particular, the gay students had an insight into the contradictory constitution of a naturalized heterosexuality that was structured through ambivalent misogyny and homophobia. In this way, gay students were able to occupy positions of power that allowed the contestation and inversion of heterosexual power. As Matthew, a young gay man, illustrates:

Matthew: The RE teacher said one day in class that teenage boys go through a homosexual phase just like earlier on they go through an 'anti-girls phase'. All totally sexist of course, no mention about the girls' sexuality. I told him, I didn't think boys did go through phases. I said that if boys go through an 'anti-girls phase' it was a long phase because men were always abusing women all of their lives. I meant straight men, but I didn't want to upset him too much. Then lots of the girls started talking about how horrible men were and why did they act like that. The teacher was mad. It was gays that were supposed to be the problem and I turned it round to show the way it really is. Straight men are dangerous to us all, women and gays.

Ethical Questions: Whose Side Are We On?

A specific strength of qualitative work with its focus on located meanings is that it facilitates the development of substantive areas and research questions in the ongoing development of the research design (see Reay, 1996). There are specific issues here for male researchers' work on male participants' experiences of the social world. Male ethnographers of young men's schooling have systematically failed to acknowledge the implicit male knowledges, understandings and desires that we share with male participants' schooling biographies. *The Making of Men*, with its particular emphases and absences, may be read as a form of male bonding, both in terms of the research process and the selected representations of young and adult masculinities and femininities. A more nuanced account might employ subtler categories than those of the social groups of class, gender, sexuality, ethnicity, disability etc., in discussions of the identification of the researcher with specific student masculine styles within the schools. For example, educational researchers of sub-ordinated social groups appear to find it easy to identify with students' rejection of the authoritarianism and disciplinary regimes of schooling (Willis, 1977). This makes interesting reading in terms of the inter-generational biographical similarities and differences across and between social categories in the history of ethnographies of schooling.

During the 1960s, Becker (1967) answered his question 'Whose side are we on?' by suggesting that the researcher must choose between the 'subordinates' and the 'superiors' perspectives (see also Gouldner, 1975). In earlier field work (Mac an Ghaill, 1991), for *The Making of Men*, a main problem was not whose side the researcher *was* on but rather whose side he *appeared* to be on. Drawing upon identity politics and the new politics of cultural difference raises specific difficulties in answering Becker's question in the 1990s in England. On the one hand, male and female students at Parnell School developed their identities within the context of materially structured asymmetrical relations of power that constitute hegemonic gender divisions and heterosexual arrangements. The choice of female students' and gay students' critical experiences of heterosexual masculinities suggests an identification by the author with subordinated social groups. Furthermore, it needs to be added that it is currently fashionable for the new politics of cultural difference theorists to be highly critical of what they call 'essentialist identities', without giving sufficient consideration to oppressed social groups: that the construction of collective identities may act as an important political mobilizing force within specific social sites and at specific historical moments. At the same time, in taking up the suggestion by the new politics of cultural difference that identities are characterized by contradictions, the response of the researcher to a dominant group with whom he or she does not identify becomes more complex. This was made clear in *The Making of Men* in relation to a group of white, English, middle-class, male students, who called themselves the Real Englishmen. Their name served as a triple signifier, with reference to their parents' political position on gender, sexuality and ethnicity which, as they indicate below, were highly problematic inter-generational issues for them.

> *Robert*: We have been emasculated. Our feminist mothers have taken away our masculinity. When I was younger, my mum would sit around with her friends and say bad things about men all the time. And then someone would say what about black men. And then they had to be anti-racist, so black men were not included. And they'd hang around with these guys, who treated them like shit. The guys couldn't have respect for them, they had no respect for themselves. And at the same time I was an anti-racist by the age of four. It just does your head in.

> *Ben*: The teachers and our parents when they talk about racism always say white people mustn't be racist to blacks. That's fine. But they won't say anything when Asian and black kids are racist to each other.

Adam: But no-one asks about us. The older generation don't ask what's it like for us to live with a lot of black kids who don't like us. No one says to the black kids, you have to like the whites. They'll tell them to fuck off.

These students might be viewed as a dominant group with whom a researcher, informed by critical theory, might be expected not to identify. However, empirical work informed by the new politics of cultural difference suggests the limitations of positioning them as one-dimensional oppressors. Within the context of the increasing criticism against anti-oppressive initiatives, such as feminism and anti-racism, these young men as a gendered, sexual and ethnic political majority, as well as being the children of feminists, embody central contradictions in providing a critique. Most significantly, they raise key questions about principles of inclusion and exclusion of gendered and ethnic majorities, that underpin anti-oppressive education.

These tensions remained throughout the study and raise the issue of how academics represent research subjects' accounts, without claiming as an 'expert insider' to *really know* the whole picture in contrast to the latters' incomplete, contingent part truths (Clifford and Marcus, 1986). I would agree with Evans (1992), who has written of the need to rethink how we represent and describe research participants and how we conceptualize their thinking and subjectivity. He suggests that:

> This would involve some experimental writing; searching for different ways of describing the complexity, the multidimensionality, the organisation and disorder, the uncertainty and incongruities of the social worlds that we and others inhabit. It would also mean resisting the temptation to produce texts which contain 'flat' rather than 'rounded' characters. (p. 245)

In attempting to do this, it was difficult both to make a reading of what was going on in the young men's schooling experiences and how this reading was communicated to others.

Conclusion

We may be in 'New Times' in conditions of late modernity with the accompanying rapid social and cultural change, but there is no disciplinary consensus about the meaning of this change. Sociology has not made up its mind about the French philosophers, who have provided frameworks for the development of identity politics and the new politics of cultural difference. British educational theorists, in taking up the new politics of cultural difference, with its focus upon diversity and contradictions, have tended to downplay or erase the big issues of state power, political economy, social class divisions and institutional exclusions. At the same time, it is not clear what the meaning of these new social and cultural theories is for methodology and more specifically for doing research in social sites, such as schools. Interestingly within this context Westwood (1992), in arguing the case for transformative research to be informed by the politics of post-modernism, suggests:

> Thus, critique and counter-critique in relation to the scientism and technicism of research paradigms come together in transformative research agendas which are situational, given context and framed by local conditions. In making 'the grand narratives' problematic, however, this does not mean that the big issues of poverty, racial discrimination, violence, sexism, hunger, disease, unemployment and myriad other issues disappear into local agendas. What it does mean is that they are not constructed in a totalising, universalising discourse which colonises and pathologises these political issues. (p. 193)

In re-evaluating methodological and epistemological issues in the research project *The Making of Men*, this chapter has sought to illustrate that holding onto the tension between identity politics and the new politics of cultural difference is productive in carrying out research. The chapter is written at a time of a political, cultural and methodological uncertainty, in which the 'old politics and identities have been in decline, but the new have still to emerge. In this sense the [chapter] describes a transition, rather than offering a definitive new position' (Rutherford, 1990, p. 23).

References

BECKER, H. (1967) 'Whose side are we on?' *Social Problems*, **14**, pp. 239–47.

BHAVNANI, K.K. (1991) *Talking Politics: A Psychological Framing for Views from Youth in Britain*, Cambridge: Cambridge University Press.

BRITTAN, A. (1989) *Masculinity and Power*, Oxford: Blackwell.

BUTLER, J. (1993) *Bodies that Matter: On the Discursive Limits of 'Sex'*, London: Routledge.

CAPLAN, P. (ed.) (1987) *The Cultural Construction of Sexuality*, London: Tavistock.

CLIFFORD, J. and MARCUS, G. (eds) (1986) *Writing Culture: The Poetics and Politics of Ethnography*, Berkeley, CA: University of California Press.

COHEN, P. (1997) *Rethinking the Youth Question: Education, Labour and Cultural Studies*, London: MacMillan.

CONNELL, R.W. (1989) 'Cool guys, swots and wimps: The interplay of masculinity and education', *Oxford Review of Education*, **15**, 3, pp. 291–303.

CONNOR, S. (1993) 'Gay gene located by researchers', *The Independent*, 16 July, p. 1.

DAVIES, B. (1993) *Shards of Glass: Children, Reading and Writing Beyond Gendered Identities*, St. Leonards, NSW: Allen and Unwin.

EVANS, J. (1992) 'Subjectivity, ideology and educational reform: The case of physical education' in SPARKES, A. (ed.) *Research in Physical Education and Sport*, London: Falmer Press.

FINN, D. (1979) 'Learning to Labour: How working class kids get working class jobs', Unpublished Paper presented to the Fourth Dutch conference on the sociology of Education, 11/12/06, Utrecht.

FROSH, S. (1994) *Sexual Difference: Masculinity and Psychoanalysis*, London: Routledge.

GOULDNER, A. (1975) *For Sociology: Renewal and Critique in Sociology Today*, Harmondsworth: Pelican.

HALPIN, D. and TROYNA, B. (1994) *Researching Education Policy: Ethical and Methodological Issues*, London: Falmer Press.

HAMMERSLEY, M. (1994) 'Ethnography, policy making and practice in education', in HALPIN, D. and TROYNA, B. (eds) *Researching Education Policy: Ethical and Methodological Issues*, London: Falmer Press.

HAYWOOD, C. and MAC AN GHAILL, M. (1995) 'The sexual politics of the curriculum: Contesting values', *International Studies in the Sociology of Education*, **5**, 2, pp. 221–36.

HAYWOOD, C. and MAC AN GHAILL, M. (1996) ' "What about the boys?": Regendered local labour markets and the recomposition of working class masculinities', *British Journal of Education and Work*, **9**, 1.

LATHER, P. (1986) 'Research as Praxis', *Harvard Educational Review*, **56**, 3, pp. 257–77.

MAC AN GHAILL, M. (1991) 'Young, gifted and black: Methodological reflections of a teacher/researcher', in WALFORD, G. (ed.) *Doing Educational Research*, London: Routledge.

MAC AN GHAILL, M. (1994) *The Making of Men: Masculinities, Sexualities and Schooling*, Buckingham: Open University Press.

McCARTHY, C. (1990) *Race and Curriculum*, London: Falmer Press.

McKIE, R. (1993) 'The myth of the gay gene', *Observer*, 18 July, p. 21.

MIDDLETON, P. (1992) *The Inward Gaze: Masculinity, Subjectivity and Modern Culture*, London: Routledge.

PARKER, A., RUSSO, M., SOMMER, D. and YAEGER, P. (1992) *Nationalisms and Sexualities*, London: Routledge.

RAAB, C. (1994) 'Where we are now: Reflections on the sociology of education policy', in HALPIN, D. and TROYNA, B. (eds) *Researching Education Policy: Ethical and Methodological Issues*, London: Falmer Press.

RAMAZANOGLU, C. (1992) 'On feminist methodology: Male reason versus female empowerment', *Sociology*, **26**, pp. 207–12.

REAY, D. (1996) 'Insider perspectives or stealing the words out of women's mouths: Interpretations in the research process', *Feminist Review*, **53**, pp. 55–71.

SKEGGS, B. (1994) 'The constraints of neutrality: The 1988 Education Reform Act and feminist research', in HALPIN, D. and TROYNA, B. (eds) *Researching Education Policy: Ethical and Methodological Issues*, London: Falmer Press.

SPIVAK, G. (1988) *In Other Worlds: Essays in Cultural Politics*, New York: Routledge.

STANLEY, L. (1994) 'The knowing because experiencing subject: Narrative, lives and autobiography', in LENNON, K. and WHITFORD, M. (eds) *Knowing the Difference: Feminist Perspectives in Epistemology*, London: Routledge.

STANLEY, L. and WISE, S. (1983) *Breaking Out: Feminist Consciousness and Feminist Research*, London: Routledge and Kegan Paul.

WALFORD, G. (ed.) (1991) *Doing Educational Research*, London: Routledge.

WALLER, W. (1976) *The Sociology of Teaching*, New York: Wiley.

WALKERDINE, V. (1990) *Schoolgirl Fictions*, London: Verso.

WEEKS, J. (1989) *Sexuality and Its Discontents: Meanings, Myths and Modern Sexualities*, London: Routledge.

WESTWOOD, S. (1992) 'Power/knowledge: The politics of transformative research', *Studies in the Education of Adults*, **24**, 2, pp. 191–98.

WILLIAMS, A. (1993) 'Diversity and agreement in feminist ethnography', *Sociology*, **27**, 4, pp. 575–89.

WILLIS, P. (1977) *Learning to Labour: How Working Class Kids Get Working Class Jobs*, Hants: Saxon House.

WOLPE, A.M. (1988) *Within School Walls: The Role of Discipline, Sexuality and the Curriculum*, London: Routledge.

10   The Profession of a 'Methodological Purist'?

Martyn Hammersley

During the past ten years I have been engaged in a methodological investigation of the standards by which social and educational research ought to be assessed. In this chapter I will sketch the origins of this work, the course it has taken, and the reaction to it of some fellow researchers. In particular, I will address the criticism that the approach I have adopted amounts to 'methodological purism'.

Clarifying Standards and the Process of Assessment

My current preoccupation with methodology probably stems, in large part, from involvement in an Open University course in that area during the late 1970s (Open University, 1979). As the only qualitative researcher on the central course team, I found myself having to defend my approach in discussions with sceptical colleagues. Working on this course forced me to think much more carefully than I had done before about methodological issues. And one of the effects was that I came to realize that the assumptions on which I had previously relied were not as compelling as I had once thought. In particular, I concluded that the criticisms directed at quantitative research by qualitative researchers often apply just as powerfully to their own work; and that some of these, if taken to their logical conclusions, undermine all research. Equally important, I recognized that many of the criticisms directed at qualitative research had considerable force, and that the usual defences against them were problematic.[1]

One focus of these methodological reflections concerned the capacity of qualitative research to produce theory. Emphasis on theory as a goal has been very common, often being used by qualitative researchers as a defence against criticism that their findings are not generalizable. However, looking carefully at a range of qualitative work led me to conclude that there was little sign of systematic pursuit of theory. While analytic induction and grounded theorizing were frequently appealed to in the literature as ethnographic strategies for theory development and testing, there were very few examples of their explicit and thoroughgoing application.[2]

At this point an opportunity arose to explore what was involved in developing and testing theory through qualitative research, in the form of a research project concerned with the impact of different modes of external assessment on pedagogy in secondary schools. Our initial intention in this research was to apply grounded theory, and later we also explored the possibility of using analytic induction. However, we ran into some serious problems (Hammersley, Scarth and Webb, 1985; Hammersley, 1992a). On the basis of this experience, I spent considerable time reading the literature about theory building in the social and natural sciences, and tried to clarify what qualitative research would need to do in order to pursue theory effectively. As part of this, I examined the sequence of studies by Hargreaves, Lacey and Ball on streaming, banding, and other forms of differentiation in schools, which seemed to be the best available example of a systematic attempt to develop and test a theory via mainly qualitative research; though these studies also display some of the ambiguities characteristic of qualitative researchers' orientations to theory (Hargreaves, 1967; Lacey, 1970; Ball, 1980; Hammersley, 1985). This model guided the later stages of our research on examinations and pedagogy, though with rather disappointing results, primarily as a consequence of measurement problems that seemed irresolvable and the sheer complexity of the causal processes involved (see Hammersley and Scarth, 1986). The effect of this experience was to throw me back into further methodological reflection.

An important aspect of our research was that in order to capture differences in pedagogy and their effects we had felt it necessary to use quantitative as well as qualitative data.[3] This led me to reflect on the similarities, and the relationship, between qualitative and quantitative approaches to social and educational research. I began to think that the same general standards of assessment ought to apply to both, since their goal is the same: the production of knowledge. I therefore set out to investigate in more depth the criteria put forward by quantitative methodologists. I found their work instructive in many respects, particularly as regards the problem of measurement. Here especially, I decided, there were ideas that needed applying to qualitative research.[4] I also came to recognize that qualitative researchers frequently make causal claims and therefore cannot avoid the problem of how to validate these — so that the literature on causal analysis in quantitative research also carries some important lessons for them (see, for example, Hage and Meeker, 1988).

At the same time, I found serious problems with the treatment of central concepts like validity and reliability in the quantitative methodology literature. In particular, it treated reliability as equivalent in character and status to validity, and it fragmented the latter into different types (face validity, content validity, construct validity, predictive validity, etc.). It seemed to me that reliability measures are merely an indirect means of assessing validity; and that validity is all of a piece — a finding cannot be true in one sense and false in another. Moreover, much of the thinking about these concepts betrayed the continuing influence of positivism, and in particular of operationism, in ways that were not defensible. For example, there was a tendency to *define* validity in terms of correlations among different measures, and thereby to confuse the definition of concepts with their operationalization (Hammersley, 1987a). I also became critical of the influential distinction between internal and external validity. This, too, seemed to misrepresent the nature of validity, in particular because it failed to recognize the difference between theoretical inference and empirical generalization (Hammersley, 1991a).

Arising out of this, I began to investigate the methodological debates that had taken place about quantitative and qualitative approaches in the past. I looked, especially, at the work of Herbert Blumer, who had been an important critic of quantitative research and an advocate of 'case study' in US sociology (Blumer, 1969; Hammersley, 1989a). Several conclusions emerged from this. One was that the common tendency to contrast two traditions or approaches to the study of the social world (quantitative versus qualitative, positivist versus interpretive, etc.) is fundamentally mistaken. This is illustrated by the fact that a large amount of research in the past, and even today, combines both kinds of method and data. Also significant is that the arguments put forward in favour of quantitative or qualitative research in the 1930s and 1940s were significantly different from those presented in the 1960s and 1970s. Indeed, sometimes the same argument was to be found on one side of the debate at one point and on the opposite side at another, an example being advocacy of phenomenalist or realist ontological assumptions (see Hammersley, 1992b, Chapter 9, and 1996).[5] Furthermore, these arguments drew on nineteenth-century debates about science and history, where multiple positions were to be found: the distinction between hermeneutic and neo-Kantian approaches, and between these and later phenomenological and pragmatist ideas, were just as important as the contrast with positivism, the latter itself changing significantly between the nineteenth and twentieth centuries. Exploration of these different views, and the debates among them, revealed how complex the issues involved are, and how crude and ineffective many of the more recent discussions have been.

A second conclusion from this work was that there are internal contradictions within the thinking behind much qualitative research; including, for example, that underlying both grounded theorizing and analytic induction. Thus, the former seeks to combine theory and description, a project that has been central to much qualitative method. Yet these are different goals that can pull researchers in contrary directions. Moreover, most formulations of grounded theorizing and analytic induction rely on the assumption of universal laws of social life, an idea that virtually all qualitative researchers reject today. At the same time, neither of these approaches conforms closely to what is required to discover such laws. Another contradiction concerns the issue of measurement. Qualitative researchers often deny that they are engaged in measurement at all; perhaps following Blumer's argument about 'sensitizing' rather than 'definitive' concepts. Yet, like Blumer, they wish to make claims that require concepts which do more than tell us 'in which direction to look'. However, whereas Blumer was all too aware of this problem, contemporary qualitative researchers do not seem to recognize it.[6]

While I was engaged in this work, in the late 1980s, the literature on qualitative methodology grew very rapidly, and much of it began to display a radical break with earlier commitments. Where previously there had been an emphasis on a scientific approach and the central task of documenting social reality, increasingly the model of science came to be rejected and so too did the commitment to realism. The sources of this change were diverse, coming from both within qualitative research and outside.

Internally, the constructionism implicit in labelling theory, and the influence of ethnomethodology, often led to the idea that what research produces is just one more account, one more view of the world, not different in character or function from the perspectives of the people being studied. Some concluded from this that research texts themselves should be subject to discourse analysis, to show how these actually constitute the realities they purport to represent. Alternatively, where before the accounts of informants had been carefully assessed for accuracy as a source of information about what they referred to, some qualitative researchers now came to see the task of enquiry as 'giving voice' to those whose views of the world are not normally heard; with this apparently ruling out assessment of the validity of those views. At the same time, emphasis was placed on locating researchers themselves within the world they study, and treating their perspectives as products of their social characteristics and circumstances.

Externally, a series of influences pushed in the same directions. In particular, existential phenomenology, philosophical hermeneutics and postmodernism undermined commitment to science. All of these philosophies emphasize the fact that science takes place in the social world and is shaped by it, and for this reason they resist scientific claims to universal validity. This has led to the conclusion on the part of some social scientists that any claims about the validity of research findings must be treated as a rhetorical ploy, like all other claims to authority; in other words as a strategy for exercising power. In the context of all this, the very notion of standards of assessment was sometimes rejected (see, for example, Smith, 1993), and ambivalence and doubt about them spread much more widely. The concepts of validity and objectivity, in particular, came under sustained questioning (Lather, 1986 and 1993; Kvale, 1989).

Equally important was an increasing emphasis on the practical and political role of social research. This took a variety of forms, including advocacy of action and practitioner enquiry, attempts to legitimate partisanship on the part of researchers, and moves towards an enhanced role for the 'users' of research in shaping it (see, for example, Oliver, 1992; Gitlin, 1994; Pettigrew, 1994; Bassey, 1995; Troyna, 1995). The result of this was to promote instrumental assessments of social and educational research findings. Sometimes, perhaps under the influence of pragmatism and critical theory, what were judged to be good effects, or at least good implications, were treated as evidence for the truth of the research conclusions. Alternatively, truth was downgraded as a criterion or simply rejected as a spurious issue, in favour of a concern with direct instrumental value.[7]

These developments served to extend the range of the project I was engaged in. The very concept of methodological assessment now needed justification, at least in the way that I was approaching it. In particular, it was necessary to think through the implications of the collapse of epistemological foundationalism for educational and social research methodology. My view was that while the critics of the scientific model and of realism were correct to point to serious difficulties with the philosophical ideas that had previously underpinned both quantitative and qualitative research (and especially foundationalism), they were wrong to draw the relativist, sceptical, and instrumentalist conclusions that many of them did (see Phillips, 1989). I set out to investigate the bases for their arguments, to try to outline a more defensible realist position, and to explicate the standards for assessing research findings that followed from this (Hammersley, 1990b, 1992b and 1995).

I cannot elaborate on the conclusions of this work in any detail here, but a summary is necessary to provide a background for the discussion of its reception that follows. Of central importance is validity as a standard of assessment and my account of how this should be judged. I argue that in the absence of a foundation of data whose own truth is given beyond all possible doubt, there are three steps involved in assessing the validity of knowledge claims:

1   The first question that we must ask about a claim is how plausible it is, in the sense of how likely to be true we judge it given what we currently take to be well-established knowledge. In the case of some claims, though rarely if ever the central ones of a study, they will be so plausible that we can reasonably accept them at face value until further notice, without needing to know anything about how researchers came to formulate them or what evidence is available in support. In most cases, though, claims will be insufficiently plausible to be accepted at face value and may even be quite implausible in these terms. Indeed, the more implausible, the more newsworthy they are.

2   A second question we may need to ask is whether it seems likely that the researcher's judgment of matters relating to the claim is accurate, given the nature of the phenomena concerned, the circumstances of the research, the researcher's characteristics and orientation, etc. I have called this 'credibility'. In assessing credibility we make a judgment about the likely threats to validity involved in the production of a claim and the likely size and direction of their effect. As with plausibility, there are knowledge claims whose credibility is such that we can reasonably accept them without more ado until further notice, but here again this is unlikely to be true of the main claims of a study.

3   Where we conclude that a claim is neither sufficiently plausible nor sufficiently credible to be accepted at face value, we require evidence to be convinced of its validity. When we examine the evidence, however, we have to employ much the same means to assess its validity as we applied to the claim itself: we must judge *its* plausibility and

credibility. Furthermore, we may require additional evidence to establish the validity of this first level evidence, which we again judge in terms of plausibility and credibility, and so on.

I have argued that this is also the process by which we assess the accuracy of information in everyday life. However, I have suggested that scholarly research is distinctive in that what is treated as true in this context depends on the judgments of the relevant research community, a community that ought to be governed by distinctive norms, notably what Merton refers to as 'organised scepticism' (Merton, 1973, Chapters 12 and 13). I interpret this norm to mean that knowledge claims should be assessed on the basis of what would be accepted as plausible or credible by most members of the research community; that where there is disagreement we have an obligation to try to resolve it by searching for common ground; and that where disagreement persists on a substantial scale within a research community all members must indicate the uncertain validity of this knowledge claim when they use it, even though they may themselves confidently believe it to be true or false.[8]

Methodological Purism?

From the start, some of the responses to my methodological work from fellow qualitative researchers were rather critical. Very early on, responding to a paper I had given on the importance of theory-testing in ethnography, a colleague commented that what was being presented was a kind of perfectionism, putting up standards that no qualitative study would ever be able to satisfy. A more oblique form of criticism has been repeated inquiries about when I am going to do some empirical research again! The suggestion is that instead of writing about it, I should *demonstrate* how it ought to be done. Built into this, I think, is the implication that methodological investigation is not proper research, and/or that if I were to try to do some empirical work along the lines proposed I might find it impossible to meet my own criteria.

I have some sympathy with these criticisms. I accept that the main point of methodological work is to improve empirical research and our interpretation and use of it: methodology has very limited value in itself. And, as I have already explained, my methodological reflections actually arose out of a project in which failure to achieve the main goal was our experience; so I am all too aware of the difficulty of meeting the requirements I have identified. At the same time, I believe that this criticism stems, to some extent, from an empiricism which continues to inform the thinking of many researchers, whereby knowledge is 'found' in the field rather than produced through the collective work of research communities, so that criteria of assessment are seen as unproblematic or irrelevant. Also, an important distinction is often ignored between standards that are difficult, or even impossible, to satisfy, but which may be necessary; and standards that are more demanding than they need to be for us to establish the validity of conclusions with reasonable confidence. While methodological ideals should certainly be tempered with practical realism, we must not simply give in to expediency, treating what we currently do as all that can be done or as automatically satisfactory (Hammersley, 1987b and 1993b).

Some other reactions to this methodological work have been much more negative. They arose, not surprisingly perhaps, when I and others began to assess particular qualitative studies (Hammersley, 1986a, 1990a, 1991b, and 1993a; Foster, 1990b, 1991, 1992, 1993a, 1993b, 1993c; Gomm, 1993 and 1995). The trigger for the most severe reaction was the work of Peter Foster, whose PhD I had supervised. He carried out an empirical study of multicultural/ antiracist policy in a secondary school when he was employed at the Research Unit on Ethnic Relations at the University of Warwick (Foster, 1989 and 1990a). In that study, he reached the conclusion that there was little evidence of widespread teacher racism in the school he investigated, and on the basis of his experience in doing this research he became critical of some other studies that had claimed to document racism on the part of teachers. The response to his work was very hostile (Wright, 1990; Blair, 1993; Connolly, 1992; Gillborn and Drew, 1992); and a colleague, Roger Gomm, and I became involved in subsequent debates and started work with Foster on a book examining research on educational inequality generally (Foster, Gomm and Hammersley, 1996). In the course of these debates, our position was labelled 'methodological purism' (Troyna, 1993; Gillborn and Drew, 1993; Gillborn, 1995, Chapter 3).

One way or another, this dispute relates to many of the methodological issues that I had been preoccupied with earlier. However, it has not done much to resolve them, not least because the arguments of the critics of 'methodological purism' are unclear in important respects. In some places they seem to question the very idea of seeking to reach agreement in the assessment of research findings, this goal being taken to reflect a 'crude positivism'. For instance, Gillborn (1995) has argued that a major problem arises when critical scrutiny of empirical studies:

> . . . translates into a debate about whether a case is 'proven beyond reasonable doubt' [. . .]. This suggests the possibility of identifying a critical mass of evidence, beyond which a case should be accepted as proven, but where anything less is rejected. Such an approach is 'authoritative, closed and certain' where a more helpful approach might seek to open up the complex and contingent nature of social processes (see Ball, 1994). (pp. 52–3)

Gillborn claims that the methodological purists 'risk simply reifying one set of assumptions over another'; and that 'what seems plausible and credible to some might appear to be wildly optimistic or even politically motivated propaganda to others' (Gillborn, 1995, p. 53). Thus, '[. . .] there is no single standard, no "significance test" for qualitative data' (Gillborn and Drew, 1993, p. 355). Here, criticism of methodological purism seems to imply a relativistic position, in which judgments about the validity of evidence are 'the product of a particular (class-related, gendered, and culturalist) perspective' (Gillborn, 1995, p. 63). This would suggest that general agreement about the validity of findings is impossible, and that its pursuit is undesirable. However, this position involves a pragmatic contradiction since the critics assume the existence of agreed standards of assessment in their own critiques of quantitative research and of the work of Foster (Troyna, 1991; Gillborn and Drew, 1992).

So, it may be that what is at issue is my particular account of the form assessment should take, rather than the need for agreed standards. Thus, my colleagues and I are accused of applying '*crude and absolutist* notions of plausibility and credibility' (Gillborn, 1995, p. 53; emphasis added). It is not clear what crudity and absolutism amount to here, but there seem to be two versions of this argument. First, there is the familiar charge that the standards are too high. Thus, we are criticized for setting 'unattainable requirements' (Gillborn and Drew, 1993, p. 355), for requiring 'research on social injustice to be based on data which are not amenable to alternative interpretations' (Troyna, 1993, p. 168). At the very least, this argument is overstated: we do not require that research be based on data that are not open to alternative interpretations, only that researchers show that *their* interpretation is more convincing than *competing ones*. In this context, it is important to recognize the distinction between accepting something as true when it is beyond *reasonable* doubt, and accepting as true only what is beyond *all possible* doubt (Hammersley, 1989a and 1990b). Of course, the idea of reasonable doubt raises the question of what constitutes *sufficient* evidence to establish the validity of knowledge claims, and it is my view that there is no general answer to this question. It is a matter of judgment in particular cases. But in order to maximize progress towards sound knowledge, such judgments must take place in the context of a research community devoted primarily to assessing the validity of findings and operating on the basis of 'organized scepticism'.

The other criticism of the approach to assessment I proposed is that using plausibility as a basis for judging validity produces assessments that are politically conservative, this being at odds with what is taken to be the 'critical' mission of sociology. I have examined the notion of 'critical social research' in a number of places (Hammersley, 1992b, Chapter 6; 1995, Chapter 2, and 1995), suggesting that its rationale is misconceived. In particular, the question must be asked: how do critical researchers justify the knowledge *they* claim to have on the basis of which they declare *others'* views to be ideological? As far as I can tell, there is no convincing answer to this question. Indeed, 'ideology' serves largely as a device for explaining away views with which critical researchers disagree (Hammersley, 1981).

However, the argument that reliance on judgments of plausibility involves a conservative political bias is one that needs to be addressed. If it were true, it would indicate a fundamental defect in the approach I have proposed. But I think it can be demonstrated that it is not. While there is a bias of a certain sort built into the ideal operation of research communities, it is not one that is likely to operate in any *particular* political direction; indeed, it is likely to be found frustrating by all sides. This bias amounts to the fact that the onus is laid on those who put forward knowledge claims, whether positive or negative, to establish their validity beyond reasonable doubt in terms found cogent by the research community at large. The effect of this is to make more difficult the validation of *any* knowledge claim.

Now, of course, it is very likely that some of the knowledge claims accepted by a research community are false, and that some which are rejected are true; and it may be that *which* are accepted and *which* rejected reflects the distinctive social characteristics and circumstances of researchers. No research community can be representative in every way; and in at least one respect all of them are inevitably unrepresentative — precisely because their members are researchers. However, while research communities must be open to membership irrespective of gender, 'race', social background and political views, they do not need comprehensively to represent the wider society in their make-up in order to satisfy the methodological ideal. All that is required is that they are sufficiently diverse in assumption and attitude to generate the organized scepticism that is required for their effective operation. Research communities do not work by referenda. Indeed, in relation to many knowledge claims most members of the relevant research community do not express public views about them.[9] Rather, in publicly reviewing research reports a few researchers (likely to be different ones on different occasions) act in the name of all, and are expected to make judgments according to considerations that any member of the community would take into account; judgments that can of course themselves be challenged. Equally important, the *initial* response to disagreement must be to engage in discussion designed to resolve the dispute by finding ground that is common to both parties, from which agreed conclusions about the relevant knowledge claim can be reached; and, of course, this may involve carrying out further research, as well as reanalysing existing data. It is not suggested that research communities operating in this way can *guarantee* production of the truth; there are no guarantees. The argument is simply that they offer the best prospect of producing sound knowledge; though they do so at considerable cost, notably in terms of the slow pace at which knowledge is produced.

There are undoubtedly problems with the approach to the assessment of social and educational research that I have put forward. But to some extent at least it must be judged against the available alternatives. One of the most frustrating features of the debate about methodological purism is that the critics are not explicit about their own methodological assumptions. At times they seem to revert to some kind of empiricism, as when Foster is accused of overlooking the racism that was 'under his nose' (Connolly, 1992, p. 142). At other times, they appeal to critical theory, standpoint epistemology, and/or postmodernist relativism (see, for example, Gillborn 1995 and Troyna 1995). Yet none of these seem viable, and the critics do not even address the well-known problems associated with them (Hammersley, 1992b, Chapter 6, and 1995).

Of course, the debate about methodological purism is reflexive in character. It is not just *about* how researchers ought to behave but is also an instance of that behaviour. One might therefore conclude that the critics are simply acting on the basis of a different conception of the proper role of the researcher. There is evidence for this in some cases. An example is an article by Gillborn and Drew, replying to a response that Gomm and I had made to their critique of Smith and Tomlinson's *The School Effect* (Smith and Tomlinson, 1989). In our article we expressed agreement with some of Gillborn and Drew's criticisms but raised doubts about others. By contrast, their article begins with a quote from Wellman's book *Portraits of White Racism* (1977) which is used to suggest that we are racists (see Gillborn and Drew, 1993). They then write the following:

> We do not intend simply to respond to each of the criticisms levelled against us by Hammersley and Gomm (1993); that would be tedious and, more significantly, let *them* define what is important in relation to research on 'race' and ethnicity. (pp. 354–55)

And while they address some of the specific points we raise, they do this only to illustrate 'the kind of tactics that characterise [Hammersley and Gomm's] position'. Their main concern is 'the wider project' of which our 'attack' is part (Gillborn and Drew, 1993, p. 354).

The militaristic metaphors and analogies — attack, tactics, criticisms 'levelled against us', not letting the opposition define what is important and thereby choose the terrain for the battle — are striking here, and perhaps indicate commitment to 'the long march through the institutions', whereby the researcher's primary task is to challenge ideology, within and outside the research community. However, the foundations of this approach have long been in doubt as a result of both internal and external criticism; including that of feminists and postmodernists. Even aside from this, though, given that one of the central themes of the critical tradition is the need to question taken-for-granted assumptions, that tradition can offer no justification for simply dismissing the arguments of those who question *its* taken-for-granted assumptions. To do so is indeed to adopt a position that is 'authoritative, closed and certain'.

Perhaps, though, the criticism of methodological purism operates at an even more fundamental level. It may be that the critics regard methodology, at least of the kind that I am engaged in, as irrelevant to their work. There is a widespread tendency to reject the idea of methodology as an enterprise that is even partially autonomous from research, on the basis of a kind of pragmatism that emphasizes how enquiry is actually done rather than the 'reconstructed logics' to be found in methodological texts (Hammersley, 1992b; Troyna, 1994). It is possible that this is what motivates Drew and Gillborn's comment in a recent contribution to the debate, quoting Becker, that: 'methodology is too important to be left to the methodologists' (Drew and Gillborn, 1996; Becker, 1970: 3).

What this statement means, though, is not very clear. Becker calls it a 'trite paraphrase of a cliché', and as such the message is presumably that *all* researchers must be concerned with methodology. Few would deny this. However, Becker goes on to criticize specialized methodological writing in American sociology of the 1960s, *not* for being specialized but rather for its quantitative bias, and for focusing on a narrow range of problems that are believed to be amenable to the reduction of sociological practice to following procedures. Yet, it is difficult to see how this criticism could be applied to my work, given that I question key elements of quantitative as well as of qualitative approaches, and that I have emphasized the role of judgment within the context of organized scepticism, rather than claiming that findings can be tested in some direct and absolutely conclusive way. Nor have I focused on a narrow range of problems; quite the reverse. It is also worth noting that Becker's major complaint in this article is about the neglect of important problems in the methodological literature, one of which is the question of why sociologists do not apply well-known safeguards to protect their conclusions from threats to validity. Here it seems that Becker is himself in danger of being labelled a methodological purist!

The debate about methodological purism raises some crucial and difficult issues facing social and educational research. However, the critics do not seem to have engaged with those issues. Instead, the term has been used as little more than a rhetorical device designed to dismiss the arguments of those who raise awkward questions.

Conclusion

Ten years is a long time to spend on any research project, and especially a methodological one. As I explained, part of the reason it has taken so long is that new problems have opened up, and in some ways these are more intractable than the original ones, for example relating to the social role of the educational researcher. Responding to reactions against my work has also taken time and, for the reasons explained, has been rather less productive than it might have been. However, those reactions have, above all else, underlined the importance of the issues with which I have been preoccupied. So, too, have recent trends towards the external control of educational enquiry (Pettigrew, 1994; Norris, 1995; Hargreaves, 1996; Hammersley, 1997b). In my view, the politicization of research, whether by Right, Left or Centre, threatens to destroy it. A central element of my methodological work has been to explore how researchers ought to use what autonomy they still have to pursue their profession.

Acknowledgments

I am grateful to Jeff Evans, Peter Foster, Roger Gomm, Donald Mackinnon and Geoffrey Walford for comments on earlier drafts of this paper.

Notes

1 I suspect that the seeds of these doubts were sown earlier, when I read Cicourel (1964) and came into contact with ethnomethodologists, around the time I was try- ing to do ethnographic research for the first time (see Hammersley, 1984). Interest- ingly, some of my colleagues on the Open University course subsequently became much more sympathetic to qualitative research and even started doing it themselves.

2 Internal criticism of qualitative work for its failure to pursue theory effectively has quite a long history (see, for example, Glaser and Strauss, 1967 and Lofland, 1970). For detailed discussion of grounded theory and analytic induction, and references to the literature dealing with them, see Hammersley (1989a).

3 The studies of Hargreaves, Lacey and Ball, and some other early ethnographic research, had also used quantitative data, but there had been a gradual drift away from this.

4 One of the influences leading me to this conclusion was the argument of Evans (1983), who had been one of my colleagues on the Open University methodology course.

5 Phenomenalists argue that we can have no knowledge of objects beyond experi- ence, beyond phenomena as they *appear* to us. Realists argue that experience can be used to infer the existence and nature of objects or processes that cannot be directly experienced.

6 On the problems of 'theoretical description' see Hammersley (1992b, Chapter 1); and on sensitizing and definitive concepts, see Hammersley (1989b).

7 Denzin's recent book *Interpretive Ethnography* incorporates many of the trends outlined in this and the previous two paragraphs (Denzin, 1997).

8 Perhaps I should underline that this is an account of how I believe research commun- ities *ought* to operate; I am not suggesting that this is how they always *do* operate.

9 On the fallacy of applying the concept of participatory democracy to research, see Hammersley (1993c, pp. 433–4).

References

BALL, S.J. (1980) *Beachside Comprehensive*, Cambridge: Cambridge University Press.

BALL, S.J. (1994) 'Some reflections on policy theory: A brief response to Hatcher and Troyna', *Journal of Education Policy*, **9**, 2, pp. 171–82.

BASSEY, M. (1995) *Creating Education through Research*, Newark: Kirklington Moor Press, in association with the British Educational Research Association.

BECKER, H.S. (1970) 'On methodology', *Sociological Work: Method and Substance*, Chicago: Aldine.

BLAIR, M. (1993) 'Review of Peter Foster: Policy and practice in multicultural and antiracist education', *European Journal of Intercultural Studies*, **2**, 3, pp. 63–4.

BLUMER, H. (1969) *Symbolic Interactionism*, Englewood Cliffs NJ: Prentice Hall.

CONNOLLY, P. (1992) 'Playing it by the rules: The politics of research in "race" and education', *British Educational Research Journal*, **18**, 2, pp. 133–48.

DENZIN, N.K. (1997) *Interpretive Ethnography*, Thousand Oaks, CA: Sage.

DREW, D. and GILLBORN, D. (1996) 'Hammersley and Gomm — A reply', *British Socio- logical Association Network Newsletter*, **66**, October.

EVANS, J. (1983) 'Criteria of validity in social research: Exploring the relationship between ethnographic and quantitative approaches', in HAMMERSLEY, M. (ed.) *The Ethnography of Schooling*, Driffield: Nafferton.

FOSTER, P. (1989) 'Policy and practice in multicultural and anti-racist education', Unpublished PhD thesis, Open University.

FOSTER, P. (1990a) *Policy and Practice in Multicultural and Anti-racist Education*, London: Routledge.

FOSTER, P. (1990b) 'Cases not proven: An evaluation of two studies of teacher racism', *British Educational Research Journal*, **16**, 4, pp. 335–48.

FOSTER, P. (1991) 'Cases still not proven: A reply to Cecile Wright', *British Educational Research Journal*, **17**, 2, pp. 165–70.

FOSTER, P. (1992) 'What are Connolly's rules? A reply to Paul Connolly', *British Educational Research Journal*, **18**, 2, pp. 149–54.

FOSTER, P. (1993a) 'Teacher attitudes and Afro-Caribbean achievement', *Oxford Review of Education*, **18**, 3, pp. 269–82.

FOSTER, P. (1993b) 'Some problems in identifying racial/ethnic equality or inequality in schools', *British Journal of Sociology*, **44**, 3, pp. 519–35.

FOSTER, P. (1993c) 'Equal treatment and cultural difference in multi-ethnic schools: A critique of teacher ethnocentrism theory', *International Studies in the Sociology of Education*, **2**, 1, pp. 89–103.

FOSTER, P., GOMM, R. and HAMMERSLEY, M. (1996) *Constructing Educational Research: An Assessment of Research on School Processes*, London: Falmer Press.

GILLBORN, D. (1995) *Racism and Antiracism in Real Schools*, Buckingham: Open University Press.

GILLBORN, D. and DREW, D. (1992) ' "Race", class and school effects', *New Community*, **18**, 4, pp. 551–65.

GILLBORN, D. and DREW, D. (1993) 'The politics of research: Some observations on "methodological purity" ', *New Community*, **19**, 2, pp. 354–60.

GITLIN, A. (ed.) (1994) *Power and Method: Political Activism and Educational Research*, New York: Routledge.

GLASER, B. and STRAUSS, A. (1967) *The Discovery of Grounded Theory*, Chicago: Aldine.

GOMM, R. (1993) 'Figuring out ethnic equity', *British Educational Research Journal*, **19**, 2, pp. 149–65.

GOMM, R. (1995) 'Strong claims, weak evidence: A response to Troyna's "Ethnicity and the organisation of learning" ', *Educational Research*, **37**, 1, pp. 79–86.

HAGE, J. and MEEKER, B.F. (1988) *Social Causality*, London: Unwin Hyman.

HAMMERSLEY, M. (1981) 'Ideology in the staffroom? A critique of false consciousness', in BARTON, L. and WALKER, S. (eds) *Schools, Teachers and Teaching*, London: Falmer Press.

HAMMERSLEY, M. (1984) 'The researcher exposed: A natural history', in BURGESS, R.G. (ed.) *The Research Process in Educational Settings*, London: Falmer Press.

HAMMERSLEY, M. (1985) 'From ethnography to theory', *Sociology*, **19**, pp. 244–59.

HAMMERSLEY, M. (1987a) 'Some notes on the terms "validity" and "reliability" ', *British Educational Research Journal*, **13**, 1, pp. 73–81.

HAMMERSLEY, M. (1987b) 'Ethnography for survival? A reply to Woods', *British Educational Research Journal*, **13**, 3, pp. 309–17.

HAMMERSLEY, M. (1989a) *The Dilemma of Qualitative Method: Herbert Blumer and the Chicago Tradition*, London: Routledge.

HAMMERSLEY, M. (1989b) 'The problem of the concept', *Journal of Contemporary Ethnography*, **18**, pp. 133–59.

HAMMERSLEY, M. (1990a) 'An assessment of two studies of gender imbalance in the classroom', *British Educational Research Journal*, **16**, 2, pp. 125–43.

HAMMERSLEY, M. (1990b) *Reading Ethnographic Research: A Critical Guide*, London: Longman.

HAMMERSLEY, M. (1991a) 'A note on Campbell's distinction between internal and external validity', *Quality and Quantity*, **25**, pp. 381–7.

HAMMERSLEY, M. (1991b) 'A myth of a myth? An assessment of two studies of option choice in secondary schools', *British Journal of Sociology*, **42**, 1, pp. 61–94.

HAMMERSLEY, M. (1992a) 'The researcher as reflective practitioner', Unpublished paper given at the British Educational Research Association annual conference, University of Stirling.

HAMMERSLEY, M. (1992b) *What's Wrong with Ethnography?* London: Routledge.

HAMMERSLEY, M. (1993a) 'An appraisal of "Labouring to learn"', in GOMM, R. and WOODS, P. (eds) *Educational Research in Action*, London: Paul Chapman.

HAMMERSLEY, M. (1993b) 'On methodological purism', *British Educational Research Journal*, **19**, 4, pp. 339–41.

HAMMERSLEY, M. (1993c) 'On the teacher as researcher', *Educational Action Research*, **1**, 3, pp. 425–45.

HAMMERSLEY, M. (1995) *The Politics of Social Research*, London: Sage.

HAMMERSLEY, M. (1997b) 'Educational research and teaching: A response to David Hargreaves' TTA lecture', *British Educational Research Journal*, **23**, 2, pp. 141–61.

HAMMERSLEY, M. and GOMM, R. (1993) 'A response to Gillborn and Drew on "race", class and school effects', *New Community*, **19**, 2, pp. 348–53.

HAMMERSLEY, M. and SCARTH, J. (1986) *The Impact of Examinations on Secondary School Teaching: A Research Report*, School of Education: Open University.

HAMMERSLEY, M., SCARTH, J. and WEBB, S. (1985) 'Developing and testing theory: The case of research on pupil learning and examinations', in BURGESS, R.G. (ed.) *Issues in Educational Research: Qualitative Methods*, London: Falmer.

HARGREAVES, D.H. (1967) *Social Relations in a Secondary School*, London: Routledge and Kegan Paul.

HARGREAVES, D.H. (1996) 'Teaching as a research-based profession', Teacher Training Agency Annual Lecture.

KVALE, S. (ed.) (1989) *Validity Issues in Qualitative Research*, Stockholm: Studentsliterature.

LACEY, C. (1970) *Hightown Grammar*, Manchester: Manchester University Press.

LATHER, P. (1986) 'Issues of validity in openly ideological research', *Interchange*, **17**, 4, pp. 63–84.

LATHER, P. (1993) 'Fertile obsession: Validity after poststructuralism', *Sociological Quarterly*, **34**, 4, pp. 673–93.

LOFLAND, J. (1970) 'Interactionist imagery and analytic interruptus', in SHIBUTANI, T. (ed.) *Human Nature and Collective Behaviour*, Englewood Cliffs NJ: Prentice Hall.

MERTON, R.K. (1973) *The Sociology of Science*, Chicago: University of Chicago Press.

NORRIS, N. (1995) 'Contracts, control and evaluation', *Journal of Education Policy*, **10**, 3, pp. 271–85.

OLIVER, M. (1992) 'Changing the social relations of research production?', *Disability, Handicap and Society*, **7**, 2, pp. 101–14.

OPEN UNIVERSITY (1979) *DE304 Research Methods in Education and the Social Sciences*, Milton Keynes: The Open University.

PETTIGREW, M. (1994) 'Coming to terms with research: The contract business', in HALPIN, D. and TROYNA, B. (eds) *Researching Education Policy: Ethical and Methodological Issues*, London: Falmer Press.

PHILLIPS, D.C. (1989) 'Subjectivity and objectivity: An objective inquiry', in EISNER, E.W. and PESHKIN, A. (eds) *Qualitative Inquiry in Education: The Continuing Debate*, New York: Teachers College Press.

SMITH, D.J. and TOMLINSON, S. (1989) *The School Effect*, London: Policy Studies Institute.

SMITH, J.K. (1993) *After the Demise of Empiricism: The Problem of Judging Social and Educational Inquiry*, Norwood, NJ: Ablex.

TROYNA, B. (1991) 'Children, "race", and racism: The limitations of research and policy', *British Journal of Educational Studies*, **39**, 4, pp. 425–36.

TROYNA, B. (1993) 'Underachiever or misunderstood? A reply to Roger Gomm', *British Educational Research Journal*, **19**, 2, pp. 167–74.

TROYNA, B. (1994) 'Reforms, research and being reflexive about being reflective', in HALPIN, D. and TROYNA, B. (eds) *Researching Education Policy: Ethical and Methodological Issues*, London: Falmer Press.

TROYNA, B. (1995) 'Beyond reasonable doubt? Researching "race" in educational settings', *Oxford Review of Education*, **21**, 4, pp. 395–408.

WELLMAN, D.T. (1977) *Portraits of White Racism*, Cambridge: Cambridge University Press.

11   The Director's Tale: Developing Teams and Themes in a Research Centre

Robert G. Burgess

> I should not have entered the world of research contacts with such naivety. Despite that nearly all my previous work had consisted of investigation in person, or sometimes supervision of the individual work of students, I should not have underestimated the extent to which this was a different world, a world in which my perception of academic research and the management of scholarship would need realignment. (Wakeford, 1984, pp. 131–2)

These opening remarks are drawn from an autobiographical statement written by John Wakeford over 10 years ago about the management of team-based social research. His comments echo my own experience, not only in managing a research team, but also in establishing a range of teams in a research centre. For most researchers in the social sciences the conduct of social research focuses on the work of the lone scholar. This is epitomized in our experience of working on a doctoral thesis where the student works alone with a supervisor and is often engaged in small-scale empirical studies. Certainly, this was my experience in the 1970s. Subsequently, academics engaged in empirical social research often continue to conduct their studies themselves. Indeed this was my own experience in the 1980s when I decided to engage in a re-study of the school that I had initially studied in the 1970s (Burgess, 1987). In addition, I had also developed a research team, composed of one researcher and one secretary, who worked with me on a project concerning the mentally handicapped in residential homes (Candappa and Burgess, 1989). This was my only experience of team-based research in 15 years.

The opportunity to establish a research centre in the 1980s gave me the chance to think about a number of issues in the social sciences which I had not encountered before. In addition, it gave me the opportunity to develop major strands of social research that would take up a series of intellectual challenges and intellectual problems that I had begun to think about. However, I needed a range of projects to engage in such work. The consequence of taking the opportunity to develop a research centre was that I automatically became involved in a world of sponsorship and research grants, the development of teams of researchers and research careers, and fundamentally, the development of a series of substantive and methodological interests that could be explored across a range of research projects. But how was all this to be developed and to what extent has it been achieved? It is the purpose of this chapter to explore some of these themes by focusing on my involvement in the development of the Centre for Educational Development, Appraisal and Research (CEDAR) at the University of Warwick over a 10-year period.

Developing a Research Centre

In the academic year 1986–87 the then Faculty of Education at Warwick established a working party to think about the possibility of establishing a new research centre. The remit of the group was to explore the possibility of establishing a centre that would encapsulate a series of major themes which were considered by members of the working group to be high on the policy agenda. The themes identified were: assessment, appraisal and evaluation. I had been invited to be a member of the working group so that it had representation from the Faculty of Social Studies. During the course of our discussions it was argued that the Centre should draw on the expertise available at Warwick in two faculties, Education and Social Studies, and in turn that the Centre should focus on contemporary issues in educational research. However, it was clear that the way in which these issues and themes could be moulded together would be a decision of the new Director. Subsequently, I was invited by the then Director of the Institute of Education at Warwick to have discussions with him about the possibility of taking on the Directorship of the Centre. It was to be a half-time post whereby I would be seconded for half my time from the Department of Sociology to establish the new Centre, which would be physically located in the Faculty of Education, but intellectually located as a social science/education activity. The opportunity was considerable. Here was the chance to develop a range of academic enquiries around topics that had been of central interest to me. The detail of the Centre was such that as long as the topics assessment, appraisal and evaluation were included, I was free to develop my interests through the Centre.

At that stage, I realized that funding would have to be obtained, but I had not thought through the consequences of finding funds from a range of bodies: local education authorities, trusts, charities and the Economic and Social Research Council. Instead, my concern was to get the intellectual content of the Centre right and in turn, to think of a title for the Centre that would reflect the work that was to be developed. I was convinced that if I brought together social science and education, it was important that there should be a focus on basic and applied research. Secondly, I was of the view that research activity should also underpin any educational development work in which members of the Centre might become involved. Finally, I considered that such work also needed to bring together, not only a range of academic staff in the University, but also practitioners who would engage in research — a theme that I had worked on in earlier years (Burgess, 1980).

Having thought through the topics that would be included in the Centre, I turned to thinking about a title. This proved much more difficult. It was evident that any title would quickly be shortened, so an acronym was essential. It took several evenings to play around with a range of words that would reflect my interests and the main intellectual themes of the Centre, and in turn would also accurately reflect the kinds of activities that would go on within the new Centre. It was on this basis that the acronym CEDAR was developed as it included one of the topics (appraisal) that had been listed as part of the research agenda by the original working party. Secondly, it included the words educational development, which picked up notions of inservice training and teachers engaged in research, and finally the all important word research to signal that fundamental work would be conducted which would allow Centre staff to make links to a range of disciplines in the social sciences and education. On this basis, CEDAR was established and was ready to open as a cross-faculty, multidisciplinary centre from 1 October 1987. The aims of the Centre were well summarized in its early documentation which stated:

- the Centre conducts basic and applied research in the field of education and training. The activities of the Centre, therefore, include work on issues and problems that confront schools, colleges and educational personnel;
- policy questions;
- and basic research on theories and methods of research and evaluation. Such a range of research work involves CEDAR staff in a variety of activities including:

  (a) studies of appraisal, assessment and evaluation which link to theory, policy and practice;
  (b) inservice and development work with headteachers, teachers, advisers, inspectors, trainers and staff in further and higher education;
  (c) theoretical and methodological studies that are appropriate for the analysis of educational settings.

  Research is central to all CEDAR's activities and is related to policy and practice.

The agenda for the Centre, therefore, brought together a series of themes — theory, methodology, policy and practice — which could be developed through a range of studies, some of which would be in the fields of assessment, appraisal and evaluation and others that would take up educational topics within and beyond the study of schooling (a theme that I had explored in earlier work to demonstrate that education was not co-terminus with schooling; Burgess, 1986).

The Centre was poised to open on 1 October, but there was still much to be done. Sponsorship had to be obtained in many different forms, staff had to be appointed, and most importantly, projects had to be established that would link to some of the themes. It was this task that was clearly a crucial element for the role of Director.

Sponsorship

Whenever researchers talk about sponsorship, the conversation immediately turns to research grants and, in the case of research centres, this usually means core funding from a research council. In CEDAR's case there were more fundamental issues to get established. First, it was important that the Centre had a physical presence and, from that point of view, rooms needed to be allocated. But even this was not easy. Where should the Centre be located? In Social Science or in Education? In turn, once it had been decided that it would be physically located in Education, in what area? Here sponsorship was essential and it was the then Director of the Institute of Education, John Tomlinson, who agreed to allow CEDAR to have two rooms within the allocation of rooms granted to the Institute. Secondly, if the Centre was to have a physical presence, it needed good communications. Rooms and furniture might be one thing, but equipment, a telephone and notepaper also had to be made available. Once again, the Institute of Education came to the rescue as an initial supply of notepaper was purchased on CEDAR's behalf. Thirdly, equipment came from the Sociology Department, who loaned the Centre an electric typewriter (with a broken key) that was no longer in use in the Department. With this initial endowment CEDAR started life, but if it was to develop, staff needed to be recruited. The first task was to have someone who would work alongside the Director and a Centre Secretary was, therefore, seen to be essential for this to occur. But how was such a post to be funded? An application was made to the University's Research and Innovations Fund in order to pay for a Centre Secretary and also to have a small amount of money that could be used for travel, xeroxing, postage and telephones. The sum of £5,000 each year was allocated to the Centre for a two-year period. This allowed the position of Centre Secretary to be advertised on a part-time basis and by late October 1987 it was possible to have a secretary who spent two-and-a-half days per week working for the Centre. In addition, the university also seconded the Director by giving an additional half-lectureship to the Department of Education so that they could repay Sociology for the loss of half a member of staff.

Having put in place some staffing, it was important to attract research grants. The first grant to be held in the Centre came from the West Midlands Examination Board and allowed the Centre to examine an aspect of educational assessment in its first project. However, the late 1980s was also the time when local education authorities still had money to spend on a range of educational evaluations. In particular, it was government policy to require local education authorities to evaluate much of their work with the result that an independent evaluation was often a condition of an LEA receiving a grant. From CEDAR's point of view this was fortunate, as it not only gave the opportunity to obtain an income stream from which staff could be appointed, but also provided an opportunity to take up one of the other themes that was outlined in its original plan, namely educational evaluation.

This was the work that needed to be done in the academic year 1987–88 when one project was in place from 1 January 1988. During the course of that academic year I visited a range of local education authorities across the country talking about the services that the Centre could provide and the projects that we could offer. The result was a series of project grants from Salford, Solihull, Coventry, Warwickshire and Buckinghamshire, but sponsorship came not only in the form of grant income, but also in the form of staff, as many of the local authorities were enthusiastic about having staff trained in the areas of research and evaluation. This allowed CEDAR to exploit a further theme in its original manifesto and took up an area in which I had direct experience and expertise — teacher-based research. While this was to become an important feature of the Centre's work, it was also an important element involved in developing research staff and creating a series of teams.

Creating a Team or Teams?

While it has been traditional within the natural sciences and engineering for researchers to be trained to work in teams, even when doing doctoral work (Pole, Sprokkereef, Burgess and Lakin, 1997), this has been rare within the social sciences. Indeed, the experience of the lone researcher is recorded in numerous autobiographical accounts of the research process in the social sciences (see, for example, Bell and Newby, 1977; Burgess, 1984b; Bell and Roberts, 1984; Burgess, 1990; Walford, 1987 and 1991). In CEDAR this was no exception. My experience had been predominantly in the lone research mode or in working in a very small team. With the creation of CEDAR, I had an opportunity to develop work on a much larger canvas, but if my plans were to be achieved, funding was essential. Within research centres funded by the ESRC the Director is given a budget and has an opportunity to appoint a core staff for periods up to five years in the first instance. In a 'soft money' centre such as CEDAR, it is dependent upon the Director and, in turn, other staff to generate research income in order to recruit academic and secretarial staff. On this basis, the choice of staff in CEDAR was critical to the operation. The staffing profile in the first ten years is detailed in Table 11.1.

From the beginning it was important to think of the recruitment of a range of academic staff. First, researchers who could work on individual projects, but who had the ambition and the ability to work in a research centre on a range of activities. Secondly, teachers and other professionals seconded from full-time positions to work in CEDAR alongside research staff. Thirdly, academics who wanted visiting status in the Centre, but who would work alongside permanent academic staff. Fourthly, academic visitors from other countries who wanted the experience of working in the UK and who would be prepared to

Table 11.1: CEDAR Staffing 1987–96

	1987	1988	1989	1990	1991	1992	1993	1994	1995	1996
Academic Staff (inc Associate and Visiting Fellows)	1	7	11.5	12	12	11	13	16	12	12
Secondments	—	3	—	1	—	1	1	—	—	—
Consultants	—	1	—	1	2	3	1	1	2	1
Secretarial Staff	1	5	5	4	4	4	5	5	4	3
				(plus temporary clerical staff)						
TOTAL	2	16	16.5	18	18	19	20	22	18	16

Notes:
1. Academic Staff are expressed as full-time equivalents.
2. The Centre has a database that contains the names of over 100 consultants on whom the Centre can draw to work on short-term projects or specialist aspects of major projects.
3. Consultants are used when the Centre is offered work that requires additional support alongside 'core' staff.

work on CEDAR projects. In this respect, the academic staff in the Centre consisted of those who were appointed to full-time positions, those who were seconded for periods of time and visitors. The seconded staff and the academic visitors were not on the payroll but participated fully in projects. In addition, a number of consultants were also hired in order to assist Centre staff in periods when there was a large volume of work.

The initial staff who were appointed to the Centre had to be recruited within the budget of a series of small-scale qualitative projects. This automatically placed constraints on the kind of people who could be recruited. First, they needed to be people who could work effectively as a team. Secondly, they needed to have the background which would allow them to meet some of the objectives of the Centre. Among the staff appointed in 1988, only one person had previously worked as a full-time researcher. All the others had some teaching experience in their backgrounds (often in schools and occasionally in colleges) and had successfully completed a master's degree. Many were also looking to register for doctoral studies.

At first glance this may be seen as problematic: however, it was turned to an advantage. The aims and objectives of CEDAR meant that we required individuals with research skills who would also be credible in schools. In addition, we needed people who were wanting to develop a research repertoire and, therefore, could be moulded to the kind of projects and methodologies that were to be the focus of the Centre. These were the criteria that were kept in mind when making the initial appointments and have served us well. Of the staff that were appointed in 1988, one person stayed for five years, working on a range of projects which involved having contracts as long as two years and as little as one month. Nevertheless, during that period the individual was never unemployed and worked on a range of projects that linked together methodologically as well as substantively. In this respect, staff in CEDAR acquired a range of research experience and a variety of skills through the work that was taken on in a range of projects that were predominantly sponsored by local education authorities. Indeed, three more members of staff have remained at CEDAR throughout the period. Two of them hold joint posts with the Sociology Department within the University. It might appear that these staff spend half their time on research and half their time on teaching. However, in practice these appointments ensure that the individuals can spend two-thirds of their time devoted to research activities and allows them to take forward a range of projects and project work, building on their earlier experiences. Indeed, many staff who have worked in CEDAR have now achieved a doctorate and have moved to positions in higher education institutions in Britain and overseas. In that sense, CEDAR has built up a network of individuals to complement those who have stayed at Warwick. But what kind of substantive and methodological work has been developed?

Developing Substantive Themes

The pattern of funding within a centre such as CEDAR means that there is a danger that the Director and his staff are always seeking projects that will fund staff time to keep people in full-time employment. Such an activity could be mindless. The result would be a research centre that was little more than a labour exchange. This was not the way in which CEDAR wished to develop and, as a consequence, the work has always focused on a series of major themes, which are illustrated in Table 11.2.

While CEDAR has covered a range of projects about education over the years from nursery schooling to higher education, there have also been a number of central themes that are summarized in Table 11.2. In the first three years of CEDAR's existence, local education authorities needed evaluations conducted on inservice education and training. It was my view that this was an area that had not been examined by social scientists in any depth. Indeed, one social scientist told me that it was such low-level work that I should not bother to take it on. For me, this underlined the challenge. It was an area that could be explored productively in order to look at the different dimensions of inservice work. It also had several other attractions. First, it allowed us to look at inservice activity as an academic endeavour which subsequently could then be picked up through development work which would be underpinned by our research. Secondly, the evaluations involved working across several local education authorities. The approach which was taken involved case studies that allowed us to develop multi-site case-study investigations. Thirdly, while there were a number of individuals working in different authorities, these people could constitute a team that could learn from one another, especially in the early

Table 11.2: Major themes in CEDAR work 1988–97

1   Inservice evaluation → Supply Teachers → Professionalism, Teacher Professionalism and Training in Higher Education

2   Legal Education → Work Place Education → Higher Level Vocational Qualifications

3   GCSE Coursework → Coursework and the Use of Libraries → Primary School Libraries → Further Education Libraries → Public Libraries and Ethnic Minorities

4   Postgraduate Education and Training in the Social Sciences → Postgraduate Education and Training in the Natural Sciences and Engineering → Postgraduate Education and Training in Business Studies and Engineering Within Ten European Societies

days. An added bonus was that researchers and teachers seconded from local authorities also worked on these evaluation projects, thus bringing together different kinds of expertise.

On the basis of this work there was a further challenge through the writing process. First, the research team were required to produce reports that would be accessible to teachers and members of local authorities (Morrison, 1989; Galloway, 1989; Newton, 1989; Connor, 1989). However, this only told part of the story. In my view a volume was needed that brought together our experience from across a range of projects. We were fortunate to be able to continue to work together to explore our data and the approach that we had used in different sites when we subsequently produced the volume, *Implementing In-Service Education and Training* (Burgess, Connor, Galloway, Morrison and Newton, 1993). The publication of this work was not the end of the story. Two of the researchers (Galloway and Morrison) decided that they wished to explore some of the implications surrounding teacher supply that had arisen in their interviews in the different authorities. As a consequence, they devised a project that looked at supply work among teachers in a range of local authorities. It extended the work that had been done in the initial inservice evaluation and moved forward by linking with a literature on teachers, teaching and teacher professionalism. The project was proposed to the Leverhulme Trust and resulted in funding for two years for both researchers and allowed them to develop a series of publications, including the supply story (Galloway and Morrison, 1994), which not only broke new ground with regard to the substantive area but also led to methodological developments through focusing on the use of diaries. In turn, further work of a comparative kind has also been planned to take place in the future, thus developing a line of research enquiry from inservice evaluation studies.

Another strand in CEDAR's work was the idea that education was not to be equated with schooling. In these circumstances, I looked for ways in which CEDAR could develop a variety of different work which took us outside of schools. This line of inquiry is exemplified through studies on legal education and workplace education. It could be argued that these are disconnected projects, however, legal education has led to an interest in this substantive area whereby two further projects are being developed. One project looks at legal training and another focuses on vocational training among solicitors. Meanwhile, a study of workplace education has also fed into our knowledge of continuing professional development and training. Seemingly disconnected themes are, therefore, linked together across a range of projects.

Another line of inquiry that has been developed in the last 10 years has concerned libraries in different phases of the school system. However, its starting point came through some work that the Centre conducted on assessment. The first grant obtained by CEDAR concerned the introduction of coursework in GCSE. Subsequently, material in the popular press indicated that students in schools that had introduced GCSE coursework were having considerable difficulties, given the inadequacies of school libraries. It seemed to me that this was an area for investigation and gave rise to the first proposal on libraries which concerned the use of libraries in GCSE coursework. Having completed a project on secondary school libraries, the terrain moved to consider the use of libraries, the distribution and dissemination of knowledge within secondary and primary schools, and, in turn, further education. This concern with libraries also generated an interest between ourselves and another centre (the Centre for Research in Ethnic Relations), which was interested in the ethnic dimension in library use — a research problem that had been generated out of the professional interest of a member of staff in the other centre. It was possible for CEDAR, with its track record in research on libraries in schools, to link with the professional expertise available in CRER on ethnicity and on libraries to produce a project proposal that focused on public libraries and their use by ethnic minority groups. In addition, CEDAR has also been able to successfully tender for a library project that focuses on the use of libraries in the context of lifelong learning — a topic that not only links to the school-based work that has been done, but also forward into further and higher education and the concept of the learning city.

Several of the lines of enquiry have touched in some ways on post-school education. For example, the way in which studies concerning evaluation have subsequently led to developments in the field of training in higher education. Here there is a link with another important strand of CEDAR work which partly stems from an academic interest and partly out of personal experience. I have always advocated that the sociological study of education cannot be restricted to schooling (Burgess, 1986). Accordingly, I was interested in conducting a series of studies in higher education. An opportunity arose through an ESRC programme on postgraduate education and training to look at postgraduate study. This area not only fitted intellectually, in terms of post-school education, but also fitted with my personal interest in postgraduate education that stemmed from my experience as a supervisor, as a member of the ESRC Postgraduate Training Board and in turn as the individual who founded the Warwick Graduate School. In this respect, developing projects in the field of postgraduate education and training brought together intellectual interests, professional experience and personal interest.

A line of development has appeared in the Centre's work since the early 1990s, when we have engaged in studies concerning postgraduate education and training in the social sciences (Burgess, 1994a) and subsequently in the natural sciences and engineering (Pole et al., 1997; Sprokkereef, Lakin, Pole and Burgess, 1995). In turn, I was of the view that we needed to set our predominantly UK work in a broader context. This was encouraged by the appointment of a member of staff from Continental Europe who encouraged the Centre to think more about ways in which projects could be broadened to include an international dimension. One area in which this seemed possible was the area of postgraduate education and training. Here I developed a network of sociologists and educationalists from a range of European countries in order that a 10-country study could be developed on postgraduate education and training in Europe, focused on policy-making and case studies of postgraduate training in departments of business studies and engineering. However, the project also contained two other components. First, the development of an international team of social scientists engaged in case-study work. Second, a programme of training in qualitative methods. In this respect, the programme of work on postgraduate education and training brought together substantive, developmental and methodological interests that are a part of the Centre's portfolio of work.

Developing Methodological Themes

In the last 25 years I have been engaged in sociological studies that have used qualitative methods in general, and ethnographic methods in particular. This resulted in a wide range of papers in the 1980s that brought together qualitative work in relation to educational studies (Burgess, 1984b, 1984c, 1985a and 1985b). In addition, I had also written a volume that focused on methodological developments drawing on my work in Sociology and Education (Burgess, 1984a). It was this focus that allowed me to develop a range of methodological work within the Centre. Ethnography, case study and teacher research had all figured in my earlier work. Now these could be developed through a series of projects. There are three particular areas of significance in relation to methodology. They are the use of multi-site case study, the development of diaries and life histories, and the conduct of teacher-based research.

The studies on which I have been engaged in the 1970s and 1980s have focused on the detailed ethnography of one institution (Burgess, 1983; Burgess, 1987). However, when I was engaged in small-scale studies in CEDAR it became evident that no funding body would provide a sufficient grant in order to employ any individual researcher to engage in a detailed ethnography. As a consequence, methodological innovation became important. No longer could case study be equated with 18 months' fieldwork. Instead a range of case studies needed to be developed. In these circumstances, proposals coming from the Centre have focused on the development of multi-site case study. Here, there are several points at issue. First, the development of fieldwork across a range of sites. In some projects this has involved as many as 24 sites. Secondly, the ability to make comparisons between different sites; for example, on the project on Libraries and GCSE coursework, comparisons have been made between four different secondary schools and their library policies (Phtiaka, 1995), and in the case of primary school libraries, the comparison has again been between different sites (Morrison and Scott, 1994). Thirdly, there was the issue of generalization and the extent to which multi-site case study could lead to generalization within the social sciences. These have been some of the issues that have been explored within our projects. However, there has also been another dimension to multi-site case study and that is the development of the research team.

Individual researchers have engaged in individual studies focused on one local authority. Certainly, this was the case in the early inservice evaluations. However, the team of Burgess, Connor, Galloway, Morrison and Newton meant that studies could be conducted across different local authorities and institutions so that case studies could be compared by a team of researchers who worked together. In these circumstances, the team needed to control the topics that were to be investigated, the ways in which the investigations would be conducted and the results reported. At this level, two important dimensions of methodological work were being explored: the use of comparison in multi-site case study work and the methodological lessons that need to be learnt by members of a team working together on a common topic.

However, methodological innovation takes many forms. In my earlier fieldwork I had often looked at the potential of the fieldwork diary and the participant's diary. Now CEDAR had the opportunity to conduct a variety of research through which we could begin to explore different ways in which diaries could be used within different projects. For example, the project concerned with supply teachers led Galloway and Morrison to develop different ways in which teachers could record the context of their work in among many other professional and domestic duties. It was this development that led to them making a contribution to the British Sociological Association's Annual Conference on Methodological Developments within Sociology that was subsequently published in one of the Association's conference volumes (Galloway and Morrison, 1996). In turn, methodological development around the diary has also occurred in a project about food and nutrition in schools, where I have worked with Marlene Morrison on the adaptation of the diary for use with pupils of different ages. How, for example, could we develop a food diary, and how might the food diary be used with primary school children? This has been a methodological area that has been developed within the project, discussed at a range of meetings and published in a volume of material that has been used for teaching purposes by the Open University (Burgess, 1994b). Yet another development has involved the use of life history materials from a project that Christopher Pole has developed on black teachers. Further, historical work is taking place through a project concerning teacher education in the period 1945–72 that is being conducted by Michele Dowling. In this respect, the development of methodology has been an essential feature of many projects, so that the Centre's contributions to the social sciences and education come, not only through a substantive discipline or a substantive topic in the social sciences, but also through methodology.

Another feature that has also been important to the Centre has been the way in which research in the field of education is disseminated and used. This resonates with a topic which was widely discussed in the 1993 White Paper 'Realising Our Potential' (HMSO, 1993). Certainly, for researchers in education, a central problem has been the extent to which research can be developed and used by teachers — a theme developed by Lawrence Stenhouse in the mid-1970s (Stenhouse, 1975) when he argued that teacher development needed to be based on research development. Subsequently, I followed up this theme through a series of articles and work with teachers (Burgess, 1980). In CEDAR there have been opportunities for teachers to become part of several research teams, for teachers to engage in research and for teachers to be trained through our development programmes in a range of methods and techniques in order to conduct evaluations in their own schools and to research their own practice. Indeed, this is the theme that has now come back in the late 1990s and is firmly on the research agenda in regard to the way in which researchers, not only conduct, but also disseminate their work and get their work into the public domain for use by teachers.

Some Problems in Developing and Directing a Research Centre

This account has been based upon different kinds of evidence: sociological, educational, methodological and developmental. It also includes personal experience of research and research management. Together it points to a range of knowledge and skill demanded of those who direct research centres. The task is exciting and demanding but does involve risk and is not unproblematic.

Developing a research centre requires a skilled staff: academics who can work on their own projects and secretaries who can support academic activity. It may sound easy but the reality is much more difficult. The academics who are recruited to a centre such as CEDAR need to have substantive and methodological skills, the ability to work as members of a team and the ability to make links between a range of studies. Without these skills it would be difficult to remain as a member of CEDAR when the researcher has to take on a range of projects covering diverse, substantive topics. Indeed, staff have often had to juggle the demands of different projects simultaneously, as it does not always work that individuals can be employed full-time on one project. Similarly, secretarial staff are often working on more than one project making research appointments for academic staff, keeping transcriptions up to date and meeting deadlines for the delivery of final reports to sponsors. The task is exacting for all concerned.

Working in this academic 'hot-house' often involves risks. Relatively few staff have permanent contracts, yet it is essential for those who work in the

Centre to be re-engaged, not only for their own livelihood and to establish a career but also to offer continuity of experience to the Centre in developing themes. If this is not achieved, new staff have to be appointed which involves a large investment of time from the Director and other more senior staff in providing training.

This may appear puzzling and some readers may ask: 'Do those staff appointed to the Centre need training?' Here, the kind of work determines the need to adapt skills that have been acquired. For example, researchers who have engaged in long-term studies need to know how to develop short cuts whilst maintaining methodological rigour in short-term multi-site studies. Learning to do case study in one institution is useful preparation for multi-site case study but the time-scales are shorter across numerous sites. In these circumstances, the researcher needs to know how to make the most of short, intensive field trips and how to use data that are drawn from numerous sites.

In turn, there are also demands made of the Director. First, income has to be generated from a range of projects in order to maintain continuity of employment for a range of staff. As a consequence I may be involved in a range of projects for a very small number of days contributing to project design, research, access and writing. This has produced challenges when managing qualitative studies where I have not gained first-hand experience of the sites by conducting fieldwork. In these circumstances my task is closer to that of secondary data analysis. In addition, project writing may involve linking together the work of disparate team members who have a range of skills and writing expertise. Indeed, the volume on *Implementing In-Service Education* (Burgess et al., 1993) was one such challenge with researchers and seconded teachers who had not produced a book before. The challenge involved getting the team to work together, to focus on key conceptual areas across a range of projects and to write in a way which brought coherence to the study. Certainly, this book was a long time in the making and took longer than any other authored volume in which I have been involved.

Finally, there are demands on time for any centre director — establishing new projects while finishing others, appointing new staff while developing the careers of established staff, marking out new areas of research which link with established projects, and maintaining research networks while establishing others. The role of research director is never dull and involves the skills of academic, researcher, personnel manager, and quasi-accountant in equal measure. Here, academic credibility is essential as the other roles are acquired through 'on the job' training and 'learning by doing'. In short, the director is the juggler in the team!

A Decade of Achievement?

In writing this chapter, I have been forced to select from the numerous projects that we have conducted in CEDAR over the last 10 years. There have been many projects that have been omitted from view that have contributed substantively and methodologically. For example, work on records of achievement (Pole, 1993) which developed our interest in a substantive field led to further work on multi-site case study and also made a contribution to data analysis (Burgess, Pole, Evans and Priestley, 1994). In this respect, when the Centre is evaluated, what needs to be considered is the way in which a range of activity that has taken place brings together a methodological core in the social sciences, a series of substantive interests in education and in turn a body of development work with teachers. These three strands have formed important points of development in CEDAR's work. But how has this been achieved? Much depends on the mix of academic and secretarial staff, bringing together those who are developing an academic record as researchers, professionals who wish to engage in research and international visitors who conceptualize the work in a wider arena and provide CEDAR with points of contact world-wide. This is an important feature of the Centre and will continue to be important as the work develops.

But what is the way forward? What are the key topics on the agenda in the future? Certainly, CEDAR has employed contract researchers, many of whom have gone on to full-time jobs elsewhere, as research staff in other institutions or as academics that bring together research and teaching. Many of those individuals now demonstrate through their teaching and research the themes that have arisen in CEDAR's portfolio: a focus on methodology, especially qualitative methodology, and an interest in a range of substantive topics in education that are not restricted to schools and schooling. At CEDAR, in common with many other 'soft money' centres, there is still the problem of finding ways in which to develop research careers, to build intellectual challenges and to develop research teams, so as new appointments are made to the Centre, the portfolio of activity develops. New methodologies can be devised and new sets of findings can contribute to the academic development of sociology and education, as well as the development of policy and practice.

Acknowledgment

This chapter draws on the work of all staff who have worked in CEDAR over a decade and to whom I am very grateful for the ways in which we have developed a range of research ideas together. In producing this chapter, I have been fortunate to have the excellent support of Karen Stokes who is our third Centre Secretary — a crucial role in any Centre.

References

BELL, C. and NEWBY, H. (eds) (1977) *Doing Sociological Research*, London: Allen & Unwin.
BELL, C. and ROBERTS, H. (eds) (1984) *Social Researching*, London: Routledge.

Robert G. Burgess

BURGESS, R.G. (ed.) (1980) 'Teacher-based research', *Insight* (special issue), **3**, 3.

BURGESS, R.G. (1983) *Experiencing Comprehensive Education: A Study of Bishop McGregor School*, London: Methuen.

BURGESS, R.G. (1984a) *In the Field: An Introduction to Field Research*, London: Allen & Unwin.

BURGESS, R.G. (ed.) (1984b) *The Research Process in Educational Settings: Ten Case Studies*, London: Falmer Press.

BURGESS, R.G. (ed.) (1984c) *Field Methods in the Study of Education*, London: Falmer Press.

BURGESS, R.G. (ed.) (1985a) *Strategies of Educational Research*, London: Falmer Press.

BURGESS, R.G. (ed.) (1985b) *Issues in Educational Research*, London: Falmer Press.

BURGESS, R.G. (1986) *Sociology, Education and Schools*, London: Batsford.

BURGESS, R.G. (1987) 'Studying and re-studying Bishop McGregor School', in WALFORD, G. (ed.) *Doing Sociology of Education*, London: Falmer Press.

BURGESS, R.G. (ed.) (1990) *Learning from the Field*, London: JAI Press.

BURGESS, R.G. (ed.) (1994a) *Postgraduate Education and Training in the Social Sciences: Processes and Products*, London: Jessica Kingsley.

BURGESS, R.G. (1994b) 'On diaries and diary keeping', in BENNETT, N., GLATTER, R. and LEVACIC, R. (eds) *Improving Educational Management Through Research and Consultancy*, London: Paul Chapman, pp. 300–12.

BURGESS, R.G., CONNOR, J., GALLOWAY, S., MORRISON, M. and NEWTON, M. (1993) *Implementing In-Service Education and Training*, London: Falmer Press.

BURGESS, R.G., POLE, C., EVANS, K. and PRIESTLEY, C. (1994) 'Four studies from one or one study from four? Multi-site case study research', in BRYMAN, A. and BURGESS, R.G. (eds) *Analysing Qualitative Data*, London: Routledge, pp. 129–45.

CANDAPPA, M. and BURGESS, R.G. (1989) '"I'm not handicapped, I'm different": "Normalisation", hospital care and mental handicap', in BARTON, L. (ed.) *Disability and Dependency*, London: Falmer Press, pp. 69–83.

CONNOR, J. (1989) *Implementing INSET: A Case Study of a Local Education Authority*, CEDAR Report No. 3, Coventry: University of Warwick.

GALLOWAY, S. (1989) *Identifying INSET Needs: The Case of Solihull Schools*, CEDAR Report No. 5, Coventry: University of Warwick.

GALLOWAY, S. and MORRISON, M. (eds) (1994) *The Supply Story*, London: Falmer Press.

GALLOWAY, S. and MORRISON, M. (1996) 'Researching moving targets: Using diaries to explore supply teachers' lives', in LYONS, E.S. and BUSFIELD, J. (eds) *Methodological Imaginations*, Basingstoke: Macmillan, pp. 34–57.

HMSO (1993) *Realising Our Potential*, London: HMSO.

MORRISON, M. (1989) *School-Focused INSET: A Case Study of Salford LEA*, CEDAR Report No. 2, Coventry: University of Warwick.

MORRISON, M. and SCOTT, D. (1994) *Libraries for Learning*, London: British Library.

NEWTON, M. (1989) *Evaluation Strategies in School Focused Training*, CEDAR Report No. 4, Coventry: University of Warwick.

PHTIAKA, H. (1995) *The Beginning of a Beautiful Friendship: The School Library and the GCSE*, London: British Library.

POLE, C. (1993) *Assessing and Recording Achievement*, Buckingham: Open University Press.

POLE, C., SPROKKEREEF, A., BURGESS, R.G. and LAKIN, E. (1997) 'Supervision of doctoral students in the natural sciences: Expectations and experiences', *Assessment and Evaluation in Higher Education*, **22**, 1, pp. 49–63.

SPROKKEREEF, A., LAKIN, E., POLE, C. and BURGESS, R.G. (1995) 'The data, the team and the ethnograph', in BURGESS, R.G. (ed.) *Computing and Qualitative Research*, London: JAI Press, pp. 81–104.

WAKEFORD, J. (1984) 'A Director's dilemma', in BURGESS, R.G. (ed.) *Field Methods in the Study of Education*, London: Falmer Press, pp. 131–8.

WALFORD, G. (ed.) (1987) *Doing Sociology of Education*, London: Falmer Press.

WALFORD, G. (ed.) (1991) *Doing Educational Research*, London: Routledge.

12 The 'Last Blue Mountain'? Doing Educational Research in a Contract Culture

Valerie Wilson

This chapter has outlined some of the main problems that can impede good fieldwork. Each researcher faces their own personal 'last blue mountain barred with snow', and has to deal with it. Flecker's pilgrims had the right idea, because they set out undeterred by mountains saying 'surely we are brave'. The good qualitative researcher can emulate the pilgrims, and struggle across the 'last blue mountain'. (Delamont, 1992, p. 49)

Background

As I have become more familiar with educational research literature, an identifiable gap emerges. The available literature could be divided into two discrete areas: firstly, numerous 'how to do' books aimed at helping the lone postgraduate student complete an academic thesis, for example Cohen and Manion (1994), which have been written in a 'readerly style' (Sumara and Luce-Kapler, 1993); and secondly, collections of papers on particular research methods typically recording conference proceedings or drawing together previously published papers on specialist topics edited by a well-known educational researcher (Burgess, 1985), also written in an authoritative manner. Management of educational contract research was conspicuously absent; so too was any inkling that the research process was anything but smooth with published accounts of disagreements tending to focus on inter- rather than intra-team conflict (Troyna, 1994). Rather surprisingly, Brown and Wake (1988), in their book published on the 60th anniversary of the founding of the Scottish Council for Research in Education 'to celebrate professional researchers', exclude any reference to the terms and conditions of researchers' employment. Additionally, a search of the ERIC system using the key words 'managing research' yielded not a single reference.

Why, when so much funded research is undertaken within teams of contract researchers, which perforce require managing to produce a research output, have researchers been so silent on this particular topic? How are researchers to make sense of this situation when they find themselves — as Lather (1993) argues 'poised at the end of the twentieth century in search of a discourse to help chart the journey from the present to the future' (p. 673) but also sur-rounded by 'a shift in responsibility from representing things in themselves to representing the web of structure, sign and play of social relations' (Derrida, 1978, quoted in Lather, 1993, p. 675)? I began to wonder whether there was a way of managing an educational research project within the confines of time, resources and funder's expectations, which does not surrender to 'conformative evaluation' (Stronach and Morris, 1994) but leads to new ways of seeing the 'mundane acts of compromise and invention in contract evaluative research' (Stronach, Allan and Morris, 1996).

This, then, is the subject to be explored: a search for insights into the management of the contract research process through a detailed exploration of a particular project. The purpose is two-fold: firstly, to describe briefly the experiences of conducting an evaluation of the entrance examination to a national organization; but primarily to explore the metaphorical peaks, crevasses and avalanches which may engulf the contract educational researcher. I utilize the experiences gained from the project to explore reflectively the issues which await the unwary, and ask the reader to engage in a 'writerly' way by filling in the spaces in my text with their own research experiences.

Beginnings

The chapter has a number of beginnings. Firstly, I read *Touching the Void* by Joe Simpson: ostensibly, an account of two men climbing in the Andes but primarily a story of human relationships. The two climbers recount their per-ceptions of that crucial moment when one cuts the rope which connects them in their joint endeavour to climb a mountain. The remainder of the book becomes a fight against the peaks, crevasses and avalanches which stand between the climbers and safety. Interestingly, the metaphor of mountain climb-ing is utilized by Delamont (1992) to describe barriers to fieldwork in educa-tional settings. She suggests that the researcher may, as in Flecker's poem, perceive the difficulties as the 'last blue mountain barred with snow' which faced the pilgrims. Delamont's metaphor is very attractive, almost seductive, in its evocation of an image of one final hurdle which the researcher/pilgrim must surmount and then all will be revealed. However, perhaps, it is Simpson's picture of 'just another mountain', fraught with dangers, which better reflects the reality of the contract research process.

But, however evocative of a more leisurely research age the metaphors used by other writers are, do they really help us understand the current reality which research teams face? As researchers we espouse the value of experien-tial learning and the concept of *constant comparison* (Glaser and Strauss, 1967) to describe the process by which data, concepts and insights from one research project are carried over to inform new ones, yet we hide our personal experiences within a language which abounds with metaphors, is often 'dense' or impenetrable, and demonstrates a degree of self-censorship to the point of mendacity. For example, in an otherwise exciting paper on the concept of 'transgressive validity', Stronach et al. (1996) provide not even a passing reference to the management of their research team. Are we to assume, rightly or wrongly, that three researchers (Stronach, Allan and Morris) eschewed managing 'these rhetorical spaces — otherwise called projects, contracts, programmes or evaluations' in favour of deconstructing their meanings in terms of another metaphor — the games researchers play? They identify at least three games which researchers may play: the first is the traditional game based upon a lengthy apprenticeship and long-term research projects; the second, using condensed fieldwork is simply an abbreviated form of the first game; and, finally, the third game represents a desire to develop new rules to meet the new situation. While recognizing the inherent stress for 'players' schooled in one game who are transferred to a second or third game, Stronach et al. (1996) neglect the pressures and conflict which may exist within teams: the very possibility has been subsumed within the post-modernist discourse demonstrated in their article.

However, my primary aim here is not to criticize other researchers but to compare my management of a funded evaluation — my research team's effort to climb just one more mountain — with a retrospective account of the evaluation process. It is both retrospective and contemporary. The former tells the story of a research project; it details the challenges, compromises and shortcuts which I *knowingly* undertook as an integral part of my pragmatic and performative role as a manager of research contracts. On the other hand, my retrospective concerns will, I hope, be more than just a post hoc justification of my own behaviour, and will develop some insights into the interrelationship between contract research and the construction of meanings at a time when notions of linear progress and modernity have been seriously undermined.

And finally, I wish to reflect on the conventionality of many reports of educational research including ones which I have authored. If reporting educational research is to be meaningful, then perhaps, at least within a book aimed at the research community, some of the conventions of research reporting may legitimately be challenged or even abandoned. In this chapter, I wish to write a more 'writerly text' (Sumara and Luce-Kapler, 1993) to fill with my own reflections taken from my research notes written during the evaluation to fill gaps in the literature. Data from a specific evaluation will be juxtaposed, some might argue conflated, with extracts from my fieldnotes, analytic memos, and retrospective reflections shared with the project's research officer, who wishes to remain anonymous. Sumara and Luce-Kapler (1993) suggest that reading is rarely a passive activity but that as we read, we constantly 'rewrite' the text. They argue that:

> Understanding our work in education as a 'tangle of texts' is profound for it suggests that all of our actions within that work are comprised of a mosaic of texts which are constantly being written, re-written, read and re-read. Working as an educational researcher, then, entails critically reflective re-writing

and re-reading of the day-to-day phenomena which present themselves to us.
(p. 388)

Ironically, the more usual 'readerly texts' in education are at the same time
both comfortable and controlling. They lead the reader logically, predictably,
often in a linear fashion, through the research process, leaving little space for
the reader to make his or her own textual connections between the stories and
images presented. In contrast, Sumara and Luce-Kapler (1993) argue that 'writerly
text' is less predictable. It calls on the reader to engage with the text 'to more
deliberately bring to the reading his or her own experiences as a way of
filling . . . the gaps in the text'. The linear development of the research will to
a certain extent provide one strand to which the reader may cling. However,
this will be interspersed with other data, and also another researcher's opinions gathered from informal interviews with the research officer and his written responses to my earlier draft of this chapter. This technique appeals to the
reader as a researcher to engage at a different level with the researchers as the
research team attempted to fulfil a research contract.

Just Another Mountain

My previous employer, an organization dedicated exclusively to educational
research, must compete for contracts and the evaluation upon which this chapter
is based is one such project. It was won in 1995 by competitive tendering and
located within my programme as a research manager. The aim of the evaluation was to examine the role and effectiveness of a standardized entrance test
within the recruitment process to a national organization, and recommend, if
necessary, ways in which the test might be improved. The researchers were
required to take account of:

- the current core duties of the job;
- the skills and aptitudes required;
- the standard training provided to recruits;
- the need to ensure equal opportunities;
- the efficiency and cost-effectiveness of applying and marking tests.

This was the remit provided by the funder for a short-term (5 months) evaluation with a maximum of £15,000 funding beginning in July 1995. It was a
typical example of what Stronach et al. (1996) refer to as the 'quick and dirty'
type of educational contract evaluation. Compare this with earlier social scientists. Recalling his work in the 1950s, Bailey (1977) reflects that:

> I now realise that I lived in a Garden of Eden . . . when I first went to India,
> those who paid for the research asked only if I seemed qualified to carry it
> out. They did not ask whether it was useful, or to whom it was useful. Whether

that research was into contemporary social change, or an archaeological dig, or an inquiry into the sixteenth century Tamil proverbs, no one seemed to care. We were to make a contribution to knowledge: no further justification was required. To raise questions about 'relevance' would have been to brand one-self as 'rackety', 'unsound' and a person likely to falsify the evidence. (p. 39)

Why did an educational research organization bid for such an under-funded project which clearly lay outwith its area of expertise? Part of the answer lies in the uneasy relationship between researchers and policy-makers where the former are seen to inhabit 'know-how' organizations within a knowledge economy in which, as Lyotard (1984) suggests, 'knowledge is no longer the subject but in the service of the subject' (p. 36). Additionally, as researchers move from one 'know-how' organization (Svielby and Lloyd, 1989) to another, their credibility is legitimized by their ability to generate more and larger contracts which both purchase their existing 'know-how' and allow them to build up more capital. The contract becomes the mechanism by which know-ledge is generated, but the epistemological basis of the knowledge is rarely articulated as researchers make pragmatic adjustments to the new situation. And the available space for negotiation is confined as I discovered. My own log of events taken from fieldnotes and marginal comments appended to team memos demonstrates my own thoughts about the bidding process:

> To say that I feel ambivalent towards this proposal is an understatement. I'm not interested in the topic, I don't want to work with the organisation, the project isn't doable within the allocated resources and I definitely don't need another project to manage. But I know that if I don't turn this unfinished proposal into a winnable contract, then one research officer, with wife, three kids and a mortgage to support, will be out of the door. Do I really have a choice? (Fieldnotes, April 1995)

My research officer recalls a different story. In a written response to this chapter, he argues that there were benefits in our completing the proposal:

> We could provide complementary expertise and we needed to know the proposal in depth. I was happy to be involved . . . I needed a new contract. (Research Officer's memo, May 1996)

The Illusive Peak

In reality there was no choice: another mountain had to be climbed. As Walford (1991) points out, books on research methods often represent the research process as logical or scientific, when the reality centres around 'compromises, short-cuts, hunches and serendipitous occurrences'. In reality, we (my researcher officer and I) took the proposal, reshaping and refocusing it, adding words such as *reliability* and *validity* (borrowed from a positivist paradigm with which neither of us felt comfortable) but which were clearly implicit in the commissioning brief. This provided a psychological gloss which had been absent from the first draft written by a senior manager, and also created for ourselves an impossible task. The project design was ambitious. It was composed of four stages: preliminary sensitizing interviews; analysis of extant examination and recruitment statistics in eight regions; case studies of two regions; and data feedback of emerging themes to informants in eight regions. And all the time we worked on the proposal, although we developed our complementary skills and knowledge, we knew that we increased the chances of success and neither of us dared to contemplate what it would actually be like to undertake this research in an area we knew nothing about. How would we develop sufficient knowledge to complete a project in five months from a zero contextual knowledge base by utilizing the skills of one part-time research officer? My fieldnotes recall:

> I don't want to work for X [the funder] . . . we have an obvious mismatch here. I know I am only doing this for [the research officer's] sake and I'm not sure that it will do any of us any favours. This is the tyranny of the short-term. (Fieldnotes, April 1995)

In any account of a research project, the researchers must decide how much to reveal and how much to censor knowingly for fear of hurt or embarrassment. Troyna (1994) argues that reflecting on reflections in qualitative research, which may often assume a 'confessional quality', is more usually engaged in by established researchers whose position in the research community protects them from the possible consequences of their reflections. This clearly does not apply to less well-established researchers and, therefore, published revelations do not represent the range of researchers currently engaged in educational research, especially contract research. Also, as Walford (1991) points out, self-censorship is commonly employed largely to avoid harm to others (in this case, the future employment prospects of a contract researcher), a threat of libel action, or the reluctance on the part of the researchers to reveal quite all that occurred. He notes that:

> In all the collections published there is, for example, a complete lack of comment on any sexual relationships that may have been a part of the research process, yet it is difficult to believe that these have been entirely absent. (Walford, 1991, p. 5)

But what of gender and that other human relationship — friendship — both of which may obfuscate the research process? My research officer and I had never worked together before: he was transferred to my team in order to avoid redundancy. Fortuitously, we immediately established a rapport and felt comfortable working with each other, which was further strengthened during periods of fieldwork. Through the vagaries of contract research employment, it could very well have been otherwise. This was a non-sexual professional relationship. We found it was easy to laugh at the inherent sexism of one case-study organization which issued a memo informing respondents that I was his assistant. Neither of us was Scots by birth but both had been educated in Scotland and had lived in the country long enough to be acutely aware of its political, social and cultural sensitivities. When our funder issued guidelines, we both knew from past experiences what to expect. A formal advisory group meeting would be convened; our role was mainly to listen to the advice offered, identify the limits of what was acceptable to the funders, while simultaneously trying to maintain our professional integrity. These are the implicit rules of contract research.

Traversing the Glacier

In practice, the research team was now composed of one 3/4 time research officer, 10 per cent of my own time as principal researcher, and an unspecified amount of time from a senior manager. The pressure was intensifying. I had suspected that the project as originally designed was not 'doable' within the existing resources of time and money. This quickly became apparent as we struggled to keep up with the established timetable. I had to devote more time to this project than had been costed, neglecting other projects, and felt locked onto a fieldwork treadmill which left me physically tired and emotionally unprepared for the exigencies of research in an unfamiliar context. Our analytic memos — a symbolic vestige of the 'old game' — chart the team's progress. I record that one respondent was particularly difficult.

> He [the respondent] walked in telling me immediately . . . how stupid and naive my questions are. Silverman's notion of 'impression management' flashes across my mind and I begin to sense that the roles have been reversed. 'Where are your written terms of reference,' he demands, 'I knows what your game is.' Am I even playing a game? . . . All I wanted him to do is answer the questions so that we can get the six o'clock train back to Edinburgh . . . (Fieldnotes, November 1995)

And as the pressure intensified, fieldwork sites began to merge into each other:

> Another day, another group of respondents. We arrive late. There isn't time to think: the interviews and focus groups are following one after another . . . If I hear another behavioural event, I might scream. Curses on McBer Associates for developing this form of interviewing. . . . I think I am in overload. All I want to be is a 'hit and run' researcher. (Fieldnotes, November 1995)

That complex mix of pressures and emotions which may assail the research interviewer has been identified by other researchers (Lee, 1993). Lee argues that while some methods, such as the survey method, assume that social phenomena have an external, stable and verbalizable reality, this is an inappropriate way of conceptualizing the dynamics of sensitive or threatening research interviews. The social researcher differs from many other professionals who 'practise on their own territory, work within set time limits, and can usually call on therapeutic support'. As a consequence, researchers are often left 'to cope with the stresses and strains of interviewing as best they can' (Lee, 1993). I would also suggest that there has been a tendency for more senior, and hence experienced, researchers to withdraw from data collection activities — thus distancing themselves from the inherent stresses of that part of the research process. For example the description offered by Measor and Woods (1991) of their collaboration, which must be typical of many teams, details their respective roles: fieldwork and first drafting by Measor, a research assistant, and grant applications and final report writing by Woods, a professor.

In our project, I gradually realized that the research could not be completed within existing resources and requested the finance manager to transfer the research officer to a full-time contract. We were beginning to pay a heavy price as a consequence of an unrealistic research design and too many other projects to be managed concurrently. But there were some good times too. The days spent driving around districts while respondents talked us through their jobs using a *protocol analysis* technique (Burgoyne and Hodgson, 1984) worked well. And we all enjoyed the resultant role confusion when we were not recognized as educational researchers mapping competences. Interestingly, this stage coincided with our organization's temporary removal to an open plan office while our own building was renovated. My research officer recalls this period as 'golden days'. He writes:

> . . . my working relationship with [the principal researcher] improved and I got to know the rest of her team. This period was exhilarating for me . . . with most people happy to see some informality and novelty brought to meetings and coffee times was one of the most popular changes. (Research Officer's memo, May 1996)

Amazingly, stages of the project were successfully completed without team roles being explicitly clarified. There are obvious grey areas on the boundaries between different jobs: research assistant, research officer and principal researcher's roles are often defined only through the development of working practices within individual teams. On short projects or with inexperienced teams (and the contract research culture is inimical to the development of experienced teams), these areas of ambiguity may be sources of potential conflict as the researchers are driven on to complete the contract. My research officer recalls his own discomfort:

> . . . the first occasion for a degree of anxiety arose because I sometimes feel uncomfortable drafting reports 'for others'. As a junior contract researcher I

feel (rightly or wrongly) that I am writing for somebody else, i.e. the senior researcher, and inevitably that cramps my style. I therefore tend to write too much so that the senior can just delete the text rather than add . . . [the principal researcher] completed the report as there was no time for passing drafts back and forward. (Research Officer's memo, May 1996)

However, despite our problems, the interim report was presented on time — one of the 'project milestones' by which contract researchers are judged. The requirement to present an interim report on a five-month project, I would argue, represents another aspect of the foreshortening of the research process identified by Stronach et al. (1996).

The Gathering Storm

We struggled on towards the final report, concurrently working on multiple research projects, attempting to sequence and coordinate aspects of a research process which had become disaggregated, and losing any sense of a coherent whole. In such circumstances, the concept of teamwork takes on new meanings. Our own experiences are confirmed by Measor and Woods (1991) who suggest that teamwork in research, while often recommended, may sometimes cause difficulties or even be counterproductive in certain instances. They describe the basis of successful collaboration in their own professional partnership as:

> First, we had different knowledge bases. This enabled us to have a wider range for the formation of ideas and for interpreting material. We were also able to act as a check and a balance on each other's work. Ideas had to be argued out for the other, and this tested them out. This approach we would argue, is a creative formula . . . We would argue that collaboration provides a sound basis for creativity, rigour and lucidity. (p. 68)

They identify the importance of team members sharing certain basic interests and values. But time for sharing is rarely costed into a research contract and, in contrast to their experiences, our discomfort intensified as the research 'progressed'. The proposal had been over-ambitious. The second period of field-work generated approximately 40 individual behavioural event interviews and numerous focus group interviews collected by 3 different researchers which now required transcribing and analysing. The research officer recalled that:

> The pressure mounted and I asked [the principal researcher] for some help with the analysis and a couple of meetings left me with a stack of literature and my own devices on generating categories . . . The project meetings can also be useful, but they never seemed to take place, other than as impromptu discussions after hours when I rather wanted to get away to have a life. How can you say that when time is of the essence and your contract is nearly up? (Research Officer's memo, May 1996)

The research officer complained bitterly that one of the prime sources of the literature review was incomprehensible and inappropriate for the current research in a Scottish context; while the other researcher could not understand why we didn't instantly see the connections. For my part, I was caught in the resultant cross-fire. Memos passed back and forth — all of which should have contributed to our understanding, but in reality could not be accommodated in our abbreviated model of research. By the end of November, with the final report due on the 5 December, I was near despair.

At the Bottom of the Crevasse

With only five days to go, and the report incomplete, I could not see how it would all end. The juggling of disparate stages and projects, the slippage from the agreed timetable and our different positions seemed irreconcilable. Strauss (1987) suggests that:

> Undoubtedly, the most difficult skill to learn is 'how to make everything come together' — how to integrate one's separate, if cumulative, analyses. If the final product is an integrated theory, then integrating is the accurate term for this complex process. This is why the inexperienced researcher will never feel secure in how to complete an entire integration until he or she has struggled with the process, beginning early and ending only with the final write-up. (p. 170)

I began to have serious doubts about how even an experienced researcher could 'pull it all together' with a team under such pressure to perform? With only five remaining days, the report was still in pieces. Ball (1991) describes a process of bringing it all together through what he refers to as *familiarization*. This he accomplishes by highlighting and cutting up transcripts and finally sitting on the floor of his study sorting data into different envelopes. This degree of familiarization with the data is denied the contract researcher. There is literally no time in a short project to engage in 'grounded theory' (Glaser and Strauss, 1967), but researchers hold onto the concept as another vestige of an earlier game. At that stage in the project, I made the pragmatic decision, unilaterally and with no consultation, to take data home and write until the report was complete. There was little time for familiarization or in-depth analysis. My sole concern was to write the report in a clear, concise format thus fulfilling the terms of our contract.

At the bottom of the crevasse, it is hard to imagine that things can get worse. But in contract research, there is one more act to perform: the contract researchers must be declared redundant. Gone were grand notions of social theorizing: we were operating at the level of reports, jobs and mortgages. In their report, Measor and Woods (1991) note that:

> . . . research projects do not always operate on the high plane of creativity.
> There are low points, for example if access is blocked, or if complex ethical
> difficulties arise. There can be periodic concern over where the research is
> going and exhaustion and worry in the draining slog of writing up. (p. 68)

It is comforting to know that what I was experiencing was the exhaustion
which accompanies the 'draining slog of writing up'. The whole of the last
week prior to submitting the project report took on a nightmarish quality. My
fieldnotes recall that at 4:30 a.m. with three days to go before the report was
due, and two other project presentations to make:

> I'm very tired. I have now been writing more or less continuously since 9.00
> a.m. the previous day. I don't think that I have ever written so much in such
> a short time — 6,000 words in less than a day. (Fieldnotes, 3 December 1995)

The Final Moraine

Wednesday 13 December was the final hurdle — the project presentation to
the funder. My fieldnotes say that:

> I am tired and late (having only returned on the night shuttle from London)
> and literally have to run to be on time . . . I'm not certain how the report will
> be received . . . I don't want to go through this again. (Fieldnotes, 13 December 1995)

The research officer, who had already left by this stage, returned in an advisory capacity for that final meeting. He recalls feeling 'confident in the report'
and felt that the funders 'got a lot for their money'. We left the meeting: it was
a strange mixture of sadness for the one made redundant but also euphoria
and relief that we had 'pulled it off' once more.

Down at Last

And where do we go from here? Different realities and different mountains?
For the research officer it has meant learning to cope with a 13-month period
of unemployment and eventually a change in career direction. Outwardly, he
remains sanguine, calling in from time to time to be with the team of which he
is no longer a member. One of his last memos to me reflects on the 'steep
learning curve' which was required of our team in order to complete the project.
    And what of the report and the status of the knowledge produced? Bassey
(1995) argues that in carrying out research 'the purpose is to try to make some
claim to knowledge; to try to show something that was not known before'
(p. 14). But this does not necessarily imply that there is a knowable 'it' out
there for which research teams search. Certainly in this project, there was a

genuine dilemma for the funder: could they publish a report which provided new insights into a process which appeared to disadvantage certain groups of applicants? Surprisingly, the report has now been published and new tests are being devised to provide a more equitable selection instrument.

But why is doing educational research so difficult for contract researchers? Burgess (1994) suggests that many researchers make the false assumption that standard procedures utilized in basic research can be applied to funded or contract research. He argues that 'the principles might be the same; that is to collect data that are reliable and valid. However, the means by which this is done may be different' (p. 64). We see from the example discussed in this chapter that there are sufficient methodological similarities for researchers to move from one 'game' to the other simply by accelerating their performance. In fact, many contract researchers received their induction into research on longer contracts within the university sector.

But differences are not attributable to speed alone. Stronach and Morris (1994) paint a picture of 'conformatory research' in an age of 'policy hysteria' in which the research team colludes with the funder to produce an evaluation which confirms the policy direction already taken. In earlier work, Bailey, (1977) identified the role of masks as an attempt by the academic researcher/ player 'to present in a bold, simple, indeed, caricatured fashion some side of himself [sic] or his policies that will captivate his supporters and intimidate his rivals' — an attempt to take control by imposing on others definitions of self. This may indeed be one of the silent collusions which occur — educational researchers have been redefined as contractors rather than academics — however, it is only a partial interpretation of the dynamics of managing a contract research project. Bailey goes on to suggest that cultural systems are sets of ideas (myths) about what is desirable but these are essentially fragile creations. He argues that:

> Any set of people who interact with one another regularly are likely to have diverse beliefs (whether about goals, the nature of the environment, or the best way of matching goals to environment) some of which stand irreconcilably in contradiction with one another. Efforts to impose definitions on each other lead to instability . . . (Bailey, 1977, p. 198)

I would argue that there is instability in all research teams — a tension which in certain circumstances leads to creativity — which becomes an acute problem for contract researchers. Invariably they are under-resourced, coping with competing research priorities, and deprived of real authority by the nature of their employment contract.

Research experiences are not a set of free-floating skills but are grounded in a particular network of complex social relationships to which we give meaning. For my research officer and me, these included the values of a Scottish Puritan work ethic (perhaps, even parochialism) married to a contract research culture in which we attempted to 'make the best' of the situation. And that is where the story rests. As Miles and Huberman (1984) remarked, 'epistemologies don't get the research done' and one might add 'and neither do ontologies'. The contracts continue to stack up, the deadlines (more metaphorical mountains) appear. Lather's (1993) search for 'obsessive validity' and Stronach et al.'s (1996) exploration of 'transgressive validity' have a hollow ring for contract researchers operating with the 'new discourse' of contracts, findings and customers.

I suspect that our experiences are not unique. I have attempted to present them here as a more complete, and I hope not too pessimistic, picture of a research project which foregrounds the dynamics within a contract research team rather than the more usual sanitized published accounts. I also recognize that accounts such as this, which attempt to 'tell it like it is' as opposed to those based upon 'normative cookbooks' (Troyna, 1994), may be just as misleading, and also suffer from delusions of grandeur that somehow this may represent the 'whole story'. I don't know the 'whole story' of how to do educational research, or even whether there is a 'whole story', analogous to Plato's forms, waiting to be discovered. But I do know that I don't believe anymore in 'blue mountains'. All I can see is the enervating sight of another 250 Munroes,[1] and in order to keep going it may occasionally be necessary (as Simpson experienced) to cut the rope which joins team members so that the team lives to climb again.

Acknowledgments

This chapter deals with an actual funded project and identifiable researchers. I am grateful to the project research officer for adding his perspective and also to William Richardson, at Sheffield University for his helpful comments on an earlier draft. However, the views expressed here are mine and do not reflect the opinions of either the funder or my previous and current employers.

Note

1 The term given to Scottish mountains over 3,000 feet high which has led to the activity of 'Munro bagging' *viz.* attempting to climb all such mountains.

References

BAILEY, F.G. (1977) *Morality and Expediency*, Oxford: Blackwell.
BASSEY, M. (1995) *Creating Education Through Research*, Kirkington Moor Press: BERA.
BALL, S. (1991) 'Power, conflict, micropolitics and all that!' in WALFORD, G. (ed.) *Doing Educational Research*, London: Routledge.
BROWN, S. and WAKE, R. (1988) *Education in Transition: What Role for Research?* Edinburgh: SCRE.

Burgess, R.G. (1994) 'Scholarship and sponsored research: Contradictions, continuum or complementary activity?' in Halpin, D. and Troyna, B. (eds) *Researching Educational Policy*, London: Routledge.

Burgess, R.G. (1985) *Strategies of Educational Research: Qualitative Methods*, London: Falmer Press.

Burgoyne, J.G. and Hodgson, V.E. (1984) 'An experiential approach to understanding managerial action', in Hunt, J.G. et al. (eds) *Leaders and Managers: International Perspectives on Managerial Behaviour and Leadership*, New York: Pergamon.

Cohen, L. and Manion, L. (1994) *Research Methods in Education*, 4th Edition, London: Routledge.

Delamont, S. (1992) *Fieldwork in Educational Settings: Methods, Pitfalls and Perspectives*, London: Falmer Press.

Derrida, J. (1978) 'Structure, sign and play in the discourse of human science', *Writing and Differences* (translated by A. Bass), Chicago: University of Chicago Press.

Glaser, B.G. and Strauss, A.L. (1967) *The Discovery of Ground Theory: Strategies for Qualitative Research*, Chicago: Aldine Publishing Co.

Lather, P. (1993) 'Fertile obsession: Validity after poststructuralism', *The Sociological Quarterly*, **34**, 4, pp. 673–93.

Lee, R.M. (1993) *Doing Research on Sensitive Topics*, London: Sage Publications.

Lyotard, J.F. (1984) *The Postmodern Condition: A Report on Knowledge* (translated by G. Bennington and B. Massumi), Minneapolis: University of Minnesota Press.

Measor, L. and Woods, P. (1991) 'Breakthroughs and blockages in ethnographic research: Contrasting experiences during the changing schools project', in Walford, G. (ed.) *Doing Educational Research*, London: Routledge.

Miles, M.B. and Huberman, A.M. (1984) *Qualitative Data Analysis: A Sourcebook of New Methods*, Beverley Hills, CA: Sage Publications Ltd.

Stronach, I., Allan, J. and Morris, B. (1996) 'Can the mothers of invention make virtue out of necessity? An optimistic deconstruction of research comprises in contract research and evaluation', *British Educational Research Journal*, **22**, 4, pp. 493–508.

Stronach, I. and Morris, B. (1994) 'Polemical notes on educational evaluation in the age of "policy hysteria"', *Evaluation and Research in Education*, **8**, 2, pp. 5–19.

Svielby, K.E. and Lloyd, T. (1989) *Managing Knowhow: Add Value by Valuing Creativity*, London: Bloomsbury Publishing Co.

Sumara, D.J. and Luce-Kapler, R. (1993) 'Action research as a writerly text', *Educational Action Research*, **1**, 3, pp. 387–95.

Troyna, B. (1994) 'Reforms, research and being reflective about being reflective', in Halpin, D. and Troyna, B. (eds) *Researching Education Policy: Ethical and Methodological Issues*, London: Falmer Press.

Walford, G. (ed.) (1991) *Doing Educational Research*, London: Routledge.

13   Compulsive Writing Behaviour: Getting It Published

Geoffrey Walford

Introduction

In his classic study of life in a psychiatric hospital, Rosenhan (1973) describes the way that covert sociologists who took notes within the hospital setting were fully accepted as patients by the medical staff. The researchers' constant note-taking of every activity that occurred was taken as sure proof that they were insane! Such 'compulsive writing activity' could only be a sign that these pseudo-patients were really as mad as the rest of the inmates.

Now Rosenhan, of course, believed that the sociologists were sane and were only taking part in the rational activity called sociology, but I have my doubts. There *is* something insane about the way qualitative sociologists spend so much time writing. They write before they start generating data in the field, they write profuse fieldnotes while they are undertaking the research and, finally, they write endless articles and books about their findings and (increasingly) the process of doing research. In most cases very few people will read any of this writing. If this is sanity, then how does it differ from madness?

In this chapter I wish to write about my own 'compulsive writing activity' linked to my research on the political processes that influenced legislation on sponsored grant-maintained schools. My focus will be on that writing activity concerned directly with publication, but this cannot be separated from the earlier forms of writing both prior to and during the 'data construction' phase of the research. For me, 'writing' and 'publishing' are not distinct activities that occur at the end of the research period, they are continuously present in the design and practice of the research. The compulsive need to write and publish helps structure what is done in the field, and the decisions made at all stages of the research.

The chapter starts with a consideration of the structure and constraints of the academic publication marketplace and the way in which these influence the publication process. This is followed by a broad outline of the particular research topic that has been the subject of much of my recent writing and publishing. Next comes a description of how particular articles and books linked to the project were eventually published and the form in which this occurred. Some general points are drawn in conclusion.

184

My objective in this chapter is to demystify some aspects of the academic publication process, such that new writers in particular will have a more realistic view of how publication occurs. I hope that readers of research will also benefit from a greater understanding of how academic research articles and books come to be selected for publication and are structured by forces far beyond the purely academic. However, unlike several recent books (for example, Derricourt, 1996; Eggleston and Klein, 1997; Thyer, 1994), my aim is not to provide helpful hints about 'how to get published' for new academics, but to give a personal account of some aspects of my relationship to the process of writing and publication.

The Academic Publishing Marketplace

The vast majority of academic books and journal articles are produced because someone believes that there is money to be made by doing so. With very few exceptions, book and journal publishers operate within a highly competitive marketplace where the single most important criterion for publication is the likelihood of short- to medium-term profitability.

There has been considerable recent research into the economics of the school textbook and how the requirements of the market constrain and influence what is published and thus the content of school textbooks (e.g. Apple and Christian-Smith, 1991; Apple, 1996). There has been less research that has focused on the marketplace at the university and academic level — but the influences are no less real. It is essential to recognize that, within a capitalist economy, academic publishing is not separated from any other form of publication. Publishers exist, and shareholders invest in publishing houses, because they wish to make a good return on their investment. Quality alone is insufficient to ensure publication; a manuscript has to have a large enough potential market for the publisher to recoup costs and make a profit.

The profit-related demands of publishing are most clearly seen in book publishing. Books are recognizable products that are traded and available in shops in a similar way to baked beans or breakfast cereals. The manufacturers of books wish to make as much overall profit as they can and price each book according to their expectations of how well it will sell. If they believe a book will have a narrow appeal, and the major part of the market is likely to be academic libraries, a decision might be made to produce only hardback copies. The price charged would be high but, even with small sales volume, a worthwhile profit could be achieved. In contrast, the expectation of a wider potential market may lead to a decision to print both hardback and soft-cover, with the hope that a cheaper edition will lead to sufficiently large sales to achieve the maximum profit.

Just as baked beans or breakfast cereals have to be packaged in particular sized boxes, so books have to be of a certain length and structure. For example, few commissioning editors will think about publishing an academic mono-graph of 30,000 words or one of 150,000. One would be too thin to be priced cheaply enough to get sales, while the other too fat to be produced econom-ically. For most publishers the ideal length is between 80,000 and 100,000 words, or about 200 or so pages. That is the rough 'size' that buyers expect 'a book' to be. That is the product that they have become accustomed to and socialized into buying; the product that has gradually been constructed by printers and publishers. The original physical limitations of printing and binding have led to a recognizable product that is within certain size and design limitations — a product that fits neatly on a bookshelf, a product that can be held in the hands relatively easily, a book that looks and feels like 'a book'.

The influence of the profit motive within book publishing is self-evident, yet similar, although more complex, considerations apply to publishing within academic journals. Journals are usually started by enthusiasts who wish to leg-itimize a particular developing field of knowledge. A new journal might be a by-product of meetings of a group of academics interested in similar issues, or it could be the entrepreneurial initiative of a small group wishing to enhance their own statuses or careers. Whatever the initial impetus, while the group itself may initially finance the journal, if it wishes the journal to expand its circula-tion, it soon has to convince an external body to invest.

Within educational publishing there are now several specialist academic journal publishers (such as Carfax, and Taylor and Francis) and other more generalist publishers (such as Routledge, and Blackwell) who publish educa-tional research journals. All do so because they can make a profit. And it has the potential for being a very profitable business. In contrast to popular jour-nals, contributors to academic refereed journals are not paid for their articles, much of the work of producing each issue is donated free by editors, reviewers and the authors themselves, and the serial nature of the publications means that once the initial subscription has been sold, the buyers will usually continue to purchase the product. Brand name loyalty is high. While the details depend on pricing decisions and the peculiarities of particular markets, the sales level at which journals become profitable is surprisingly low. Once 300 or so sub-scriptions have been made profits can usually start to flow.

Most academic refereed journals have an editor and an editorial board, with the editor having a vital role as academic gatekeeper (Simon and Fyfe, 1994). Generally, when a manuscript is sent to the editor she or he will quickly assess if it is relevant to the aims of the journal and looks worth reviewing. Two or three referees are then chosen (often including someone from the editorial board) and are sent copies of the manuscript. They then assess the article and write back to the editor with their views about the desirability of publications and any changes that they believe to be necessary before publication can pro-ceed. It is common for there to be disagreement between reviewers and, when this happens, the editor will adjudicate with or without a further opinion being sought.

A straightforward decision to publish is rare. Much more common is the decision to reject the article or publish subject to changes being made. In the latter case the author will be sent copies of a selection of what reviewers have written about the paper and be asked to revise in the light of their suggestions. As is shown later, it is not uncommon for the comments from different reviewers at this stage to be somewhat contradictory. The author is left to try to make sense of multiple demands.

In a similar way to book publication, the decision about publication of articles in academic journals is not made purely on academic grounds. Editors work within the constraints and rhythm of the journal production process. They have to find sufficient articles to fill the planned number of issues each year. As with books, each issue has to be of an acceptable size — usually about 130 pages for Carfax or Taylor and Francis journals. This means that the decision to publish is influenced by the flow of articles submitted to the particular journal. Submitted articles compete with each other for space, so that when many articles are being submitted the standard of the papers accepted rises. In contrast, in times of scarcity, editors are forced to publish articles about which they may have considerable doubts. Most editors try to smooth the flow of articles by building a stockpile of articles ready for future publication, but authors object if the wait between acceptance and publication becomes too long. Few editors like to have more than about a year's worth of articles waiting to appear in print so there are sometimes fluctuations in the standard of papers accepted in most journals.

Why Do Academics Publish So Much?

While the publishing industry is structured around profit, monetary gain is certainly not the prime motivation for the academic author. A particularly generous publisher might give authors 10 per cent of the net price of a book. This might be about £1.00 per copy. As most academic books are rated highly successful if they sell more than 2000 or 3000 copies, the amount that an author gains cannot be a prime motivation. In terms of the rate of pay per hour of writing, most authors would be far better off serving drinks behind a bar!

With academic journal articles, the authors are not paid anything at all. They spend time researching and writing, they produce manuscripts to set length and style requirements, they modify what they have written in accordance with referees' comments, and even act as proofreaders for their printed article. Yet they receive not a penny from the publisher!

There are clearly other motivations. One is that most academic writing is done by people already in full-time work where there is at least an implicit contractual requirement that they publish. Academics are usually required to 'teach and conduct research' and publication is seen an essential part of the latter. Moreover, at least in the initial stages of a career, there is often perceived to be an overriding need to 'publish or perish'. The academic on a short-term contract is unlikely to have it renewed or to be able to find another academic job elsewhere unless he or she has several articles published or in press. Obtaining a permanent job or promotion within academia are highly dependent upon a substantial and significant record of publications. This direct pressure to write is at its most evident for academics at the early stages of their careers, but the regular Research Assessment Exercises within the British higher education sector have increased the pressure on established academics to continue to get published once they have obtained an established post. The current expectation for the Research Assessment Exercise is that every academic will produce at least four significant publications within each assessment exercise period of about four years.

But many established academics produce far more than this. Many well-known academics within education (such as some of those with chapters in this book) are producing several books and dozens of academic articles within each assessment period. It is hard to believe that the pride of seeing one's name in print is sufficient to encourage such overproduction. There is a real sense in which this is 'compulsive writing behaviour' — it certainly is for me.

Researching the Development of Policy on Sponsored Grant-maintained Schools

The main purpose of this chapter is to provide some examples that illustrate some aspects of my relationship to the process of writing and publication. These examples will draw upon my recent research into the development of policy on sponsored grant-maintained schools, so it is necessary to first give an outline of that research.

The research discussed here was conducted between 1987 and 1995, and focused primarily on the activities of a particular pressure group, the Christian Schools Campaign, whose aim was to obtain state funding for existing private evangelical Christian schools. Although national, the Campaign never had more than a handful of active workers. However, it achieved considerable success by working with other groups campaigning for funding of their own schools and by closely associating with several powerful and prominent individuals on the political New Right. While there is no necessary ideological agreement with those on the New Right, the aims of the Christian Schools Campaign coincided with the Right's wider project of encouraging a greater diversity of schools and a greater market orientation towards schooling (Sexton, 1987). As a result, the Christian Schools Campaign had a strong influence on legislative changes in the 1993 Education Act that enabled these Christian schools to apply to become a new form of state-funded, grant-maintained school (Walford, 1995b).

Since the 1944 Education Act almost all religious denominational primary and secondary schools in England and Wales have been an integral part of the state-maintained system. Religious schools within the state system have the status of voluntary schools, where all of the everyday running costs and teachers' salaries are provided by the state. For voluntary-aided schools, the church organizations pay 15 per cent of any new capital expenditure. At present about 28 per cent of primary pupils and 17 per cent of secondary pupils are in voluntary schools.

However, the vast majority of these voluntary schools are Church of England or Roman Catholic schools, with a very few Methodist and Jewish schools. The current pattern thus reflect the social and religious character of the 1940s rather than the 1990s. As Britain has gradually become more multi-ethnic and more religiously diverse, there has been growing pressure to establish new schools to serve these new groups. In theory it has long been open to followers of other Christian denominations or religious faiths to establish schools that could then be taken into the state-maintained system as voluntary schools. Yet, in practice, in spite of clear demand for such schools, there were no state-supported Muslim, Sikh, or Hindu schools in Britain. Neither were there any state-supported schools representing any of the smaller Christian groups or denominations.

The 1993 Education Act for England and Wales opened the way for new state-supported, grant-maintained schools to be established which reflect particular religious or philosophical beliefs. Additionally, existing faith-based private schools can apply to become re-established as grant-maintained schools. The legislation that allows these new faith-based, grant-maintained schools can be seen to have been strongly influenced by the continued campaigning from an interlocking network of pressure groups that represent a range of 'reluctant' private schools — in particular the Christian Schools Campaign that represented about 65 private evangelical Christian schools.

My original interest in the new Christian schools developed from my long-standing research focus on the private sector. During the 1980s I had written about elite private boys' boarding schools (Walford, 1986 and 1987), and I had followed that with several article and books about the private sector (e.g. Walford, 1989 and 1990). I began to recognize that there was great diversity within the private sector and that very little research had been conducted on the smaller and more idiosyncratic schools. I attended some meetings of various groupings of small private schools and began to visit a few, but my interest intensified as a result of attempts in the House of Lords to amend the 1987 Education Bill such that 'opting-in' was included as well as 'opting-out'. The amendments had little chance of success and were duly rejected, but they generated considerable publicity. It was evident that many of those involved would continue with their campaign.

I decided that I would attempt to follow the campaign and also find out more about the 'new Christian schools'. The research project passed through several stages. At first it was very much a 'background' project to my other activities, where I collected newspaper cuttings, visited a few schools, attended some meetings (including a three-day meeting of these schools), conducted some interviews, and published an early article based on this work (Walford,

1991). Intensive activity did not really start until I obtained a small two-year grant from the Nuffield Foundation in early 1992. Following the award of this grant, more schools were visited, headteachers, teachers, politicians, officials and academics involved with the pressure group were interviewed and a further crop of meetings attended. A questionnaire survey of the schools was also conducted which eventually drew a response rate of 83 per cent (Poyntz and Walford, 1994). Further articles and a book have since been published (Walford, 1994a and b, 1995a, b, c and d).

The Publishing Process: Some Examples

I have had colleagues approach me with an article they have written and ask me to suggest journals to which it might be submitted. I find this bizarre. To me, it is rather like writing a letter and, only after completing it, deciding who should receive it. While it may be true that ageing Aunt Joan may be interested in some of the same things as your bank manager, it is highly likely that both the content and style of letters to each of them will be substantially different.

My writing, and to a great extent the conduct of the research itself, is always structured around particular books and journal articles that I wish to write. I always have in mind a particular 'outlet' for everything I write, and it is only if a piece is rejected by that journal or publisher that I have to search for another that is as similar as possible to my original preference.

From the point when I received the Nuffield Foundation grant, I decided that I wanted to publish four or five academic articles about the work and then revise them and add some new material to form a book. In particular, the pressures of the regular higher education Research Assessment Exercise led me to feel that I 'needed' to have several publications in highly respected academic journals, but I also wished to have a complete book as an outcome. In my mind, as the research progressed, I divided the various parts of the research into articles, each linked to a particular journal.

Educational Studies

One article was straightforward. With Colin Poyntz (who was a social sciences undergraduate working with me for a year) I conducted a survey of the 60 or so new Christian schools then in membership to the Christian Schools Trust. This was a necessary preliminary to any further work and the results of the survey could be easily shaped into an article that presented both a quantitative and qualitative description. This type of article almost writes itself and the structure broadly follows the physics reports of experiments that I wrote when I was 13. The traditional format of experiment, method, results, conclusion, was echoed in this paper by introduction, research methods, results, conclusion.

The only slight development of structure was that the results were presented under four sub-headings covering different aspects. *Educational Studies* seemed an appropriate journal to aim for and, to my surprise, they accepted the article with no amendments required (Poyntz and Walford, 1994). I later learned more of the unusual way in which the editor and editorial board of *Educational Studies* go about their task. In contrast to practically all other refereed academic journals in education, with this journal, if the Editor in Chief judges a manuscript to be worthy of refereeing, a copy is sent to all members of the six-strong editorial board. The board meets three times each year to decide which of the articles they have read since the last meeting should be included in the next issue. Only very rarely is an article from the previous period held back for the next, so the law of supply and demand is starkly evident. While the articles published are each reviewed by many more people than in comparable journals, the decisions made about publication are highly dependent on the quality of the papers submitted during the last four-month period. In my case, I guess I was lucky. Mine was one of the eight papers selected for that issue, but then, unusually and for reasons unknown to me, was held over for the next issue.

Journal of Education Policy

The next article about the research was the result of an unexpected victory for the Campaign during the passage of the 1992 Education (Schools) Act. The main purposes of this Act were to introduce the offices of Her Majesty's Chief Inspector of Schools for England and for Wales, to provide for regular inspection of schools, and to give the Secretary of State powers to require schools to publish information. In practice, it was the Act that led to Ofsted (the Office for Standards in Education) and more detailed league tables of examination results. The Christian Schools Campaign saw the Act as another way of raising a debate about religious schools. Through contacts in the House of Lords, principally Lord Northbourne, they introduced amendments that related to the inspection of spiritual, moral and cultural values and to the publication by schools of information on the spiritual, moral and cultural values that each school was trying to promote. This was done to challenge what they had come to see as the 'myth of religious neutrality' which accepted the idea that schools could either be religious or religiously neutral. The campaign believed that it was not possible for schools to be religiously neutral, and that schools always present their own spiritual and moral values either overtly or covertly. Those involved in putting forward the amendments had no expectation that any of them had a chance of being accepted.

The recent panic about declining values and morality, and the now widespread acceptance of the importance of teaching appropriate values in schools, makes it difficult to remember that in 1992 the idea that schools could and should be 'morally neutral' was widespread. This was the basis of the American ideal of separation of church and state and many educationalists argued that it should be emulated here. What was interesting was that, quite unexpectedly, the Lords agreed with the amendments and there was about an hour of one-sided support for the Act to include the inspection of values. There were no speeches against and only three expressed any hesitations. Faced with such determination, and in spite of the perceived difficulty of inspecting values, the government of the day was forced to re-think. It eventually introduced its own rather similar amendments that led to a fundamental change to what was to be inspected.

What interested me was why this had happened. I decided to investigate and write an account that tried to understand that particular decision-making process. I soon recognized that I did not fully understand the procedures of the House of Lords and House of Commons, so I first had to read some elementary books on the British political system. Next, I had to delve into the Parliamentary Reports in the local law library and interview various people about their activities. I learned a great deal about the workings of Parliament that I had not known before. Then I attempted to relate what I had found to existing models of decision-making. Rational models clearly did not fit, but it seemed to me that two theories were particularly helpful — micropolitics, derived from Stephen Ball's (1990) work, and the 'garbage can' model from Cohen, March and Olsen (1972). The latter idea is based on the metaphor of viewing the opportunity to make a choice as an open can into which participants can 'dump' problems or solutions. 'Solutions' are seen as products looking for choice opportunities and a group of problems to which to fit. In highly politicized settings, opportunities are seized as they present themselves and as events unfold. Here, I decided, the Lords were using the 'solution' of inspection of values to answer a 'problem' about school league tables. They wished to emphasize that education was to be seen as more than just examination results, and agreeing to the Northbourne amendments allowed them to express that view.

The article that I wrote for the *Journal of Education Policy* was largely a blow-by-blow narrative account with an additional section where I discussed the theoretical models of decision-making and argued that the 'garbage can' model gave considerable insights into the case. I gave the article the rather over-clever title of 'The Northbourne amendments: Is the House of Lords a garbage can?'. I now think it was an inappropriate title for two reasons. First, it does not tell the reader what the article is about. Only those readers who already have a deep knowledge of the topic will be guided to read it. Second, it assumes that readers know that I am playing with the idea of a 'garbage can' and that there is a theoretical model with that name. I was advised to not include the paper in my list of publications for the last higher education Research Assessment Exercise as readers might think that it was a flippant and highly critical article about the House of Lords.

In due course the editor of the *Journal of Education Policy* sent me comments from two reviewers. Although both reviews recommended publication subject to revision, they were very different. The first, unusually, was hand-written. It was about 200 words long and, although there were some helpful suggestions, there were several parts of the review that I simply could not decipher. The writing was so bad that I, and other people who I showed it to, could not understand what was being suggested. I took account of what I could read and ignored the rest.

The second review was a stark contrast. The reviewer had clearly taken a great deal of time and effort to give suggestions and indicate areas where he or she believed changes should be made. In about 800 words the reviewer made several significant suggestions for improvement as well as going through the paper page-by-page correcting errors, inconsistencies and unclarities. The tone of these comments can be judged from the opening words:

> I think this paper may be publishable subject to revision, although the case is not of great interest unless its theoretical side, and the link between theory and the case study, are both considerably strengthened. In particular, the interpretation (p. 19ff) is underdeveloped . . . The 'garbage can' model is not very well explained or applied. The case itself is not of sufficient interest, so the success of the article must rest on the theoretical insights to which it might give rise, and that is where the paper is weak. I will point this out later on in itemising where I think revisions should be made. The reason I am spending time on these details of wording, etc. is that I would like to encourage the author to resubmit the paper.

The last sentence of this introduction was important to me. Without it, the review would have felt very critical. As it was, although I felt that the case in itself *was* of considerable interest as a narrative account, I was more than willing to follow the suggestions made by the reviewer. There were more than 60 points of detail which included deleting an extra 's', instructions about how to address a Baroness, and several pointers to where further explanation or clarification was required. There were also more substantive suggestions about the general content and structure of the article. I was genuinely very pleased to receive such full comments and wrote to the editor to ask that my thanks should be communicated to the reviewer.

I usually try to make any revisions to articles very quickly. Indeed, some-times I have returned a revised manuscript the next day. In this case I took three months over it. I hope both reviewers was satisfied with the final product (Walford, 1995c).

British Educational Research Journal

The next article came from a gradual recognition of a contradiction that I saw as the research progressed. As I visited the various new Christian schools and talked with those involved in the Christian Schools Campaign, I saw the open, honest and very positive way in which most of them viewed schooling. While these schools were technically private schools, they were far from being elitist and exclusive. Most served working-class families who were worried about the schooling that was locally available for their children. These parents simply sought what they believed was in the best interests of their children and were prepared to make considerable financial sacrifices for their children to attend these schools. More surprisingly, most of the schools were open even to children of different religions, and several Muslim parents preferred to send their children to schools where religious belief was respected rather than to what they saw as secular state-maintained schools. These parents and activists were not natural friends of the New Right, yet their activities were in accord with the desires of the New Right, and the Christian Schools Campaign was working with leading figures on the Right such as Baroness Cox, Stuart Sexton and John Marks to achieve their aims. I saw a severe contradiction here between ends and means which I believed would provide the basis for an interesting article. I thought that the *British Educational Research Journal* would be appropriate for an article of this nature that outlined the history of the campaign and highlighted the contradictions. By that time the 1993 Education Act had been passed and the campaign could be seen as having been successful. Yet, while the immediate objectives had been achieved, I predicted that many of the potential results of the legislation would be in contradiction to the beliefs held by most of the parents and activists from the Christian schools.

Somewhat unusually I received only one set of comments from the reviewers. I assume that the other reviewer was prepared to have the paper published as submitted, but the first reviewer bluntly demanded some amendments before the paper was to be accepted. The paper could be published after:

1   more details of the research methodology are included
2   the CSC is located in relation to other Christian initiatives, e.g. on p. 9 in relation to the ACE schools studied by O'Keefe
3   comparisons are made (e.g. p. 29) with European policies for funding religious and other schools of sub-cultural maintenance
4   more references are made to relevant social theory
5   the claims made on p. 28 and 29 about inequality and deepening social and ethnic divisions are justified (at least by reference to other literature) rather than just asserted
6   the paper's significance for wider debates about choice and diversity is clarified.

Some other minor, but very helpful, comments were made on detailed presentation.

This list of suggestions presented me with several difficulties. As someone who had taught research methods for about sixteen years, it was the first point that gave me the most angst. It was easy to expand what I had written on methodology, but slightly shameful that I should have to be asked to do so. I